Critical Muslim 40

Biography

Critical Muslim is published quarterly by C. Hurst & Co. (Publishers) Ltd. on behalf of and in conjunction with Critical Muslim Ltd. and the Muslim Institute, London.

All editorial correspondence to Muslim Institute, CAN Mezzanine, 49–51 East Road, London N1 6AH, United Kingdom.
E-mail: editorial@criticalmuslim.com

C. Hurst & Co (Publishers) Ltd., New Wing, Somerset House, Strand, London, WC2R 1LA

ISBN: 9781787385986 ISSN: 2048-8475

To subscribe or place an order by credit/debit card or cheque (pounds sterling only) please contact Kathleen May at the Hurst address above or e-mail kathleen@hurstpub.co.uk

Tel: 020 7255 2201

A one-year subscription, inclusive of postage (four issues), costs £50 (UK), £65 (Europe) and £75 (rest of the world), this includes full access to the *Critical Muslim* series and archive online. Digital only subscription is £3.30 per month.

A Cataloguing-in-Publication data record for this book is available from the British Library

Critical Muslim

Subscribe to Critical Muslim

Now in its tenth year in print, *Critical Muslim* is also available online. Users can access the site for just £3.30 per month – or for those with a print subscription it is included as part of the package. In return, you'll get access to everything in the series (including our entire archive), and a clean, accessible reading experience for desktop computers and handheld devices — entirely free of advertising.

Full subscription

The print edition of *Critical Muslim* is published quarterly in January, April, July and October. As a subscriber to the print edition, you'll receive new issues directly to your door, as well as full access to our digital archive.

United Kingdom £50/year
Europe £65/year
Rest of the World £75/year

Digital Only

Immediate online access to *Critical Muslim*

Browse the full *Critical Muslim* archive

Cancel any time

£3.30 per month

www.criticalmuslim.io

CM40

AUTUMN 2021

CONTENTS

BIOGRAPHY

BIOGRAPHY

INTRODUCTION:
CM@TEN

Ziauddin Sardar

The first issue of *Critical Muslim* was published in January 2012, in the heydays of the 'Arab Spring'. Anti-government protests and rebellions, starting from Tunisia, had spread across the Middle East. The issue was cheekily entitled, *The Arabs Are Alive* based on the hope that positive change will finally be ushered in the Arab world. Indeed, the whole CM enterprise was motivated by this prospect. But there were other issues and some nagging questions behind the project. The uprisings may topple the dictators, but will they dethrone the mind-set of dictatorship that is deeply entrenched in Muslim societies? What if we end up replacing one dictatorship with another — as had happened, for example, in the case of Iran after the fall of the Shah; or has happened in Pakistan numerous times. How do we move Muslim societies and cultures from imitation (*taqlid*) to original thought, from constantly looking backwards to an idealised past to looking forward, from passively accepting that 'things change' to actively changing things? A viable future for Islam and Muslims, I firmly believed, depends on looking at ourselves, our history, tradition, legacy, theology, societies and cultures, critically. To change and transform the world, nudge it towards equity and justice, we needed to engage with it judiciously.

The CM project is related somewhat to my biography and personal quests. In my early travels and encounters in the Muslim world, from the 1960s to the end of the millennium, described in *Desperately Seeking Paradise: Journeys of a Sceptical Muslim*, I met countless individuals, men and women, young and old, with a passionate, idealistic attachment to Islam. While passion can be a virtue, it can turn toxic without a modicum of critical acumen. Indeed, as the book makes clear, all varieties of Islam need a healthy dose of scepticism to avoid degenerating into authoritarian outlooks. Many readers of the book have complained that it does not have 'a proper ending'. The last chapter of the book describes the initial preparation of a journey and simply concludes with the words: 'But that's another story'. *Critical Muslim* then is that journey, the continuing story.

My companion in that last chapter of *Desperately Seeking Paradise* is the then young, and rather optimistic, British-Pakistani science journalist, Ehsan Masood. (The optimism diminished as his age increased). Ehsan and I have entangled biographies – both of us have worked for, helped, and consulted with various community organisations and magazines. And when I accepted to become the Chair of the Muslim Institute in 2009, he joined as a trustee. We reformed and re-launched the Institute as a learned society of thinkers, academics, artists, and people generally interested in ideas. There was a need for the Institute to have some sort of publication. So, it seemed natural that CM should live in the Muslim Institute. I consulted fellow trustees, the former Chair and old friend, Ghayasuddin Sidqqui, and Sharia scholar, Mufti Barkatullah, who I knew from my student days. They concurred: there was an urgent need for the kind of publication I had in mind, and that it should carry the Muslim Institute imprint. The then Director of the Muslim Institute, Merryl Wyn Davies, was also a strong supporter of the project. But there was a problem with the name. Should it be 'Critical Muslim' or could it be 'Critical Islam'? One trustee objected strongly: as believers, we cannot be critical either about Islam or about Muslims, she declared. But when the majority of the trustees agreed on the title, she resigned.

Other questions arose as Ehsan, Merryl, and I sat to work on designing and shaping CM. Should it be an academic journal or something else? We approached Routledge and got a positive response. But none of us was in favour of 'yet another academic journal that no one will read'. We wanted it to be an intellectual as well as cultural product, with reportage, art, fiction and poetry. As such, we needed novelists, poets, artists, who shared our vision to join us. At a book festival in Scotland, I came across novelist Robin Yassin-Kassab. I had read his novel *The Road From Damascus*, which had just come out, and liked it. It turned out that he had also read a couple of my books. Books bonded us. I pitched the CM project to Robin; and asked if he would join me as co-editor. Robin, a rather thin chap, scratched his reedy beard, which looks like week-old stubble, and thought. He seemed to scratch his beard persistently; and for quite a long time. Finally, he simply said: 'OK'.

Then, there was the question of finding a publisher. We approached I B Tauris without much joy. Ehsan suggested that we needed a 'brave publisher' who was not only willing to take a financial risk but was also able to face some the hullabaloos we will inevitably generate and face from certain quarters. I knew a number of publishers and editors who worked for various publishing houses – some friends, some acquaintances. But there was only one publisher I knew who fitted Ehsan's criteria: Michael Dwyer of Hurst. Michael was first introduced to me, way back in the late 1990s, by my friend, the celebrated Indian intellectual, social theorist and critic, Ashis Nandy. In those days, Ashis came to London every couple of years; and would always be invited for dinner by Michael. His wife, Rachel, who taught at the School of African and Oriental Studies (SOAS), London University (and went on to be the first and only, so far, Professor of Bollywood) would persuade him to give a lecture or two. I was invited to some of these dinners; and, in turn, I invited Michael and Rachel for 'Begum's biryani' and 'killer daal' at my place. (According to Scott Jordan, who has had quite a few dinners at our place: 'you use a criminally low number of positive adjectives to describe your wife Saliha's cooking'!). Our mutual love of classic Bollywood films and all good aspects of Indian culture and civilisation cemented our friendship. But, as Michael complained, in all the years I had known him, I had never published a book with him. Merryl pointed out that this situation had to be remedied before we could approach Hurst.

It was duly sorted. My next book, *Reading the Qur'an*, based on my *Guardian* blogs, went to Hurst. Soon afterwards, Ehsan and I presented the CM proposal to Michael. He was interested; but had a concern. He published books, not journals or magazines, which are a distinctly different speciality. So, CM was reshaped as serial books, or as we later called it, 'bookzine', each issue with a specific theme or title, published quarterly. Michael liked the idea. And we had a 'brave publisher'. At about the same time, I persuaded Samia Rahman, who had worked on a short-lived Muslim style magazine, *Emel*, and was freelancing as a journalist, to join the Muslim Institute as Deputy Director. We soon discovered that she may be petite but she is big on initiatives and enthusiasm; and the natural choice as Deputy Editor.

We spent considerable time debating what we meant by 'Critical' and 'Muslim'.

A critical spirit has been central to Islam from its inception. The Qur'an is generously sprinkled with references to thought and learning, reflection and reason. The Sacred Text denounces those who do not use their critical faculties in the strongest terms: 'the worse creatures in God's eyes are those who are [wilfully] deaf and dumb, who do not reason' (8:22). A cursory look at the life of Muhammad reveals that his strategic decisions were an outcome of critical discussions – the way he decided, for example, to fight the Battle of Badr outside Medina, or, later on, defend the city by digging a trench. The Prophet's basic advice to his followers, in one version of his 'Farewell Pilgrimage', was to 'reason well'. The scholarship that evolved around collecting the traditions and sayings of the Prophet was itself based on an innovative and detailed method of criticism. It is widely acknowledged that debate and discussion, arguments and counter-arguments, literary textual criticism as well as scientific criticism were a basic hallmark of the classical Muslim civilisation.

Yet, with the exception of a few notable reform-oriented scholars and thinkers, this critical spirit is largely absent from the Muslim world. The reasons for the evaporation of this critical thought are many and diverse. Perhaps it was all the fault of al-Ghazali, as 'a widely held view' has it: he 'strongly attacked Islamic philosophy in *The Incoherence of the Philosophers*' and, as a result, 'their role was significantly reduced in the Sunni world', along with the importance of criticism, notes Abdullah Saeed. Perhaps it was 'the well-known decree of al-Qadir in 1017–18 and 1029', that banned the rationalist Mutazalite school of thought, as the late Mohammad Arkoun suggests. As a consequence, 'to this day, the *ulama* officially devoted to the defence of the orthodoxy, refuses to reactivate the thinking introduced and developed by original, innovative thinkers in classical period'. Perhaps it was the closure of 'the gates of Ijtihad' that sealed the door to criticism: while no one actually closed the gate, it came to be treated, as Sadakat Kadri notes, 'as a historical fact rather than a poetically pleasing way of saying that jurists were no longer as good as they used to be'. Perhaps it was because Muslim societies could not develop 'legally autonomous corporate governance', Arabic thought is 'essentially metaphysical' and incapable of developing universalism, and Muslim culture and ethos is just too reverential to religious authorities, as the arch critic of the history of Islamic science, Toby Huff, has argued. Perhaps criticism died out because of a lack of any kind of state support or protection for dissent; or maybe it was due to the colonisation of much of the Muslim world. However, all of these explanations of the decline of Muslim civilisation and the disappearance of the critical spirit are partial, and some are seriously problematic, as I argued in my 2006 Royal Society lecture.

Merryl suggested we equate 'critical' with the concept of *ijtihad*, conventionally translated as 'sustained reasoning'. What we are looking for, she argued, is 'sustained reasoning and thinking to initiate Islamic reform'. For centuries scholars have been suggesting that 'the doors of ijtihad' should be re-opened. At the beginning of the twentieth century, the Iranian thinker, Jamaluddin Afghani, and Muhammad Abduh, the Mufti of Egypt, suggested that Islamic thought needed to be upgraded. The message was echoed in *The Reconstruction of Religious Thought in Islam*, the famous book by the poet and philosopher, Muhammad Iqbal. Since then, the calls for ijtihad have been repeated endlessly. But virtually nothing has been done about it. And lack of critical thought, over centuries, has allowed extremism and obscurantism to become intrinsic in Muslim societies. We all agreed that reviving the spirit of debate and discussion, objectivity and lucid thought, was our homage to the Mutazilites, the rationalist school of Islamic thought and its great philosophers and thinkers such as al-Farabi, ibn Rushd and ibn Sina. But criticism for us was not so much about 'deconstructing' but more about enhancing the subject or object of criticism. It was about moving the discourse to a higher level. Samia suggested, repeatedly, that one of our goals should be to encourage young writers, scholars and thinkers, and equip them to solve complex, social and cultural problems of our societies. Ehsan wanted us to be equally critical of both, Muslim and the West, look at the wider world and seek to synthesise what is best and most suitable not just for Muslims but the human family as a whole. Ready-made Western answers as well as excesses of modernity and postmodernism should be put under the scalpel. Robin wanted us to promote openness, pluralism, and tolerance. We all wanted CM to be a good, engaging read. And there was a consensus that the quality of writing was very, very important.

The 'Muslim' part required less discussion. A Muslim, we all agreed, is not defined by naïve pieties, attachment to rituals, or nostalgia for bygone days. The obsession with a medial notion of 'the Shariah' and obscurantist, deathly traditionalist modes of thought had to be questioned and dispatched. The embrace of destructive modernity that suppressed or relegated life-enhancing tradition to the margins, had to be overturned. Sectarianism was as much anathema to us as fundamentalism; our aim would be to offer more inclusive and pluralistic perspectives on Islam and Muslims.

After much debate and discussion, and several meetings, which, it has to be admitted, involved some raised voices if not actual shouting, we produced a mission statement, jointly written by all of us. It was printed in the first page of the first issue:

> *Critical Muslim* is a quarterly magazine of ideas and issues showcasing ground breaking thinking on Islam and what it means to be a Muslim in a rapidly changing, interconnected world.
>
> We will be devoted to examining issues within Islam and Muslim societies, providing a Muslim perspective on the great debates of contemporary times, and promoting dialogue, cooperation and collaboration between 'Islam' and other cultures, including 'the West.' We aim to be innovative, thought-provoking and forward looking, a space for debate between Muslims, between Muslims and others, on religious, social, cultural and political issues concerning the Muslim world and Muslims in the world.
>
> What does 'Critical Muslim' mean? We are proud of our strong Muslim identity, but we do not see 'Islam' as a set of pieties and taboos. We aim to challenge traditionalist, modernist, fundamentalist and apologetic versions of Islam, and will attempt to set out new readings of religion and culture with the potential for social, cultural and political transformation of the Muslim world. Our writers may define their Muslim belonging religiously, culturally or civilisationally, and some will not 'belong' to Islam at all. *Critical Muslim* will sometimes invite writers of opposing viewpoints to debate controversial issues.
>
> We aim to appeal to both academic and non-academic readerships; and emphasise intellectual rigour, the challenge of ideas, and original thinking.
>
> In these times of change and peaceful revolutions, we choose not be a lake or a meandering river. But to be an ocean. We embrace the world with all its diversity and pluralism, complexity and chaos. We aim to explore everything

on our interconnected, shrinking planet — from religion and politics, to science, technology and culture, art and literature, philosophy and ethics, and histories and futures — and seek to move forward despite deep uncertainty and contradictions. We stand for open and critical engagement in the best tradition of Muslim intellectual inquiry.

We have, since then, been rather faithful to our mission statement; and looked hard at what thrills us about ourselves and the world, and even harder at our follies and agonies. Along the way, a number of established writers and thinkers joined us, strengthening our small team. Aamer Hussein, the amiable, considerate short story writer. Abdulwahhab El-Affendi, the ever cheerful and positive British-Sudanese academic and political scientist. The quiet and pensive, literary critic and writer Boyd Tonkin. The tall and exuberant historian of South Asia, Iftikhar Malik. The courteous and intuitive historian and writer on Arabic literature Robert Irwin. The frank and resourceful playwright and art critic Hassan Mahamdallie. The gregarious and efflorescent artist and poet Alev Adil. The celebrated poet Ruth Padel. The passionate anthropologist and cultural campaigner Leyla Jagiella. The ever reliable and erudite scholar of Islam, Jeremy Henzell-Thomas. The inquisitive guru and expert on religion Bruce Lawrence. The empathetic and

A CM Editorial Board meeting, 2014. Photo: Rehan Jamil

inventive science fiction writer Naomi Foyle. The unassuming and learned academic and former government official, Peter Mandaville. The young, buoyant emerging scholar of Islam Shanon Shah (his only fault: he laughs at all my jokes!). And the even younger, adaptable and adventurous Scott Jordan, philosopher and emerging guru. All of them joined our Board and became regular contributors, advisors and guides. (Along the way, a couple of pestiferous individuals joined and then left; but let's not go into that). We met at regular 'high tea' editorial meetings – riotous affairs full of scintillating ideas for themes and content, which were vigorously debated, some discarded, some collectively endorsed.

The first four issues caused quite a few ripples. Bulk copies of the second issue were confiscated in Malaysia: apparently, the Ministry of Home Affairs did not like 'The Idea of Islam', the title of the issue, that we were exploring. Michael, a self-effacing man with a natural ability to make deals, had secured co-publishing contracts with Oxford University Press (OUP), Pakistan; and later, with Westland Publications in India. OUP were concerned by my satirical essay on beards in *CM3: Fear and Loathing*. Criticising Muslim beards, they suggested, was an open invitation to Taliban and other extremist groups to take pot shots at them. They published three issues (1, 2, & 4), and then pulled the plug. The Indian publishers were anxious about the reaction of the government of Prime Minister Narendra Modi and his band of Hindu nationalists and extremists – and did not honour their contract. But they did publish two later issues as stand-alone books: *Food in Islam* (CM26) and *Beauty in Islam* (CM27). Quite a few eyebrows were raised by the issue *Dangerous Freethinkers* (CM12); my criticism of al-Ghazali upset a few of his devotees. As my friend Anwar Ibrahim, the Malaysian intellectual and leader of the opposition pointed out 'most of Malaysia would be shouting at you in defence of al-Ghazali'. *PostWest* (CM20) was criticised because, it turns out, we are not against the West as much as we should be! And *Futures* (CM29) became the Bible of young Muslim thinkers seriously concerned about challenges and opportunities in the coming decades. And we upset quite a few academics for rejecting their contributions; largely because they could not liberate themselves from jargon and obscurantist terminology. 'It is our stand against academic clichés', Scott declared.

We faced constant low-key resistance to the concept of long-form writing, and we were urged numerous times to make the CM pieces shorter, more bite-size. But, as Samia puts it, 'we are one of the few platforms that offers such nuanced and thoughtful expositions that require length and are not bogged down with inaccessible jargon. Our appeal and success bears witness to the appetite for deep thinking, which goes against the narrative of shrinking attention-spans of readers'. However, we are constantly thinking of ways to disseminate the ideas and articles in CM in diverse formats so as not to alienate those who feel daunted by the idea of absorbing themselves in a mass of text. This has taken shape in the form of webinars and CM launches and we will continue to attempt to engage a wider range of audiences via innovative formats without compromising on standards of 'deep critical thinking' content.

Some of our contributors have gone on to turn their CM pieces into books – most notable being Medina Whiteman's *The Invisible Muslim*, Hussein Kasvani's *Follow Me, Akhi*! and Leyla Jagiella's *Among the Eunuchs*. 'We must strive to provide contributors with the space to explore issues and topics and showcase their talent, an opportunity to make their voice heard, that doesn't really exist anywhere else', says Samia. We allow those who are often spoken about and spoken for to reclaim their biographies by championing the diversity of stories that exist within Muslim traditions and lived realities.

A couple of times we came quite close to being closed. The first time, we were rescued by the Selangor Foundation, Malaysia; the second time by Aziz Foundation, London. There has also been an attempt or two to 'influence' CM with truck load of dosh, which we have rejected, and will continue to, in no uncertain terms. But we thought ourselves rather lucky to be presented with challenges that were not fatal; they gave us the strength to become an integral and undying part of the intellectual and literary landscape of the East and the West. CM is thus certainly filling a gap out there – a gap that is almost a chasm.

How the world has changed since the first issue of CM was published! The Arab Spring turned into a severe winter. In Egypt, the secularists and liberals who joined the Islamists to topple the regime of Hosni Mubarak then turned on the democratically elected government of Mohamed Morsi and the Muslim Brotherhood and ushered in a military government even worse than the previous one. The West failed the opposition in Syria and allowed Bashar Al-Asad to turn it into a killing field. The 'war on terror', which was also a war on truth – perpetuated by presidents Bush, Clinton and Obama – has left Iraq in tatters, killed 80,000 people in Pakistan alone, almost a million in Afghanistan, and returned the long-suffering state to status quo ante. The fall of Kabul had all the hallmarks of the fall of Tehran and the fall of Saigon. When future historians write the biography of the West – both as power and concept – they will identify the last decade as the beginning of the end of Western domination.

During the 2010s, the world went genuinely postnormal: contradictory, complex and chaotic. Post-truth, a product of the 'war on terror' as much as pernicious relativism of postmodernism, arrived with a vengeance; and manufactured lies became the currency of politics, international relations, and social and cultural discourse. Social media, Big Data and Artificial Intelligence became supreme, leading to what has been called 'surveillance capitalism' where human emotions, desires, likes, hopes, and aspirations became the main commodity to be bought and sold. We could communicate instantly to millions of people; but we could not communicate with each other. The US split into two warring factions, faced an attack on Congress, and drowned itself in delusional politics and social relations. For the first time, the European Union encountered a country that wanted to leave rather than join it. Indeed, rather than a bastion of democracy, the EU has become more an incubator of fascism, given that two of its members have openly far right governments – Poland and Hungary – and around a quarter of members of the European Parliament come from far-right parties. China became the dominant economic and technological power, used AI to fuel 'the fourth industrial revolution', and transformed itself into an Orwellian state. Russia turned into the enclave of former KGB agents (who continued to do what they do best), flexed its muscles, captured Crimea, and began terrorising those who objected to its politics both internally and externally. India, the so-called 'world's biggest democracy' became a totalitarian state under a far-right, Hindu nationalist tutelage. Brazil followed. NATO became a superannuated joke. Blockchain and digital currencies allowed criminals and nefarious networks to remain anonymous, and ushered an age of cyber theft, ransomware, and digital looting. Economics became a bankrupt

Aamer Hussein and Robin Yassin-Kassab listening attentively. Photo: Rehan Jamil

discipline. We experienced climate change in real time. And, then, of course, there was the pandemic.

When the first issue of CM was published, the Middle East was facing a chaotic event. Ten years later, CM40 comes out at the same time as Afghanistan is recaptured by the Taliban.

Was the chaos in Afghanistan, President Joe Biden was asked in an 18 August 2021 interview with ABC's George Stephanopoulos, 'a failure of intelligence, planning, execution or judgement'? Biden's answer: 'it was a simple choice'. But there is nothing simple about our complex, interlocked world. It was indeed, a failure of intelligence for intelligence that does not take account of complexity and contradictions is not very intelligent. (While the Taliban were only a few miles from Kabul, the Pentagon was predicting it would take three months for them to enter the city!) It was a planning failure. For a linear plan that does not consider feedback loops and the speed with which things change is not much of a plan. Complex problems cannot be implemented in simple ways; they require complex approaches that adjust to rapidly changing situations. And sound judgement needs appreciation of the postnormal nature of our time. But retreating to simple solutions is not just an American problem; it is a global issue. We should not underestimate the incompetence of judgements based on old orthodoxies and dying paradigms.

The more things change, the more they stay the same. A particularly notable contradiction is that while events and issues move at accelerating velocity, customary cultures transform at quasi-static pace. Have the Taliban changed since they were last in power some two decades ago? Perhaps. They may have learned a thing or two from their experience. But their one-dimensional view of the world, based on an outmoded notion of 'Islamic Shariah', does not bode well. If the Taliban really want to change, they could start by changing their name: from *Taliban*, that is semi-literate students, to *Makhluq Bashariin*, decent human beings with love and compassion for other creations of God. Calling yourself Mullah Hibatullah (Terror of God'), as one Taliban chief is known, and Zabiullah (Sacrifice of God), as their spokesperson identified himself, does not generate much confidence!

We have explored various aspects of postnormal times – described as 'a noisy, chaotic, confusing world' in *The Economist* television advertisement – in the pages of CM. From the shift of power to China and Asia to the last Hurrah of the West, the emergence of populism to the new varieties of racism, transformations in personal relations to values that endure, climate change, to rethinking futures – we have highlighted their complexity, dissected their inherent contradictions, and highlighted their chaotic potential. But truth moves as slowly as a glacier; and requires patience and perseverance.

Closer to home, CM faced a shattering loss with the untimely death of Merryl Wyn Davies, who did so much, in her own inimitable but sometimes irritating way, in shaping the project. As I describe in my essay, she was an intellectual companion, penetrating critic, and loyal friend for most of my adult life. A formidable intellect, she was a highly original anthropologist, a treasure-trove of irrelevant information, a walking encyclopaedia on the Indian Ocean World, and a true devotee of classic Bollywood, particularly the films of the late Dilip Kumar, which she insisted on watching without subtitles even though she did not speak a word of Urdu. (Not quite: she knew a few expletives, which came out at appropriate times).

The civil war in Syria had a devastating impact on the family of Robin Yassin-Kassab. Distressed, he became disillusioned. 'I don't see any Islamic answers to our problems. It's fair enough to say I am disillusioned with the Muslims, though I am less disillusioned with them than I am with the media, the left (in particular), or Western (and Muslim) culture in general, which prefers its own stories to working out what's really happening. I'm also disillusioned with my own capacities to do anything about it or to engage with it more than I have', he said. He retired from CM, and moved to a remote part of Scotland, full of sheep, 'silver birches, wild cherries, ash, hazels, hawthorns, rowans, field maples, Scots pines, larch, white beams and hornbeam, a walnut, a red oak, a beech, alders, elders, and a thicket of aspens'. He calls it 'Mossland'. Aamer Hussein, who is profiled by the emerging Pakistani novelist, Taha Kehar, faced serious health issues. At one point, we feared the worse; but it turns out, he is as good at arguing with God as he is with his fellow humans. 'Despite a difficult period in his life, Aamer keeps writing'; and passing his experience and wisdom to emerging writers as Kehar's essay demonstrates.

Writing biography is a Muslim art that we can trace right back to the life of the Prophet Mohammad itself. Classical Arabic biography – known variously as *akhbar* and *sira* – began with the study of the traditions of the Prophet, collecting hadith, and examining the chain of transmitters. Al-Nadim, the tenth century bibliophile, describes the *akhbaris* as collectors of reports, genealogists and authors of biographies. They were professional experts who rose to prominence during the seventh century Umayyad period. Earlier biographies concentrated on transmitters of hadith but after the Sira of the Prophet and hadith literature became substantial, the tradition of biography shifted to scholars, theologians, jurists, poets, singers, Qur'an readers, scientists, travellers, Sufi masters and other notables. Ibn Khallikan's *Biographical Dictionary*, published in the thirteenth century, is a shining example of the Muslim biographical tradition.

Reading contemporary biographies of the Prophet, Shanon Shah finds that different biographers present the Prophet in different lights. He is portrayed as 'an environmentalist, a feminist, a human rights activist, an interfaith role model, and an instinctive democrat' as well as someone who was angry, violent, or did not care much for Jews. Whether they are written from a pious or a hostile viewpoint, all biographies of the Prophet, Shah argues, need to confront a basic problem: while there is voluminous biographical literature on the Prophet, it does not 'yield many certainties, because so little can be known for certain about the Arabian Peninsula of that era'. Shah opts for a personal relationship with the Prophet, speaking to him directly, and 'paraphrasing this advice to me today'.

Biographies can reveal as much truth as they hide. In 'The Puzzling Memoir of Hanna Diyab', Robert Irwin looks at the life of the eighteenth-century Christian Maronite who travelled to Marseille, Paris, and Versailles and worked for Antoine Galland, the translator of *The Arabian Nights*. Diyab's *The Book of Travels*, which describe his travels and doubles as a memoir of youth, raises a number of issues. 'How much do some of the most famous stories in Galland's version of the *Nights* owe to Diyab? Was he perhaps the real author of "Aladdin", "Ali Baba", and "Prince Ahmed and the Fairy Peri Banou"? Why does Diyab's narrative end so suddenly?' Irwin tackles these questions; but not all questions can be answered satisfactorily. Even DNA analysis, as Jeremy Henzell-Thomas discovers, can raise more questions than it answers. He manages to trace various strands of his DNA – '31.1% North and West European, 29.5% Irish, Scottish, Welsh, 18.6% English, 11.2% Italian, 3.5% Iberian, 6.1% Central Asian (Kazakhstan, Uzbekistan) – but, in the end, has to admit: 'our biography rests on much

Robert Irwin in a contemplatative mood. Photo: Rehan Jamil

more than genes'. Henzell-Thomas suggests that we should 'conceive the core of a biography as the extent to which it unfolds the Divine imprint within the original "text" of human nature' — what in Islamic terminology is described as *fitra*, the 'primordial disposition', 'the qualities or attributes of character which the human being has the potential to "unwrap"'.

Complex lives are not easy to unwrap; and memory is subject to selection and editing. In his article on Mohammad Asad, the Qur'an and Hadith scholar, political scientist, adventurer, and author of the classic *The Road to Mecca*, Josef Linnhoff suggests that we do not have a proper biography of Asad because he is difficult to pin down. 'He defies neat classification and our tendency to sharply categorise and define scholars', Linnhoff writes. 'Is he liberal or Islamist? Progressive or reactionary? Heretical or mainstream? In Asad we see a commitment to social liberalism alongside strident anti-secularism; Mu'tazili-esque theology alongside Zahiri legal theory'. Thus, no group has claimed him as their own. But Asad's own autobiographies are somewhat contradictory, with facts edited and changed in four different editions of *The Road to Mecca*. Focusing on historical facts, Linnhoff suggests, 'blinds us from the deeper "truths" that Asad sought to convey'; and the task of future biographers of Asad is to go 'beyond half-truth, simplification, and ignorance', to discover the true multifaceted Asad and his truly monumental achievements.

Linnhoff notes that we tend to reduce rich and complex lives into simplistic binaries. Who is the real person behind the biography? The 'I' in autobiography is always open to interpretation; and narratives of other lives, selected and abridged as they always are, seldom reveal the whole picture. And sometimes, the subject hides behind veils — *nom de plumes* being the most obvious. When novelist Bina Shah agrees to interview Algerian-French writer Yasmina Khadra, well known for such novels as *The Swallows of Kabul* and *The Sirens of Baghdad*, she discovers, to her surprise and confusion, that he is a man not a woman. Khadra explains: 'during his time in the army, he became a counterterrorism expert and wrote six books under his own name. Then the Algerian Army demanded he submit his writing for authorisation and censorship. He refused, used different pen names for eleven years, then settled upon his wife's name, Yasmina Khadra, as a tribute to her love and loyalty'.

Often what appears to be the main event presents only an illusory image; the real story is often to be found on the side-lines. 'Did I really see the Taj Mahal?', asks Boyd Tonkin? Yes, no, perhaps, and maybe. He knows that he visited the Taj Mahal in Agra and Fatehpur Sikri, the nearby great fort city that was founded as the capital of the Mughal Empire. But did he actually see the great monument; or just saw a reflection of accumulated imageries?

What really confirms the visit is the classic courtly Urdu he heard, the meat-heavy Baluchi restaurant he ate at, the *hijras* he encountered on road-side cafes, and the chants of the protestors he met. 'The memorable truth of any life-event that will come to serve as a milestone of individual biography', Tonkin concludes, 'collects around its margins, not its centre'.

Boyd Tonkin checking his photos of Taj Mahal. Photo: Rehan Jamil

Sometimes, what is written on the margins can indeed be the most important part of a biography. The off-centre bits of life narratives can have a real impact on the world and play a crucial role in shaping dialogues across cultures. When I first met Hassan Mamadallie, his life as an active anti-racist was behind him. I was co-editor of the art journal *Third Text*; he was responsible for diversity at the Arts Council, which funded the periodical. We couldn't be more different from each other: his biography was rooted in Punk and the hard left movement; mine was entrenched in conservative Islam. What brought us together was something we did not talk about initially – our similar experiences not just of racism but also the heart-breaking stories of victims that we had witnessed. We became friends only when we shared these stories, a few of which he relates in his essay. When he left the Arts Council, we began a conversation about *Critical Muslim*. His Trotskyite tendency had not left him; and we disagreed on many things. But we agreed that there was a need to promote critical thought amongst Muslims, usher Muslim societies towards embracing humanism and pluralism, and give some serious attention to our pressing social and cultural problems. We should build on the intellectual and literary foundations of Islam, not hesitate to ask difficult questions, and work for positive change, Hassan said.

Critical Muslim aims to bring what is on the margins to the forefront, transform all variety of unthought into forethought. It is a two-part process: it articulates, to rephrase French philosopher Maurice Merleau-Ponty, latent meaning and calls for further, continuous reflection; and anticipates the potential hurdles and pitfalls of the unthought of the future. The goal is to rethink Islam for contemporary times, to discover anew what it means to be Muslim in the twenty-first century. We have to create a new space, beyond postnormal times, a space that could be described as transmodern. Transmodernity is a condition that is beyond tradition and modernity, but synthesises the best of both by rejecting the domineering, arrogant inflexibility that has become essential features of both. It is a space where open, plural societies with vibrant civic institutions and organisations that transparently hold their political, social, cultural, and economic conditions up to public scrutiny, that innovate as much as they value and learn positive lessons from history and tradition, thrive. It's a place where questioning and self-criticism are the norm, and consensus emerges organically from robust open debate.

'Things change'. But they don't always change for the positive. Moreover, positive change does not come overnight. It requires multi-generational effort. *Critical Muslim* is concerned with the continuous on-going process of changing things and shaping a more appropriate and desirable future for the Muslim world – and beyond.

BIOGRAPHIES OF THE PROPHET

Shanon Shah

I am a failed vegetarian. But during my vegetarian days, I conducted extensive research and spoke to many Muslims on what is nowadays euphemistically called, after the vegetarian movement rebranded itself, a 'plant-based diet'. What delighted me in my interviews and research were the numerous examples from the life of our Beloved Prophet Muhammad suggesting that he was almost vegetarian, too. I was inspired by people who pointed me to written sources showing that the Prophet ate a mostly plant-based diet and consumed meat rarely and sparingly. The Prophet is even recorded to have admonished his followers not to let their stomachs become 'a graveyard for animals' – in some traditions, this saying is attributed to his cousin, son-in-law, and close companion Ali. If he were alive today, the Prophet would probably love hanging out with pacifist vegan environmentalists.

Or would he?

According to Barnaby Rogerson, Muhammad was, 'like every desert dweller one has ever met – passionate about meat and would eat any of the five desert meats: camel, rabbit, gazelle, chicken or mutton'. Not that the Prophet was a total carnivore. Rogerson adds that Muhammad also delighted in dates, pumpkins, melons, grapes and cucumbers – basically the 'foods of the poor'. But this was accompanied by a fondness for 'chewing meat off the bone, especially the shoulder, which he would eat in his fingers'. True, the sources abundantly record that the Prophet was no glutton – he usually ate only once a day and advised others to eat moderately. But it would seem that the jury's still out on whether he was a proto-vegetarian.

It's not my purpose to adjudicate whether Muhammad was a meat-lover or a plant-eating pioneer. Rather, it's about noticing the way in which his life can be made to tell different stories about Islam and Muslims. For example, in addition to being a potential proto-vegetarian, he also could have been a proto-feminist. Just look at how he was said to be respectful, faithful and lovingly devoted to his first wife, Khadija, right until her death. Or how his youngest wife Aisha reported that he often mended his own clothes at home.

The Prophet might have also been an interfaith champion, as seen in his regard for the Negus – the Christian ruler of Abyssinia – who offered refuge to the earliest Muslims when they were persecuted in Mecca. Upon learning of the death of the Negus years later, the Prophet said to his followers: 'this day a righteous man has died. Therefore, arise and pray for your brother Ashamah.' One can also derive a model of proto-democracy and responsive government in the way that the Prophet was said to consult his companions on important decisions.

Put it all together, and you have a Prophet who was an environmentalist, a feminist, a human rights activist, an interfaith role model, and an instinctive democrat – a paragon of modern 'liberal' values. For me, for a long time this was a supremely appealing portrayal of Muhammad.

Yet this was not the image of Muhammad I grew up with in Malaysia. Our mandatory Islamic Studies classes were filled with reminders of the Prophet's likes and dislikes. He hated women who did not cover their hair, but he loved polygamy. For ages, I actually thought a Muslim man *had* to be married to more than one wife at a time – preferably four. The Prophet also did not mind if husbands physically struck their wives for 'disobedience'. And he loved cats, hated Christians, *really* hated Jews, and was disgusted with homosexuals to the point of near speechlessness.

I grew up in the grip of an authoritarian, nationalist government which cracked down mercilessly on its critics, often justifying its actions in the name of 'true' Islam. In this context, the Prophet was conspicuously silent on the detention of political opponents, human rights activists, environmentalists, and journalists without trial. Nor did he have anything to say about torture and deaths in police custody. He also seemed to have very little insight about the inhumane treatment of refugees and indigenous peoples.

It is not that I was never taught that the Prophet was gentle, compassionate, ethical, and just. But this list of virtues felt incongruent with the other aspects of Muhammad's life that were drummed into me. I internalised this uneasy, contradictory image of the Prophet for most of my formative years. Then, just before 9/11, I started trying to unlearn and relearn Islam for myself – a process that was turbo-charged after the attacks. This is when I started voraciously reading more progressive thinkers and scholars, and discovered a welcome surprise – a gentler and more enlightened Prophet for a Muslim desperately seeking paradise.

Since then, my life has become defined by this constant rediscovery and relearning of Islam's sacred texts and the life of the Prophet. A good way of explaining this phenomenon is through the work of the French sociologist of religion, Danièle Hervieu-Léger. According to her, one way to understand the function of religion is by seeing it as an expression of collective memory – a 'chain of memory'. While this memory is shaped collectively, it also produces emotions and motivations that are intensely personal and intimate. Our individual emotions and motivations, in turn, affect us collectively too. Religion can thus become a powerfully affective ingredient in the shaping of our identities.

The chain of religious transmission, however, has been ruptured by the forces of modernity, continues Hervieu-Léger. It is not so easy anymore for collective religious memory to be sustained in an unbroken flow from generation to generation. This break has occurred at several levels, from the institutional (through official religious hierarchies, schools, and state agencies) to the interpersonal (through families, community elders, and peer groups). Some of us try to keep the chain alive but, like DNA sequences that are interrupted by exposure to chemicals, infections, or copying errors, our religious memory can and does mutate.

Did I inherit a particular sequence of mutated memories about the Prophet from disruptions in my personal history and my wider social context, including those that pre-dated my existence? The answer can be found in the clues embedded in what contemporary authors disclose as their motivations for retelling Muhammad's story.

Karen Armstrong, for example, was driven to compose her biography in the aftermath of Ayatollah Khomeini's 1989 fatwa pronouncing death for Salman Rushdie. I was eleven when the Rushdie Affair erupted. I find Armstrong's introduction to her revised, post-9/11 edition particularly moving:

> I abhorred the fatwa and believed that Rushdie had a right to publish whatever he chose, but I was disturbed by the way some of Rushdie's liberal supporters segued from a denunciation of the fatwa to an out-and-out condemnation of Islam itself that bore no relation to the facts. It seemed wrong to defend a liberal principle by reviving a medieval prejudice. We appeared to have learned nothing from the tragedy of the 1930s, when this type of bigotry made it pos-

sible for Hitler to kill six million Jews. But I realized that many Western people had no opportunity to revise their impression of Muhammad, so I decided to write a popular accessible account of his life to challenge this entrenched view.

Armstrong is not alone as a Western writer who has worked hard to correct stereotypical views of Muhammad. Yet there are differences as well as overlaps in the motivations of different writers. Armstrong, for example, is concerned with pointing out the double standards in Western liberal values as a means of challenging Islamophobia. Barnaby Rogerson's biography, first published in 2003, is also a personal quest for empathy and bridge-building but from a slightly different starting point. As he explains in his preface, knowledge of 'this path, of the details of the life of the Prophet Muhammad, is vital if one is to enter the imagination of the Muslim world'. For Maxime Rodinson, Muhammad is a case study in how the specific combination of 'historical juncture', 'psychological make-up' and 'sociological conditions' of time and place can produce lasting impact 'on a world scale'. Lesley Hazleton, meanwhile, aims for a three-dimensional, humane, warts-and-all story, because 'to elide the more controversial aspects of Muhammad's life does him no service'.

Modern Muslim writers share some of these motivations, too. Ziauddin Sardar's short biography aims 'to go beyond (Muslim) hagiography and Western stereotypes to understand Muhammad and meet a remarkable human being who made history'. Omid Safi states quite frankly that his study, published in the aftermath of the Danish Muhammad cartoons crisis, is a corrective to the West's 'Muhammad problem'.

These constitute only a sample of the many retellings of the life of Muhammad within a larger corpus of works that aim to balance sympathetic and critical perspectives of Islam. But the specific subject matter covered by different bodies of work within this corpus can illuminate different aspects of the investigation. So, while modern biographies of Muhammad rely on textual sources, they primarily focus on him as a *person* compared to, say, works that introduce Islam by starting with the Qur'an as a sacred *text*. Because of this, we often get quite personal images and character traits which differ subtly from author to author. Rodinson's Muhammad is an ambitious, formidable state-builder, whilst Sardar's is a rationalist and a pragmatic humanist. Hazleton's is a visionary mystic who was profoundly shaped by early experiences of abandonment and marginalisation. Rogerson's Muhammad is full-blooded, passionate, even romantic, while Armstrong's is a unique religious and political leader who had to rise above extraordinarily challenging circumstances. These portraits of the same person often emphasise different aspects of his character and motivations. They demonstrate Safi's contention that people imagine and remember Muhammad how they want to – one Twelver Shi'a portrait chosen by Safi to illustrate this point clearly depicts the Prophet with Persian features and dress.

This variety, however, does rely on a general consensus on the basic chronology of Muhammad's biography. Born in Mecca around 570, Muhammad grew up an orphan. He journeyed with his uncle and guardian Abu Talib to Syria in the 580s and married Khadija when he was twenty-five and she was forty in what was a loving and happy union. He began receiving the Qur'anic revelation in 610. His resulting preaching contained egalitarian currents that attracted converts among the disadvantaged and hostility from the elites. Some of his early followers sought refuge in Abyssinia in 615. Khadija and Abu Talib died in 619, the Year of Sorrow, and around two years later Muhammad experienced a mystical and miraculous Night Journey and Ascension into Heaven. He led his Meccan followers in a migration to Medina in 622. The transition to Medina in the years after Khadija's death also marked the beginning of Muhammad's multiple remarriages. The turbulent growth of the nascent Medinan polity and religious community was accompanied by difficult relationships with local Jewish tribes and continuing hostility from Mecca. This period was defined by some key battles, notably a victorious Muslim campaign at Badr in 624 followed by a disastrous one at Uhud in 625. In 627, the Meccan forces tried unsuccessfully to lay siege to Medina. In the aftermath, the Banu Qurayza, a Jewish tribe, were accused of treason. Muhammad eventually led the Muslim conquest of Mecca in 630, where he was met with negligible resistance, and died in 632.

Numerous accounts of Muhammad's life have been spun from this brief biodata which, from the early centuries of Islam, were expressed through different genres of writing. The *hadith* corpus became the home of legally significant aspects of his example, whilst the *Sira* contained longer narrative elements that are closer to modern ideas of what constitutes a biography. I've been using the term 'biography' loosely so far, when the idea of a biography for us now does not exactly map neatly onto how pre-modern authors depicted the lives of key individuals. Also, material for modern biographers is often spread across different earlier genres. To make sense of these genres in Muslim contexts, the hint is in their names. 'Hadith', meaning 'talk' or 'discourse', refers to written records of the Prophet's speech and actions, focusing primarily on his ethical and legal example. A *sira*, meanwhile, is a path through life – when it is styled *Sira*, it refers to the life of Muhammad. These genres sometimes overlap, and the material found in one genre is often commented on, summarised or expanded in an adjacent genre. This mixture is unsurprising, given that Muhammad, for his followers, was a prophet who largely taught by personal example. There are also other written genres that space does not permit me to discuss. The main point is that these early written sources still constitute the building blocks of modern biographies of Muhammad.

This straightforward account conceals a problem that all biographers of Muhammad, whether they are writing from pious or hostile viewpoints, need to confront. On one hand, in Kecia Ali's words, 'Muslims have a voluminous biographical literature' of Muhammad. On the other hand, scholars generally agree that that the 'quest for the historical Muhammad' is 'unlikely to yield many certainties, because so little can be known for certain about the Arabian Peninsula of that era'. There is thus abundant material for 'polemicists and apologists and journalists and many scholars' to keep producing biographies of the Prophet, but much of it is incredibly difficult to verify or even contextualise. Besides, the modern biographical format of Muhammad's life that we are familiar with – 'a birth-through-death narrative, which pauses at marriages, battles, and revelation' – only became standard a century or two ago. This complication is also partly why standard biographies of Muhammad now sit alongside radically revisionist studies which question even the basic outlines of early Muslim history.

To return to Hervieu-Léger's analogy of religion as a 'chain of memory' that can break and mutate, it seems as though there were always multiple chains with multiple links in the story of Muhammad. This observation connects with another aspect of Hervieu-Léger's thinking – the idea that religions are products of bricolage. Imagine this – an art assignment requires students to create an elephant out of objects that they must collect from the banks of their local river. Even though they might be using random materials – shells, pebbles, broken bits of tyre, crushed soda cans, torn shoes, and other bits of flotsam and jetsam – if they apply themselves diligently to the task, we will all probably start seeing elephants. Yet depending on each artist's personal standpoint, we might discern different interpretations of an elephant, some perhaps in protest of poaching and deforestation, others as mystical symbols of majesty. In other words, while bricolage often has a spontaneous, improvised DIY ethos at its core, it is rarely haphazard. Objects that clash or might have very little value in other contexts are brought together for a purpose. They produce something that is greater than the sum of its parts.

According to Hervieu-Léger, this capacity for improvisation was always present in virtually all religious systems – otherwise they would never have been able to invent and reinvent themselves to survive. But here's where the issue of mutated or broken memories remains relevant – in our time, increasing numbers of people are insisting on their freedom to create new understandings of religion. It is thus not religious improvisation that is new, but the proliferation of demands from people of their *right* to produce and reproduce religious bricolage.

It is no wonder that we now have a plethora of narratives that portray Muhammad as an environmentalist, a state or empire builder, an animal rights activist, a human rights activist, an authoritarian theocrat, a warmonger, a democrat, a proto-feminist, a misogynist, a socialist, a capitalist, an anti-Semite, an anti-racist, an interfaith role model, a religious mystic, and a dogmatic legalist, among others. This list might sound wildly contradictory, but each of these labels can be justified based on the earliest sources. Characterisations of a cuddly Muhammad can thus be produced just as easily and validly as representations of a supposedly cruel Muhammad. Upon returning my copy of Safi's *Memories of Muhammad*, a few years ago, a progressive Church of England vicar quipped to me good-naturedly, 'he was practically an Anglican, wasn't he?'

We can choose to find this distressing because it's so difficult to identify the 'real' Muhammad, or liberating because it's so difficult to identify the 'real' Muhammad. What's comforting, to me, is that this dilemma is not something new even within Islam. As far back as the fourteenth century, the great Hanbali jurist and polymath Ibn Qayyim al-Jawziyya (d. 1350) observed, regarding the contradictory examples of Muhammad contained in the *sirah*: 'Thus, if one faction of the Muslim community were to claim in argument to possess these virtues [of the Prophet] to the exclusion of other factions or groups, another faction can appeal to the same set of virtues to make a similar claim.'

Ibn Qayyim goes on to list these different 'factions' that can lay claim to Muhammad's example, including 'those who go on raids and *jihad*', 'the poor and patient man', 'the rich and grateful man', 'the humble and self-restrained', and 'the mighty and powerful'. It is a lengthy list, but it seems to hold up quite well. For example: 'If one who eats rough food such as barley bread and vinegar were to cite his example, so too can it be cited by one who eats delicious food like grilled meat, sweetmeats, fruits, melons and so forth.' Or here's one for contemporary feminists and anti-feminists to slug it out: 'If his example is used by one who is kind and meek with his womenfolk, so too can it be used by one who disciplines them, causes them pain, divorces them, abandons them or gives them the choice to stay or to leave.' One more: 'If his example is cited by one who avoids intercourse with women in menstruation or during the fast, so too can it be used by one who embraces his menstruating wife but without intercourse or kisses his wife while fasting.' Finally, my favourite as someone who grew up in a country where the ruling regime and its largest opposition were constantly trying to out-Islamise each other: 'If his example is cited by one who shows mercy to sinners in due measure, so too can it be used by one who executes the commands of God, cutting off the thief's hand, stoning the adulterous and flogging the wine drinker.'

Ibn Qayyim closes this list by declaring neither the 'poor and patient people' nor 'the rich and grateful' as rightful claimants to the Prophet's example. Instead, he exhorts: 'those who have the highest claim to him are the most knowledgeable about his life and example, and who follow that example most closely.' This sounds like good advice, but in the light of all we know about the contradictions and uncertainties in Muhammad's biographical material, it reads like a cop-out. What does one have to do? Trawl through every single work of *Sira* or modern biography to be counted as 'most knowledgeable'?

Luckily for us, we can be guided and oriented by the critical modern scholars who have done the hard work of trawling through the volumes upon volumes of biographies of Muhammad, old and new. That is, if we really want critical guidance and orientation. I have already referred to the works of Omid Safi and Kecia Ali, with their reflexive examinations of the corpus of modern and traditional biographies of Muhammad. And so, while many contemporary biographers of Muhammad might be compelled to contextualise his story as a corrective to dominant anti-Muslim stereotypes, scholars such as Ali and Safi help to contextualise these contextualisations. For example, Ali has made me more attentive to the symbolic significance of details in Muhammad's biography that I had previously taken for granted. Take the age gap between him and his first wife, Khadija, whom the sources say was fifteen years older and whom Muhammad married when he was twenty-five. There is room for speculation here, with some sources suggesting that Muhammad might have been twenty-one and Khadija twenty-eight at the time of marriage, or that Muhammad was thirty and Khadija was forty. But the fifteen-year age gap is generally not disputed in conventional narratives. Contemporary apologetic biographies often use this 'fact' to make certain pseudo-feminist claims about Muhammad's character, usually as 'evidence that he was not consumed by lust and that he was comfortable with a powerful woman'.

Why forty, though? Ali explains:

> As anyone familiar with the biblical tradition knows, forty is a potent number. In the Hebrew bible, the flood lasts forty days, the Israelites wander in the wilderness for forty years. Jesus fasts forty days and forty nights, according to the Gospel of Matthew, before the devil tempts him. And in Muslim tradition, Muhammad is usually said to have been forty when he received the first revelation from Gabriel in the cave on Mount Hira (though a few versions put him at forty-three). One scholar suggests that the Prophet's age at revelation relies on the symbolic significance of the number forty: 'in matters involving measurement of time, this usage of "forty" is clearly devoid of specific chronological content.'

The symbolic richness of 'forty' probably also applies to Khadija. According to Ali, we can safely assume that early *Sira* authors 'were aware of the symbolic resonance of forty and, further, that they expected their readers to be aware of it as well'. This age symbolism is even more potent when it comes to the age of Muhammad's youngest wife, Aisha. According to the most revered Sunni hadith collections by Bukhari and Muslim, she was six or seven at the time of her marriage – Muhammad was fifty-three – and nine at consummation. For early Muslims, determining Aisha's age at marriage was significant because she proved to be a controversial figure later in her life. She is recorded as being envious and dismissive towards the late Khadija and fractious towards some members of the Prophet's family, and she directly challenged Muhammad on many other matters. There is also the infamous 'affair of the necklace', where she was basically suspected of being unfaithful to the Prophet and which occasioned the revelation of a key Qur'anic verse that exonerated her. Ironically, this same verse has become the basis for draconian 'Islamic' legal punishment of women accused of adultery in modern jurisdictions such as Nigeria, Pakistan, and Malaysia.

For early Sunni biographers, Aisha's age at marriage thus needed to symbolise her virginity and purity. Yet, while it preoccupied early Muslim scholars, it did not seem to discombobulate later Muslims. Neither did it drive medieval or early modern anti-Muslim polemics by Christian writers. They were more bothered by Muhammad's polygamous marriages, which they regarded as proof of his depraved lust *and* political duplicity. As recently as the 1970s and 1980s, there were very few biographies that were overly perturbed by Aisha's age at marriage.

It is the colonial encounter that planted the seeds of contention about Aisha's age. British attempts to impose family laws, including a minimum age of marriage, were resisted in parts of the Empire by Muslim activists who referred to Aisha's age as a way of exposing this interference with religious law. In turn, modern Orientalists became increasingly preoccupied with Aisha's status as a minor and their counter-arguments started picking up steam, eventually providing fodder for some truly nasty Islamophobic stereotypes of Muhammad today. I should know, because this is what caught me off guard a few years ago when I was a volunteer usher at an event at Conway Hall in London.

This was an evening debate between two Muslim speakers and two secular humanists. Before the event started, I was providing support alongside another Muslim volunteer at an information booth set up by a Muslim charity. A white English man in his fifties approached us and started grilling me about what the charity stood for. Did we, for example, work with some of the mainstream Muslim organisations that he rattled off his tongue and dismissed as 'Islamofascists'? Whenever I tried to answer in more than a short phrase, he called me an 'apologist'. Eventually, in a moment of weakness, I pulled rank by telling him I had a doctorate in the sociology of religion and knew what I was talking about. He challenged me even further, but only backed down when I explained to him the basic difference between theology and social science. While I maintained composure, I was quite shaken on the inside. My fellow volunteer then gave me a big hug and whispered, 'See the badge he's wearing?' I glanced furtively and saw what it said: 'Muhammad was a paedophile.'

My skin crawled. I wanted to break through the crowd, grab that man by the collar and yell at his face that he was a sickening Islamophobe. In hindsight, I was probably also yelling at myself for letting him rattle me. But why did he get to me? Probably because this brief encounter encapsulated what the anthropologists John and Jean Comaroff have referred to as 'the colonisation of consciousness and the consciousness of colonisation'. The Comaroffs acknowledge that for colonial conquest to work, the material subjugation of colonised populations – whether through armed incursions or exploitative trade – is often guided by an ideology that justifies, and even sanctifies, colonialism. This is the stuff of the 'battle for hearts and minds', a leitmotif that accompanies military interventions even to this day. The question is, in this cognitive and affective battle, what happens to our *consciousness* as individuals and collectively as a community? Looking at the role of evangelical Christian missionaries in South Africa, the Comaroffs argue that colonial encounters did produce large-scale transformations of the consciousness of colonised populations, but often through the accumulation of mundane conversations about everyday life.

Take, for example, the battle for water between Protestant missionaries and colonial administrators on one side and Tswana communities on the other. White Protestant settlers wanted to create a Christian peasantry – a 'lost British yeomanry' – to revive and enliven the 'desolate vineyard' of Africa. They also had to grow enough produce for their own survival. They thus started digging wells and trenches to irrigate their own fenced gardens, which set them at odds with local Tswana values and practices. For the Tswana, water was a scarce resource that, along with land, was distributed by the chief to households where women, as primary producers, had direct control over them. Tswana resistance to these disruptive settler practices included stealing their fruits and sabotaging the Europeans' efforts at watering their gardens.

This battle over material resources raged alongside an ontological struggle, since Tswana cosmology also included a repertoire of symbols and rituals that organised the management of water. This is where the European colonisers zoned in on Tswana rites of rainmaking as emblematic of 'superstition'. Missionaries and colonial administrators started regarding rainmakers as 'inveterate enemies' of Christianity and sought to eradicate the practice entirely. The stage was thus set for an existential debate, grounded by European 'reason', which produced a legitimation crisis for the Tswana. A brief excerpt between Dr Livingstone's debate with a local Kwena 'rain doctor' gives us a flavour of the exchange:

> Medical Doctor: So you really believe that you can command the clouds? I think that can be done by God alone.

Rain Doctor: We both believe the very same thing. It is God that makes the rain, but I pray to him by means of these medicines, and, the rain coming, of course it is then mine. It was I who made it for the Bakwains [Kwena] for many years...; through my wisdom, too their women became fat and shining. Ask them; they will tell you the same as I do.

Medical Doctor: But we are distinctly told in the parting words of our Saviour that we can pray to God acceptably in his name alone, and not by means of medicines.

The discussion continues, with Livingstone (the Medical Doctor) constantly putting the Rain Doctor on the back foot. The Rain Doctor tries his best to respond, yet cannot help but be drawn into the parameters of the debate which has been set by Livingstone. In recreating this dialogue, Livingstone presents himself almost as a reluctant spokesman for God and science. Yet the use of the word 'Doctor' to describe both his position and his opponent's is meant to indicate that this is a debate that is being waged on equal ontological ground. This framing of the story suggests that debates like these are what persuaded colonised peoples, despite the onslaught of colonisation, that it was worth pursuing a conversation with the Europeans and to try to acquire their superior technologies and practices.

My consciousness, too, has been dominated by conversations such as these about Islam. For rainmaking, substitute thorny issues such as Aisha's age at marriage, Muhammad's multiple marriages, the assassinations of poets who undermined Muhammad, and the killing of the Banu Qurayza. Growing up in an authoritarian, heavily censored religious environment in Malaysia, these troublesome 'facts' were transmitted via osmosis, albeit one-sidedly, through numerous channels – in my Islamic Studies lessons in school, in the government-controlled mass media, and in everyday conversations with extended family members, classmates and friends. Since moving to Britain more than a decade ago, I find that they are even more nakedly expressed here. Again, in the mass media, at the workplace, in dinner party conversations, in popular culture and literature, even amongst people I have come to regard as friends and extended family.

Often these encounters are merely annoyances, like a mosquito bite or a papercut. Rarely do they erupt into explicit showdowns with people wearing obnoxious badges. But even when I have recovered from the bruises of these more dramatic showdowns, the psychological papercuts remain a fixture of my existence. Sometimes I wonder whether I am also cutting myself because, like the Tswana, I too am often on the backfoot when I am interrogated about Muhammad's supposed violence, warmongering, anti-Semitism, homophobia, misogyny, lust – take your pick. And I find it hard to push these thoughts out of my consciousness even when I am in the safety of my own home. At times, I worry that one day I will go insane or die from a million papercuts.

Instead of spiralling into despair and self-loathing, I remind myself of three things now. First, I am and always have been a religious bricoleur. Second, there is no point being afraid or ashamed of this – the chain of religious memory was always already broken and it mutated long before I was born. Third, religious bricolage does not happen in a political vacuum. And – though I constantly get overwhelmed by arguments and counter-arguments about Islam, Islamophobia, and (post)colonialism – I have a choice in what I want to fashion out of my religious bricolage.

Perhaps the papercuts are not weakening me, but rather providing me with an invisible immunity. This is an interesting thought, considering that the very things about Muhammad's biography that vex me are described by Tarif Khalidi as 'antibodies' within the *Sira*. According to Khalidi, the first *Sira* writers incorporated 'a number of counter-stories or counter-narratives that cast a shadow of doubt over the light, purity, attestation, and temptation stories' that marked Muhammad's prophethood. This can be confusing for a modern reader of early *Sira*, who will probably 'be struck by its very rich texture, which preserves many reports about Muhammad without excising them even when they were considered false'.

Khalidi uses the term 'antibodies' to refer to 'foreign substances inside a body of texts whose obvious objective is otherwise to celebrate and glorify the Prophet of Islam'. We find these antibodies mostly in the *Sira*, whereas the hadith corpus 'gives us a far more uniform version of what Muhammad said or did'. Why did early *Sira* writers do this? Khalidi argues that, in the nascent Muslim community, these writers saw themselves as historians who erred on the side of inclusiveness. Whether or not individual writers thought that a particular incident was probable or favourable, they would include it because their first duty was to transmit the story of the Prophet as comprehensively as possible. For them, 'accepting what was transmitted was a sign of trustworthiness in a historian'. Respecting the Prophet and his followers meant demonstrating 'total honesty in transmission'. Besides, these *Sira* writers would also be aware of contemporaneous Biblical stories and contemporaries which showed that 'the lives of earlier prophets were also not entirely free of "lapses"'. Objectionable or unfavourable episodes in Muhammad's life story were thus part of the 'lapses' that marked the lives of all prophets. We must also remember that these early *Sira* writers took for granted the preponderance of the supernatural. Hence, episodes that seem bizarre or disagreeable to us as modern readers were acceptable to these early historians because they were operating within a different framework of evidence and causality.

The concept of 'antibodies', to me at least, provides a way of retracing our steps in how contemporary images and impressions of Muhammad have been informed by images and impressions from previous periods in history. Foundational to my memories of Muhammad has been the Islamist obsession with defending every uncomfortable aspect of his life, from his polygamous marriages to his supposed violence. This, in turn, is a collective response to Orientalist and colonialist polemics that seized upon the existence of these antibodies and multiplied them. I must add that the work of Orientalists is not uniform, either. Some of them drew upon studies of Muhammad as a polemical device to criticise contemporary developments within Western Protestantism or Catholicism. Others saw this as a parallel endeavour in their quest for the historical Jesus, which was fraught with complexity, too. On the whole, however, the Orientalists' attention to antibodies in the *Sira* was also nothing new – Muslims, from the earliest times, were always uncomfortable with the existence of these antibodies. And I cannot describe how freeing it is to acknowledge that I am not alone in my ambivalence about some aspects of Muhammad's biography, and that it does not make me any less Muslim. Nor does it make me a neo-colonial stooge. In fact, it puts me in some very good Islamic company, whether Sunni or Shi'a, 'mystical' or 'rationalist', and traditional or modern.

It is almost as though I have found some of the missing links in my chain of memory, although nowhere near all of them. But this is what has renewed my excitement in this personal, continually unfolding journey of religious bricolage. It is the *Sira* antibodies – or rather, the continuous tradition within Islam of grappling with these antibodies – that are the key to decolonising and reinvigorating my relationship with my prophet.

To me, one of the profoundest sayings attributed to Muhammad is captured in the modern *Sira* classic by Martin Lings:

During the return march to Medina after the victories of Mecca and Hunayn the Prophet said to some of his Companions: 'We have returned from the Lesser Holy War to the Greater Holy War,' And when one of them asked: 'What is the Greater Holy War, O Messenger of God?' he answered: 'The war against the soul.'

When I was growing up, this saying was sometimes used in my Islamic Studies classes to discipline the raging hormones of adolescent boys. Not always, but often enough for me to remember this version of it. The word that is rendered here as 'soul' is 'nafs' in Arabic, which was adopted into the Malay language as 'nafsu'. And *nafsu*, in its modern usage, accentuates lust and sensual desire as predominant characteristics of the lower soul. Basically, the Greater Jihad is to be fought against one's own sexual appetite.

Later, in my post-9/11 rediscovery of more progressive interpretations of Islam, I came across this quote by writers who used it to debunk the idea of *jihad* as violent warfare. The Greater Jihad, according to this quote, was about self-improvement and spiritual growth. I still have a lot of sympathy for this interpretation, but with renewed appreciation in the light of my reflection on *Sira* antibodies. Because if we are to accept the conventional episodes in canonical versions of Muhammad's life story, then the man who said this was probably not just reflecting upon a military campaign. By the time he said this, Muhammad had endured the deaths not only of Khadija and Abu Talib, but had buried several of his own children who died as young adults or in early childhood. This was the same man who, the sources tell us, had no mercy for the Banu Qurayza or the poets who slandered him. This is the same man whose doubts about the faithfulness of his youngest wife, Aisha, distressed him and became immortalised in the Qur'an. And this is the same man who led military campaigns in which many of his followers were brutally butchered and in which they committed some pretty horrific killings, too.

Within this context, here's how I hear him paraphrasing this advice to me today:

'Now that you've smacked down the idiot with the badge saying I'm a paedophile, it's time to do the True Work.' I ask: 'What is the True Work?' He answers: 'The True Work of confronting your inner demons. Your saboteur. Your lapses and your mistakes. Your big, messy, wonderful spirituality and humanity.' I ask: 'How do you know?' He answers: 'Because I've been there, too.'

MERRYL

Ziauddin Sardar

Illustrated by Zafar Abbas Malik

1.

'Ye, ye. Said Qi. Systi?'.

Those fortunate enough to have met Merryl Wyn Davies instantly noticed certain features of her towering personality. She was seldom seen, much like her favourite poet T S Eliot, without a cigarette in her hand; and subscribed to the Oscar Wilde dictum, that a cigarette is the most perfect of all the perfect pleasures. She was a habitual forty cigarettes – increased to sixty towards the end of her life – a day person; for her, smoking was an integral part of the very act of thinking and writing, a precursor to a sparkling conversation. And a conversation with Merryl was a noteworthy experience. She would always start with a compliment, move on to small talk, listen with considerable attention, and then ask a string of penetrating questions. You would be drawn, by her considerable wit and charm, into an elaborate and meaningful discussion. The conversation could easily lead to her Welsh origins; and the exchange would begin to simmer.

Merryl was born in 1949 in South Wales, more specifically Merthyr Tydfil, which she describes as 'the very hub and centre of the universe'. She was from a family of mixed religious heritage. Her maternal grandfather was Catholic; her maternal grandmother was a Welsh Congregationalist. And they ran away to get married in an Anglican church. Her father, John Haydon Davies, was a hospital administrator; and her mother, Maisey Davies, worked at the local labour exchange (which later become 'Job Centres') as a Disablement Resettlement Officer. The parents divorced when Merryl was still very young; and she never heard from her father or knew much about him. She and her brother, Peter, were brought up by their mother. Later, Maisey became the Director of Merthyr Tydfil Institute for the Blind and edited the Institute's *Talking Newspaper*, often rolling in both Merryl and Peter to write stories for the paper. Merryl was sent to the nearby Cwmbran High School, then located in the sixteenth-century Cwmbran Castle, from where she went to University College, London, to read social anthropology.

She was 'forever Welsh'. 'Wales', as Merryl often said, 'is the land of my fathers', which is also the opening line of the official national anthem. There are hills and mountains and valleys aplenty, and waterfalls and impressive views. But the local speciality is horizontal rain with a devilish

ability to enter up inside one's protective outer garments. It is both, as Tom
Jones sings, 'the green green grass of home', and 'wild Wales'. As she
explained in one of her columns in *Critical Muslim*,

> Wild or benign in myth and legend as well as real history this land is imbued
> with particular meaning: *hiraeth*, an untranslatable condition compounded of
> endless yearning, loving and longing, presence and absence, that underpins one's
> relationship to home and transmutes it into a moral, even some say 'religious'
> landscape. To the Welsh our land is always old and little and oh so meaningful
> because it is history in every sense of the word and this history is an ever-present
> witness to the belonging of this people to this place. The clouds of witness, all
> who have gone before, are ever with us and this being Wales they frequently
> shower and deluge us not only with rain but also with moral judgement.

Her deep sense of history, and truly vast range of historical knowledge, as
well as her concern for social justice and moral acumen, not to say her
anger at the inequalities she saw all around her, owed a great deal to her
Welsh background.

Merthyr Tydfil, Merryl would tell anyone listening, played an important
part in the industrial revolution. It was 'the very hub and centre of the
universe' because the city was the centre of the world's iron making industry
that propelled the industrial revolution. Merthyr was close to reserves of
iron ore, coal, limestone, and water, all of which made it the ideal site for
iron works. During the eighteenth and nineteenth centuries, Merthyr Tydfil
was an engine of innovation: the ground-breaking puddling method for
making wrought iron was developed in the city and acquired international
acclaim as 'the Welsh method', the famous 'Pen-y-darren' locomotive which
led to steam-powered railway was invented in Merthyr, and iron and steel
from Merthyr was exported throughout the British Empire. The iron works
and coal mines were a significant source of employment for the city, which
also saw a major uprising in 1831 against the exploitative practices and
lower wages of workers imposed by iron masters.

The city began to lose its distinction as the world's top 'Iron and Steel
Town' towards the end of the nineteenth century, and coal mines began to
close in the 1920s. The closure of steel and iron works, as well as well-
established collieries, ushered a rapid decline after the Second World War.
Much of Merryl's anger stemmed from the fact that, as she put it, 'Merthyr

was left to rot'. From the 1990s onwards, the city has been regarded amongst the worst places to live. Long term unemployment has remained persistently high and the city suffers from serious economic disadvantage.

The 'industrial brutalism', as she called it, also left its mark on Merthyr, and Merryl, through other means. She remembered and frequently recalled the fateful day of 21 October 1966. She was 17, working on the local newspaper *The Merthyr Express*, before going off to the University. 'The day of the Aberfan disaster', she wrote, 'has been, and I presume always will be, alive in my mind. It is the day when one of those naked mountains of spoil turned liquid and rampaged down the mountainside to consume all the houses in its path and the village junior school'. The disaster was caused by the collapse of a colliery spoil tip on a mountain slope above Aberfan, near Merthyr Tydfil. A week of heavy rain caused the slurry to slide downhill and engulf Pantglas Junior School and other buildings, killing 116 children and 28 adults. 'An army of volunteers digging for days where there could be no hope. Their only triumph the heart-rending discovery of little broken bodies'. I saw the volunteers digging, Merryl said: 'their look will haunt me all my days'.

Then, there was the aftermath of the Chernobyl nuclear disaster of April 1986, when northern uplands of Wales began to 'glow in the dark'. 'This remarkable feat of luminescence', Merryl wrote, 'is achieved courtesy of Chernobyl. When the radioactive cloud made its demon passage over the hills of my homeland it met that regular feature of the climate, persistent rain. This enabled large amounts of its devastating debris to make a new home on the hills and valley of my green and pleasant land'. Sheep could no longer graze safely. The livelihood of hundreds of farmers was put in peril. And local butchers, the home-grown gossip had it, had to keep Geiger counters in their shops!

The trials and turbulations of Merthyr Tydfil were written on Merryl's body. But she also imbibed the Welsh tradition of wry black humour for making sure that good cheer in adversity does not let the essence of the issue fade from the mind. She blamed England for the agonies of Merthyr – 'Wales was', after all, 'the first place to be colonised by the English'. And the English had to pay for their uncouth behaviour, cruelty and oppression, and 'foul calumnies'. Despite her overflowing love for Merthyr and all things Welsh, Merryl was not a Welsh nationalist – except when it came to rugby. She was, quite simply, a rugby fanatic; and it was on the rugby field that merciless revenge had to be taken on England, a price extracted for historic injustices. On matters of rugby, she would declare, 'I am Welsh and engage my nationalist loyalties fully'! The Welsh rugby team was 'my boys' who play rugby like angels. When the fifteen fine Welshmen with red jerseys took the field, Merryl became a fuming bull, cheering them full throated, with all the power of her nicotine-filled lungs. 'The object of the exercise', she declared,

> is to beat the English. It being a well-known dictum of old Welsh wisdom that the English deserve to be beaten, comprehensively and often. And they always are. As the saying goes, a Welsh team never loses. The other side only scores more points. Which is a rather profound statement, if you pause to reflect. For what a rugby international does is confirm the identity of a people, its culture and sense of being, this being a nation that has no formal nationhood, just a rugby team to hang on to. They play five times a year and it is that glorious sense of belonging, community, nostalgia and home which triumphs every time. It's a decent kind of nationalism, it may bruise the odd person, dislocate an odd shoulder and dislodge a few teeth but it never killed anyone by design, or sought to dominate anyone beyond putting a few more points on the score-board. It uplifts the spirit and leaves one free to be an internationalist, but one who knows where home is, for the rest of the year.

Home was a place she regularly returned to throughout her life. She was an inveterate traveller; and there were numerous other cultures to explore. While still at university, she set out with a group of students and friends to cross the Sahara Desert. It was 1968. The old caravan routes, following a series of reliable wells, circumventing difficult terrain like mountain ranges or sand seas, were still in evidence. The expedition travelled from Morocco and Western Sahara to Mauritania. It was a gruelling and dangerous track. The following year she went to Nigeria where she spent several weeks doing fieldwork. It was during these trips that she developed a passion for collecting, what she called, '*objets*'. She returns loaded with spears, drums, masks, pottery, and many other items of ethnographic variety.

After university, she went back home to join *The Merthyr Express* as a reporter before moving on to the morning radio news magazine programme *Good Morning Wales* at BBC Cymru Wales Radio. A couple of years later, she joined the BBC TV Religious programmes to begin 'a career of anthropology with pay'. She worked on the award-winning documentary series *Everyman*, which explored difficult moral issues. Merryl also worked on *Heart of the Matter*, a debate series which aired alternately with *Everyman*, and dealt with current ethical and moral controversies. Later, she moved to *Global Report*, which dealt with issues of poverty and underdevelopment in developing countries. All of this involved extensive travel which provided opportunities to acquire ever more '*objets*'.

2.

I met Merryl in April 1980 when she was living in Golders Green, London. I had just moved to nearby Colindale. On the fateful day of our meeting, she was filming an episode of *Heart of the Matter* on the Sharia at the London Central Mosque in Regent's Park. The city was going through a tumultuous period. The Iranian Embassy was under siege; gunmen had taken twenty-six people hostage, including a couple of my friends. I went to the Mosque both to pick up some news of the siege and see Zaki Badawi, Egyptian scholar of Islam and my former colleague from the Hajj Research Centre, who was now the Director of the Islamic Cultural Centre and chief Imam of the London Central Mosque. I arrived right in the middle of the shoot.

It was not going well. We introduced ourselves to each other. Merryl paused after hearing my name. 'Are you', she said, 'the author of *The Future of Muslim Civilization?*'. 'The very same', I confirmed. She appeared excited. 'I have just finished reading it', she said. There was a big beam on her face, suggesting all her problems were over. 'Would you', she said and paused, 'could you', another long pause, 'possibly', yet another pause, 'sit in the discussion and steer it in a more positive direction?'. I was reluctant. 'Muslims', Merryl explained, 'spend a lot of time trying to justify the unjustifiable and end up sounding as if they are defending the indefensible'. I joined the discussion. But Badawi, who I often referred to as 'the luminary', would not allow anyone to shine. My efforts were futile. Merryl and I exchanged contact details and agreed to be in touch.

A few months later she rang to ask for a favour. Would I help her to convert to Islam? Why would you want to do that? I remember asking her. I have never thought of myself as a *dai* – someone who goes around preaching and inviting people to convert, or as they used to say in those days, and perhaps still do, 'revert'. To invite people to 'all that is good', as the Qur'an says (3:104), you have to be good yourself. And I never saw myself as good in any way.

So, why me, I enquired. Because, Merryl answered, 'I share your vision of Islam as expressed in *The Future of Muslim Civilization*'. Oh God, I murmured to myself, this is going to be rather tiresome – best to disengage. I advised her to think again, and forget about it if at all possible.

For the first time, and not for the last time, Merryl totally rejected my advice. A couple of weeks later, she went to Regent's Mosque to see Zaki Badawi, who performed the necessary ritual.

Soon afterwards, she became a regular visitor to our house. She loved my wife Saliha's cooking – *daal* was her favourite, 'to die for' she would announce – and we would eat and talk for hours. I discovered, like me, Merryl wasn't particularly strong on rituals. She was brought up on once a week visits to the chapel, and that was about as much ritual as she could take. (Although she was big on Christmas). She covered her hair for a few months and then decided wearing the scarf was not for her. She would begin fasting during Ramadan enthusiastically but would lose the resolve half way. We both agreed that the God of Islam was an argumentative God. He wanted us to argue back; that's why He raised questions for us to wrestle with. 'Islam is about finding a way to ask questions', she said. But we also had our differences. I was concerned with the future; she was passionate about history. I was interested in how things change and how do we adjust to change. Her interest was diametrically opposite: she was focussed on what does not change, what stays the same, the 'ever present history', and how often history repeats itself. I talked about shifting values; she was insistent on 'enduring values'. The differences became a source of constant tension between us.

Merryl did not like people to ask her why she embraced Islam. But when people insisted, she would answer:

> as a convert to Islam, I have encountered integration. For me it has been a question of integrating Islam within myself (an incomplete process) and myself into the Muslim community. I have never understood Islam requires the abolition of my 'Britishness', or to suggest that the only authentic way to be a Muslim is to become the very model of a Pakistani or Arab. Islam has opened my eyes to the possibilities of living and making sense of the only environment I know, the only one in which I have the opportunity to live Islam: contemporary Britain.

Islam was, for Merryl, all about asking questions: of herself, the Muslim community, and the world. It provided her the framework in which to understand both the questions and try to generate constructive answers. Faith, for her, was a process – a process of self-definition - and 'a schooling in reason'. But to reason requires knowledge, for 'reason does not help unless you know something to reason with'. That is why, we need greater knowledge of who we are, where we are heading, where do we actually wish to go, and the diversity of what we think. She saw herself as 'a fully paid-up member' of the Muslim community. As she stated in an Annual Community Relations Lecture at Kensington and Chelsea Council,

> I, in a sense define part of the diversity that exists within the Muslim community in Britain and worldwide. But one of the other things that I also define is how much I see Islam as belonging here in Britain and being part of the landscape of Britain because what I understand of Islam as a faith is that it calls us to engage with the community where we live. It is the means by which we articulate what is enduring with what is temporal and what is here around us. That is why faith for me is the bedrock of my identity.

We talked endlessly about identity, multiculturalism, the plight of Muslims, the western representation of Islam, and had heated discussions on the Sharia. She was particularly concerned about the meaning of definitional terms, 'the naming of categories'. When Muslims use contemporary modernist terms, they often say things they do not actually mean or believe. When using traditional language, the terms and concepts of Islamic convention, different people mean different things by using the same language. The overriding example, she asserted, the lodestone for all Muslims, is Sharia. 'In essence, all Islamic discourse today as it ever was is about the meaning of, organisation, and operation of Sharia. But the question is what do people mean by Sharia, what does it include, what should it include, how do they wish to see it organised and operated in contemporary terms'. Muslims see the Sharia as a systematic view of Islam, as the body of principles, precepts, and methodology, she would roar, but what does this mean in the circumstances of the contemporary world?

The contemporary world also made its demands on me. In 1982, I joined London Weekend Television (LWT), to work as a reporter on *Eastern Eye* – an hour-long fortnightly programme on British Asian issues, broadcast on the newly established Channel 4. Meanwhile, Merryl decided to go on a long trip to the US, travelling coast to coast, by National Express. She was exhausted on her return, but that did not stop her from passing on valuable advice. She would watch each episode of *Eastern Eye* with a critical eye and then ring with her suggestions. Don't wear a patterned tie on a checkered shirt, when doing a piece to camera your eye line should be directed at the bottom of the camera lens, and, for Heaven's sake, do something about your hair (I am still working on it). Eventually, she suggested that we should do a few programmes together.

The following year she persuaded the BBC to commission a series of four half-hour shows 'exploring the way Muslims understand their religion'. It examined the key concepts of Islam, such as *tawheed* and *khalifa*, in conversation with noted Muslim scholars. Merryl worked to transform me as best as she could, selected the appropriate shirt and ties for me to wear, and forced me to get a haircut under her supervisions. The publicity shot for *Encounters with Islam*, which was broadcast in July 1984, is the only photograph of my good self where I look reasonably handsome.

Our next project was 'Inside Islam', a major series of six hour-long shows, to be filmed all over the Muslim world. Merryl travelled extensively researching the series, and we worked furiously on the scripts. Just when we were ready to start filming, the editor who had commissioned the series left for more lucrative pastures. His replacement had serious issues with me. I did not go to the right university. My accent was not suitable for the BBC. And, most importantly, a series of programmes on Islam could not be written and presented by someone who was himself a Muslim, for he could not be objective enough. The show was cancelled. Merryl was shattered.

She left the BBC soon afterwards. But it wasn't just the cancellation of 'Inside Islam' that upset her. She became disillusioned with the BBC when working on *Global Report*, where alternatives to the standard western development paradigms were never really explored. While working as a researcher on a particular programme, the purpose of which was to take an alternative view of what is development and how it can best be achieved, she found herself at odds with the producer, who was anxious to focus on women's emancipation. She was asked to find a good human story, a girl about to go off to university wrestling with family problems and cultural oppression – that amounted to a searing critique of the problem of women in the Third World. 'The only trouble', Merryl wrote, we were in Sri Lanka, the first country in the world ever to have a female head of government, where women have always had property rights, where female education is proportionally higher than anywhere else in the Third World and goes on proportionally longer. One can try and tell them that when staying in the village one was treated to long discourses on the problems of the new irrigation scheme, from two large and vociferous ladies while the seven-stone weakling male head of the household said not a word. But in the nearby tourist hotel the oppression of the women was all the rage. And that was the story they filmed. A view of development not so much found in the field as made in western ideas of what development ought to be about.

The independence of the BBC, Merryl declared,

is a polite fiction. How can an institution which champions, upholds and extolls and presents the hagiography of the British nation as beloved of the Oxbridge Englishmen ever be seen as intent on espousing ideas and attitudes dedicated to their overthrow? Especially at a time when it is trying to justify its existence to secure an increase of its funding which is set by – you guessed it – the government.

The reality of the polite fiction at the BBC works because the majority of those who work for it are genuine clones, true scions of the Oxbridge English, usually complete with public school background. Men and women who innately know the language of the raised eyebrow, the vague frown and can follow the gist of an unspoken firm intention without ever needing to ask questions or demand explanation. The whole system works this way, self-censorship hand in hand with understanding the nods and winks of what is and is not quite the done thing.

We decided to set up our own production company: ISF (Informed, Serious, Forward looking) Productions. But we had a hard time obtaining any commissions. Meanwhile, I left *Eastern Eye* to edit *Inquiry*, a monthly magazine of 'events and ideas', supported by Iran. Merryl became a regular contributor and wrote a highly opinionated column called 'Opinion': 'each month, as I write this column, I reflect on the state of the world. Each month I face the inescapable sinking sensation that the world is terminally insane. Each month I state my case, then retire bloodied but unbowed to await the next instalment'.

One particular bloodied instalment came in July 1985. A collection of traditional and, let's say, not-so-traditional, Muslim scholars gathered at

East West University in Chicago to discuss 'The Contemporary Relevance of Islam'. As Merryl wrote in a report of the conference, 'the meeting was not an exercise in proving that the contemporary relevance of Islam exists, but a search of ways in which this relevance can be made to work by Muslim intellectuals for the benefit of the *ummah*'. The emphasis was on 'making Islam the relevant problem-solving method for the complex problems of daily living in the modern world'. The participants were 'invited not to confront each other with meticulously prepared texts but to think aloud together to bring the process of devising a terminology, methodology and programme for action which took Islam as its starting point, frame of reference and intellectual aspiration'. Unfortunately, the loud thinking got off on the wrong foot. Right at the beginning of the proceedings, a distinguished Egyptian scholar from Al-Azhar University, solemnly declared: 'we have not any problems. The *ulama* have solved all our problems'. The other traditionalist scholars agreed in unison. Merryl erupted. What followed was a spectacle to behold! The not-so-traditionalists sat back and watched Merryl take on one traditional scholar after another and render them speechless. It was as though she was dissecting a corpse with great expertise and equal fury. Who is this fire-breathing dragon lady (a name that stuck), they asked?

After the meeting, some of the participants gathered in my hotel room. They were mostly my friends and regular contributors to *Inquiry*. Apart from Merryl and myself, there was Swedish Pakistani intellectual and linguist, Parvez Manzoor. The Canadian Pakistani architect Gulzar Haider. The Pakistani biologist Munawar Ahmad Anees. Artist and graphic designer Zafar Malik. And the British Pakistani architect, the late Ayyub Malik. We collectively agreed that it was our responsibility to liberate Islam from the fossilised tradition and religious obscurantism. We were all visibly shivering, not just with rage but also the abundant air-conditioning of my hotel room. We fabricated an initiation ceremony and dubbed ourselves the Ijamalis, the seekers of *ijmal*, the beauty and wholeness within Islam.

After the Chicago fiasco, Merryl started reading widely on traditional Islam. As she suffered from permanent insomnia (thanks, no doubt, to endless cups of black coffee and lavish smoking), her nights were spent reading. She went through my entire stock of Jamaat-e-Islami literature, my extensive collection on Islamic movements, Islamisation of Knowledge, and whatever else she could acquire. The more she read, the more she fumed. And she took her anger out on me.

Her fury reached its zenith when she read the works of Abul Ala Maududi, the founder of Jamaat-e-Islami. In particular, his book *Purdah and the Status of Women in Islam*. 'My blood pressure has sky rocketed', she said. I asked her to write an article for *Inquiry* on her thoughts about the book. But she refused. 'It would be unprintable', she declared. Eventually, she wrote a thundering piece comparing Maududi's ideas with that of Iranian scholar and intellectual, Ali Shariati, who she admired. Maududi, she declared, provides us with an all-embracing mechanical answer to all the problems faced by Muslim societies in modern times: 'if only you are sufficiently pious, Islam will prevail and solve all our problems'. She focussed not on *Purdah and the Status of Women in Islam* but on *Birth Control*, where his analysis is based on 'dubious proposition'. As a sociological analysis of western society, 'he gives us hysteria which is fitted out to masquerade as information by quoting indiscriminately without any context from a variety of sources', even citing 'opponents of control whose position was inspired by the eugenic debate'. 'Uninformed about science and medicine', Maududi peddles, Merryl declares, 'opinionated ignorance'.

She became equally furious when she read Akbar Ahmad's pathetic pamphlet, *Towards Islamic Anthropology: Definition, Dogma and Direction*. She rang to say that it was not just totally devoid of any original thought but some of the paragraphs in the text seemed to be a bit too familiar. The debate about Islamic anthropology seems to accept all the premises of western anthropology, she said. From the Islamic perspective, she announced, there are no 'other' societies in the sense of western anthropology. Moreover, Islamic anthropology cannot be based on a compound of social and cultural reasoning defined by the operation of one particular society as is conventional in western anthropology. Once again, I asked her to write her criticism for *Inquiry*. She produced two long articles exploring how 'a really alternative discipline' can be developed.

What would that alternative discipline look like? The question was raised at a dinner in Golders Green, hosted by Merryl. By now, it had become a convention for a small group of Ijmalis to meet once a month at her flat for dinner and debate. It included Parvez Manzoor, Ayyub Malik, Zafar Malik and myself. Merryl would prepare an elaborate, multi-course meal. Her kitchen would be full of saucepans, trays, and plates with cooked and half-cooked food, spread randomly across the length and breath. There were bits of scraps and specks all over her apron, hands, and face. On first sight, it looked like a complete mess. But somehow, order emerged out of the clearly visible chaos. One delightful dish arrived after another; and they kept arriving. The conversation – animated, heated, with a considerable amount of screaming and shouting – would start with the starters and continue till early dawn. The discussion on Islamic anthropology was particularly intense. Merryl tried to explain her position in a number of ways; she was questioned and challenged at every step. Finally, exhausted, she declared. 'There is only one thing for me to do: I will write a book so you lot can grasp what I am saying'. It would argue, she said, that there is an urgent need to acquire another way of knowing, another way of understanding the history and complexity of the world we inhabit, a world in which we are increasingly dependent on mutual recognition of our difference and diversity. She asked if I would help. I was only too eager.

And so began our life long writing collaboration. In May 1986, Merryl sat down to write *Knowing One Another: Shaping an Islamic Anthropology*. She would deliver weekly dispatches, written on an electric typewriter. I would read carefully, edit, suggest additions and subtractions, and return the pile of manuscript. I soon discovered that Merryl wrote as she cooked. Baked and half-baked thoughts and ideas were strewn all over the text. She would change her mind half way through a chapter, spike it, and begin all over again. It was all too painful. But when, after eighteen months of labour, it was complete, and Merryl declared that she was satisfied with the final version, I read the clean, freshly minted copy. And exclaimed: it is a paragon.

Knowing One Another, much like Merryl's personality, is a complex, multi-layered text. Merryl does not think that Islamic anthropology is simply the study of Muslim societies. Rather, it is a comparative, cross-cultural and historical study of all humankind, concerned with all types of human, cultural and social organisation and relations. As it studies human societies from the standpoint of an Islamic conceptual base, it must be a reflection upon Islam itself. She argues that Islamic anthropology has to be based on concepts, derived from the Quran and the Sharia, such as *adl* (justice), *istislah* (public welfare) *halal* (beneficial), *haram*, (harmful), *ilm* (knowledge) and *fitrah* (the created inherent nature of humanity). Theory

building should begin with an understanding of *fitrah*, which is unitary and the same for all humankind; it is moral nature, has passion and reason, and the capacity and capability to apprehend both the seen and the unseen. This is emphasised in the famous Qur'anic verse, 'We have created you male and female and have made you nations and tribes that you may know one another' (49:13); the study of societies and cultures, from an Islamic perspective, is essentially a commentary on, and an attempt to understand, this verse in the contemporary world. The concepts of Islam function as a system, she asserts, but not as a system with a definitive concrete form.

Islam is not culturally specific; and, as the verse indicates, it recognises the validity of diverse social and cultural forms which are themselves ways of knowing. Islam, Merryl argues is a system of 'permissible structures' which emphasise the plasticity of human nature and society in achieving normative ends by diverse forms and means. Studying other societies therefore actually extends our understanding of the potential meaning of Islamic concepts and ways in which this understanding can be applied to ordering, planning and determining the course of society in the future. Islamic anthropology therefore is not seeking merely to record diversity, or even to understand the nature of diversity. Rather, it is a study seeking to penetrate through the diversity of form demonstrated by different societies and cultures to apprehend the consonance of normative behaviour. Merryl does not call her approach to understanding societies and culture 'Islamic anthropology' or 'Islamic sociology'. She calls her enquiry, after ibn Khaldun, *Ilm ul Umran*: knowledge of human aggregation which is the organised habitation (*umran*) of the world. *Ilm ul Umran,* she asserts, carries a greater significance, a clear indication of relevant questions and is a better basis for both discourse and dialogue than is the unqualified label 'Islamic anthropology'. When the name of the discipline changes to *Ilm ul Umran,* it signifies that an entire system of Islamic thought is necessary to carry it forward; thus, it can never be an appendage to the dominant Western discipline.

The following year, Merryl and I went to Kuala Lumpur to work on an issue of *Inquiry* devoted to Malaysia. She made a bee line to Dewan Bahasa dan Pustaka, the national Language and Literature Development Agency, and interviewed a number of writers – including the noted novelist Samad Ismail, short story writer Kris Mas, the literary superstar, Samad Said, and spent time 'listening to poems of love, sweet melodies from the Garden of Grace' by the poet Kemala. I took the opportunity to reconnect with my friend, Malaysian politician and intellectual, Anwar Ibrahim. We spent some time discussing issues of tradition and modernity, the problems of Islamic movements, the lack of critical thought in Muslim circles, and the then hot topic, 'Islamisation of knowledge'. I suggested Anwar joins the Ijmalis; he proposed that the Ijmalis should organise a series of 'Intellectual Discourses' to introduce their ideas and thoughts to Malaysian academics, thinkers, and writers. Both suggestions were met with approval. The

Inquiry issue on Malaysia, with Merryl's article on Malaysian writers, was published in September 1987. But a month before, I was summarily dismissed from *Inquiry*, for writing an unfavourable review of a mediocre book by an Iranian scholar. (*Inquiry* closed soon afterwards). So, we found ourselves heading East.

3.

We organised a string of 'Intellectual Discourses' in Malaysia, anything from short seminars at universities to full fledge three-day conferences. Topics ranged from contemporary western thought to criticism of 'Islamisation of knowledge' to 'the futures of the *ummah*'. There was a memorable three-day 'visioning' workshop where we tried to persuade scholars from the International Islamic University Malaysia (IIUM) to imagine a future Muslim society with totally reformed and reformulated Sharia – and failed. For the Ijmalis, it was all cerebrally exciting, considerable fun, quite exhausting, and sometimes very frustrating.

But Merryl's attentions were elsewhere. She wanted to get back to television. And there was a newly established television channel, TV3, which offered opportunities. With Anwar's help, ISF Productions got its first commission: *Faces of Islam*, a series of twelve half-hour discussion programmes that examined contemporary problems and issues in terms of twelve Islamic concepts: *din, tawhid, kitab, sirah, Sharia, adil, ibadah, ilm, khalifa, dawa, jihad, and ummah*.

We gathered some of the most original thinkers, writers, and activists – from as far afield as Pakistan and Nigeria, Saudi Arabia and Malaysia, Sudan and Turkey, and Australia and Canada – and asked how their chosen concept applied to the problems of the modern world. After the broadcast of *Faces of Islam*, Merryl and I became consultants at TV3.

In 1988, Merryl moved to Kuala Lumpur; I began commuting between London and KL. We rented an apartment in Menarah Indah in Taman TAR, opposite Kelab Darul Ehsan, a golf and recreation club. Apart from working at TV3, we became advisors to Anwar, with added responsibilities for Merryl of writing his speeches. At TV3, our job was to bring some professionalism to the station's newsroom, train their broadcast journalists and presenters, and create some new programmes. We established the

'Seven O'Clock News', launched a business show, 'Money Matters', and tried to introduce as much objectivity in TV3's coverage as possible.

It was not an easy task. We found it difficult to get the journalists not to rely too much on press releases and government handouts. To write scripts to pictures. To even shoot sequences. I would often throw my hands in the air and give up. But Merryl persisted. She would spend hours in the newsroom rewriting scripts, coaching producers, hours in the studio directing and training newsreaders and presenters. She would work way past midnight, return to Menarah Indah for a couple of hours of sleep, and be back at TV3 before dawn. We had to constantly critique the stories that were being shot and produced; and we had to do it without anyone getting upset or demoralised, and – this is very important in Malaysia – 'losing face'.

So, we developed our own language to deal with the situation. It was a mixture of words taken from English, Malay, Chinese and other languages, jumbled together to sound like gibberish. Indeed, to outsiders it was claptrap, but for us it was patent precision. Part serious, part play, it was also a reflection of our special bond. '*Ye, ye*', was both our 'Hello!' and an indication that what follows is code. '*Said Qi*': what does Qi, the vital force of every living entity in Chinese culture (which we pronounced as ki), has to say? In other words, what is your assessment of a particular piece – a news story that has just been shot, or a particular script you have seen? The Malay word for system is simply *system*; we corrupted it to *systi*, which could have different meanings in different contexts. In the TV3 context, it meant does it work? – does the news report have enough substance to be broadcast? '*No systi*', meant it was rubbish and had to be ditched. '*Little systi*' suggested it required lot of work from us to bring it up to a professional standard. Or, as Merryl would announce triumphantly: '*we have systi*'.

We discovered that our language worked equally well when it came to dealing with Anwar and his staff. In certain meetings, we could not always express our frank opinion openly, or disagree with each other in front of others. Coded communication between us brought us both to the same page. When we were asked to undertake a task and Merryl was not sure if I actually wanted to do it, she would say: '*systi possible?*'. I would reply: '*Can be had*'. Alternatively: '*not maujood*' – *maujood* being the Arabic word for existing or present. Other terms were added to our lingo, bits from Urdu and French, and it became quite a concoction. Pretty soon, what was meant to be limited to TV3 newsroom, became, to the utter bewilderment of others, our common mode of communication.

This was the happiest period of Merryl's life; and, by now, she had become an integral part of my life. She was doing all that she loved: working for television, engaging in intellectual pursuits and heated cerebral discussions, helping to shape policies she believed in, and when the time permitted, doing the occasional piece of serious writing. She was the godmother of my three children; a role she took very seriously. They grew up under her aegis and became very close to her. She referred to my house as 'Plumpley', ye olde English name for a village in Cheshire meaning both plum and plum tree but also signifying creativity, curiosity, charm, friendliness, cheer, and social life. On every birthday of every child, she sent a special birthday fax, sometimes written in our prattle, sometimes in her own equally barmy patois. An example of a birthday greeting sent to my son, Zaid:

We Prevail!

As we forewarned, we are now EPIC, a universal blockbuster nonpareil.

As was to be expected the world now beats a path to Plumpley, lavishing us with their monetary wares and seeking what they can of our goods and services (chattels not included, batteries not needed).

Yet we the EPIC of Plumpley still remember from our humbler more modest days that this is

A DAY TO REMEMBER

A day when our esteemed free citizen moves ever onward chronologically

with grace and style included at no extra charge (as defined by the Plumpley Ministry of Financial Accounting and Crediting and usable for tax purposes).

HAPPY BIRTHDAY

NOBLE FREE CITIZEN OF PLUMPLEY

One particularly intellectual pursuit took her to Mecca. I was involved in organising an international Islamic conference entitled, 'Da'wa and Development of the Muslim World: The Future Perspective'. Organised by the Jeddah-based Muslim World League, it was held on 11–15 October 1987 with the participation of over 200 delegates from all over the world. The objective of the conference was to rethink the notion of *dawa* and broaden its scope from preaching about Islam. 'Our objective', the conference prospectus stated, 'is a course of *dawa* that tackles hunger, illiteracy, unemployment, poverty and the need for a secure and better future according to the concepts and values of Islam'. We had worked out a very detailed outline of the subjects that the conference was to cover, ranging from living environment to economic and financial development, education and human resources, managing law and order, science and technology and information, media and literature. Merryl was the only single female delegate at the conference.

She had to travel to Mecca on her own. An undertaking not permitted by the laws of the Kingdom, which required all women to be accompanied by their 'guardian'. We thus had to acquire special permission for her to be allowed into Saudi Arabia without a male chaperone. It was a letter from the King himself – Fahd bin Abdulaziz Al Saud. Merryl arrived two days before the conference, all covered up, looking like, as our friend, Zafar Malik, said, 'a kamakazee pilot'. She became the second woman to travel to Mecca on her own in recent history (the first was Lady Evelyn Cobbold who arrived in Mecca on 26 March 1933 as a personal guest of King Abdul Aziz.) She was met by the protocol officers who took her straight to Mecca Intercontinental, then located on the outskirts of the city, where the conference was being held. On arriving at the hotel, she insisted on going immediately to the haram – to visit the Kaaba in the Sacred Mosque. I was busy with conference matters and asked Zafar to take her. She entered the haram, stood in front of the Kaaba for a few moments, and then fell to her knees. 'She sobbed uncontrollably', Zafar said. She spent considerable time praying and crying.

Much to her annoyance, Merryl was confined to the women's quarters. But she wasted no time in taking charge of the group, a mixture of female scholars, scientists, thinkers, and wives of delegates, and began to, what one Saudi official said, 'mislead' them. She became a centre of attention not just amongst female participants but also from Saudi delegates and officials. She received a number of unsavoury calls in the middle of the night. We made formal complaints to no affect. But not all calls were unpleasant. She received a number of proposals for marriage. All of which she rejected out of hand – except one. She consulted with me about it. It came from Abdo Yamani.

Yamani, a short portly man, was a highly respected figure and well-known philanthropist. A native of Mecca, he went to Cornell University to study geology, taught at various Saudi universities before becoming the Minister of Information. He was also an accomplished writer with a string of books, on Islam and cultural issues, to his name. During that time, he was chairman of Dallah Al-Baraka, a Saudi multinational company established by Saleh Kamal, the founder of al-Baraka bank, who had partly funded the Mecca conference. Merryl asked me what I thought of Abdo Yamani. I recalled an incident when Yamani found himself alone in London and called me to take him out to dinner. On our walk from his hotel to a *halal* restaurant (he was insistent that it should be a certified *halal* eatery!), we came across a homeless man. Yamani stopped in front of the man. He was clearly moved by the plight of the man. He took out his wallet and handed it to him. I ended up paying for the dinner! He was, I said, the kind of Saudi (more precisely, Hijazi) one could love and respect. They say, when you can't find anyone to support a humanitarian project, you go to Abdo Yamani. And, I added for good measure, as far as humanitarian projects go, you are up there on the top of the list. Think of all the *objets* you can acquire! Merryl gave serious thought to the proposal, mulling it over for a couple of days. Finally, she decided against it. 'I can't bear to live in Saudi Arabia', she said.

The conference was a disaster. But we managed to get three books out of it. I collected a pile of papers on *dawa*, community, refugees, and communication and sent them to her with a note: 'here is a *buku* what you have writted'. She edited the papers meticulously and turned it into a book, which she called *Beyond Frontiers: Islam and Contemplator Needs*.

While we were still working on the books of the Mecca Conference, another book was published that would have a major impact on our lives: *The Satanic Verses* by Salman Rushdie. Both of us read the novel; and both of us were equally upset and angry. The Muslim community had few academics or intellectuals to defend its position; and it was not always defended in the best possible way. The situation became worse after the 14 February 1989 fatwa by Ayatollah Khomeini. We found the undiluted racism and Islamophobia that emerged, often in the guise of liberalism and freedom of expression, deeply disturbing. It repeatedly reduced Merryl to tears; on a number of occasions, she cried for days. I wrote a few columns for the newspapers, and appeared on some television programmes to defend our corner. But that was not enough. We had to do something much more. Rushdie's novel needed a proper knowledgeable response. One evening in Kuala Lumpur, a meeting was held with Anwar in his study. We discussed the novel and our potential responses till late into the night. It was finally decided that, in the best tradition of Islamic intellectual history, a book should reply to a book. It was going to be a serious task that could not be undertaken in our little Menarah Indah apartment. Anwar agreed that Merryl should go back to London and stay there until the book is written. So, in March 1989, Merryl return home to Merthyr and sat down to write *Distorted Imagination: Lessons from the Rushdie Affair*.

I have described how we wrote *Distorted Imagination*, and how it was eventually published, in some detail in *Desperately Seeking Paradise*. We knew exactly what we had to say and write. Merryl would raise questions, I would try and explore the questions, and it would become the first draft, or part, of a chapter. It would go to Merryl who would expand, add further arguments, analysis and examples, and it came back to me for a final polish. We had each bought ourselves an Apricot laptop computer: it was rather heavy, ran MS-DOS, had an orange screen, (what we considered then to be) massive 20Mb of memory, and was the first computer to use 3.5" floppy disks, rather than the 5.25" disks which were the norm at the time. Our word processor was called Wordcraft 2.00, which was easy to use but also full of sophisticated features. (The best word processor I have ever used). Envelopes stuffed with floppy disks flew between London and Merthyr. When we finished the book, it was stored on 14 floppy disks. It took well over a year during which we experienced, what I can now call, my first lockdown. I did not go out for days, and for days I resembled a mullah with an uncouth beard. Merryl gained several pounds in weight. When *Distorted Imagination* was finally published, Anwar declared it to be a 'masterpiece'.

4.

Merryl returned to KL in March 1991, a week before Anwar became Minister of Finance. She had complained that our apartment in Menarah Indah was too small; it was cluttered with our books and there was hardly any space to move. So, we moved to a new villa in Section 17, Petaling Jaya (PJ). Our TV3 commitments were reduced, and Merryl had a bit more time to travel. She went to Thailand, Cambodia, India and New Zealand to meet Muslim communities, give a few lectures, and, of course, collect *objets*. She turned one room into a video library, with a sophisticated air conditioning system needed to maintain the videos in prime condition in the unforgiving heat of Kuala Lumpur. It contained Hollywood output going back to the silent film era, British movies, television series, as well as classics of Japanese, Iranian and Indian cinema – hundreds of videos, legal and pirated. An area was devoted to displays of her *objet* collection. I was barred from this part of the house. 'Chappu', she declared, 'you are too clumsy and too prone to breaking things'.

She began to describe KL as her second home; but not secondary! She loved the place. The people. Everything about it. If I were to criticise any aspect of Malay culture, or the conspicuous absence of intellectual thought in the Archipelago, she would pounce on me. In her presence, barefaced criticism of Malays and their culture, customs, history, or food could not be tolerated. She made frequent trips to Malacca, compulsively collected books and artefacts on the history of Southeast Asia, and became obsessive with the 'Indian Ocean World'. We agreed on demarcation; and did our work in our designated area. Or, at least that was the arrangement.

It was a particularly creative period in our lives. Merryl decided to write a history of Islam from the perspective of the Indian Ocean world. I had to write an essay on Bollywood and its impact on the British Asian community for a book on Indian cinema that my friend, the Indian intellectual and cultural theorist, Ashis Nandy, was editing. I had also decided to write a critical evaluation of postmodernism. Merryl seemed more interested in what I was doing rather than her own book. She was, as Anwar has noted, 'a cinephile without equal'. She would talk about films with Anwar at great length – not just about classic Hollywood films they had seen, but to my surprise, also Bollywood movies and films of the great Malaysian director, writer, and actor, P Ramlee (1929–1973). I had to study a few selected classics of Bollywood – films of Dilip Kumar, Guru Dutt and Amitabh Bachchan. We watched these films together as I took notes. I suspected that Merryl could not follow them as they had no subtitles. When I started writing the essay, she would come and stand behind me – and laugh loudly. 'Don't you know anything about your own culture?', she would shout. And then proceed to present an analysis that would undermine all that I was saying in the essay. 'Am I writing *this*, or are you?', I would shout back. 'You should only write about things you know something about', she would exclaim. We fought constantly; and what I thought would be a relatively easy essay to write turned into a mega enterprise.

I abandoned all notions of writing while I was in KL. I would do most of my writing in my attic in London. But Merryl's video collection was a treasure trove; and her insights into film incredibly valuable. Indeed, her collection of books, videos, and artefacts had become so large that it became necessary for us to move to a larger premises. When Anwar became Deputy Prime Minister, in December 1993, the time was as right as any for a move to a bigger villa for us in another section of PJ. More *objets* were secured; and the villa began to resemble an anthropological museum.

When I mentioned that I was thinking of beginning my next book, *Postmodernism and the Other*, with an analysis of the British television series *The Prisoner* (1967), she told me not to write a word till she had her say. I considered *The Prisoner*, about a secret agent who suddenly resigned and is then imprisoned in a shadowy village from where he constantly tries to escape, to be the first authentic postmodern product. Merryl had all the seventeen episodes in her library. She was an active member of St David's Society, the organisation of the Welsh expatriates in KL. Members of the Society were invited to 'The Prisoner Weekends' during which the gathering watched three or four episodes, and Merryl regaled all, animatedly and loudly, accompanied with abundant 'food and beverage', with her take on what *The Prisoner* was all about, and the coded messages in each episode.

Meanwhile, her own project was quasi static. Whenever she interfered with my writing, I would simply yell: 'Indian Ocean World'. She would retire with a huff. It became shorthand for infuriating her. I must confess, for the sake of truth, that I took some delight in annoying her. It was often when she was fully charged up that she came out with *bons mots*.

She got as far as writing the introduction. Merryl argued that the trading world of the Indian Ocean predates the coming of Islam. It was certainly established by the first century when Indianised states emerged across Southeast Asia from the Champa states on the coast of Vietnam, to Funan in modern Thailand, and across the Indonesian archipelago, principally on Java, where the states of Majpahit and Sri Vijaya arose and held over territory on many islands as well as peninsular Malaysia. 'Arab seamen and traders were part of this trading world', she wrote,

as details of the life of Prophet Muhammad indicate. It is these long-established trading connections borne on the monsoon winds that produced the gradual spread of Islam throughout the region. The Malay world, the islands of Indonesia and peninsula Malaysia, were the place where the various branches of this extensive trading world met. Traders came in search not only of spices but also tin, precious metals and the other produce of this rich and varied region. The Indianised states of Majapahit and Sri Vijaya on Java had been centres of Hindu and Buddhist learning long before the coming of Islam. The regular monsoon winds that brought traders to this region meant they had to remain for a period of months before the change in wind direction enabled them to make their return home. It is through this pattern of regular often extended interaction that Muslim traders and travellers introduced Islam to the Malays. By 1000 Muslim trading ports begin to emerge and by 1200 a Malay Muslim state was in existence in Acheh on the northern tip of the island of Sumatra. A succession of Muslim Malay states rose to prominence in succeeding centuries. They grew through the facilities they provided traders, and their own participation in regional trade, extended their control over territory that straddled various islands and parts of peninsula Malaysia and then declined when tensions between the port city and its hinterland caused internal disruption. Another port would then begin its rise to prominence as the focus of a new state. The last great trading centre to arise was Melaka, on the Malay peninsula, a Malay Muslim state with a Malay speaking Chinese population and numerous groups of Indian traders both Muslim and Hindu. It was, according to the Portuguese writer Thomas Pires 'the emporium of all the world.' So important was Melaka that capturing the city was a major objective of the Portuguese invaders of the Indian Ocean, with whom Pires travelled and whose history he wrote. The Melaka Sultanate fell to the Portuguese in 1511. The remnants of the sultanate removed to Jahore where they established a new state. The coming of Europe imposed new constraints on the whole Indian Ocean, but Malay states continued to exist, to develop the resources of their environment that made them such a lure for colonial expropriation on a more systematic basis in later centuries.

The trading world of the Indian Ocean, she argued, was the first period in history of true globalisation.

The East coast of Africa was an integral part of the Indian Ocean trading world. In the lifetime of Prophet Muhammad, we saw that there was abundant contact between Arabia and the Horn of Africa. The Yemen had from the earliest times been connected to the region of Somalia, just as the Nile had connected Egypt to the Sudan since Pharonic times. Both of these ancient connections provided the means for Islam to spread organically through East Africa. After 900 Islam began to spread down the eastern coast of the continent into the region referred to as al-Zanj. It led to the establishment of a series of black African states in the coastal regions of Kenya, Tanzania – the name derived from the fusion of Tanganikya with the Muslim Island of Zanibar – as far south as Sofala in modern Mozambique. These coastal trading states were in contact with the interior of Africa from which they acquired such products as gold, ivory and slaves and to which they traded the produce of the whole Indian Ocean trading world. Chinese pottery is among the artefacts that have been excavated at the site of Great Zimbabwe, the stone city in the heart of the modern nation to which it gave its name. The Muslim culture of coastal East Africa was part of the wider ambit of Muslim civilisation. When Vasco da Gama made the initial European entry into the Indian Ocean in 1498 after nearly a century of Portuguese exploration around the coast of Africa his objective was to reach India. In the port of Malindi, in modern Kenya, he hired a Muslim pilot used to travelling this familiar route who guided him to Calicut. Some sources suggest the pilot was ibn Majid, a native of East Africa who was a leading authority on geography and author of some 14 books on the subject. This is most probably an apocryphal tale, but its strong irony conveys a reality European history has expunged. European expansion, seen as an epic heroic endeavour undertaken in the spirit of scientific inquiry did no more than stumble into an existing, long established and highly sophisticated world whose connective tissue was Muslim civilisation.

She couldn't concentrate on her own writing because her mind was elsewhere. The fact that Anwar was Deputy Prime Minister was not necessarily a good thing, Merryl thought; particularly under a rather controlling and increasingly cantankerous Prime Minister, Mahathir

Mohammad. The fact that he was also overseeing the Anti-Corruption Agency was even more problematic given that all levers of power were in the hands of the most corrupt person in the land. Mahathir had already dethroned three previous Deputy Prime Ministers. Would Anwar's efforts to undermine the overindulgences of Mahathir lead to his downfall?

There were serious differences between the two; and Mahathir had begun to flex his muscles.

Mahathir was a cold and maniacally shrewd politician who was not known for keeping those who had outlived their use around. Anwar's moves as Education Minister fed the Old Man's appetite for political capital, but as Finance Minister, now just at his heels, he had demonstrated an incorruptibility that was incompatible with the endemic corruption of the New Malaysia Mahathir had crafted in his own image. Merryl spent endless time talking and discussing Malaysian politics. While Anwar was keen for the top job, Merryl was even more eager to see him in the Prime Minister's office. 'It is my main desire in life', she declared.

One day, we met Anwar in his office. We talked at length about his problems with Mahathir. He said he is moving as cautiously as possible, but the sheer extent of sleaze and crony corruption of the 'old man' - named after the Old Men of the Mountain, who led the Order of Assassins - was forcing his hand. With a rather pensive look on his face, he said: 'you are not there till you are *there!*'.

The following morning, I remember rather well, I got up to see Merryl sitting at the dining table, cup of coffee in hand. She looked haggard. I thought she'd had another one of her illustrious sleepless nights. 'Meeraal', I shouted, 'are you awake?'. 'I have been thinking', she replied after a long pause. 'About the Indian Ocean World! The more you are going to think about it the more you are unlikely to write the bloody book'. 'No, no, no', she yelled.

'No'. 'I have been thinking: what could the old man do to stop Anwar from getting *there?*'

We immediately sat to work on the question. We read whatever we could find by and about the old man, local and international news stories, interviews, and profiles to try and work out how his mind works. We made extensive notes on the rumour mills around KL. We talked to friends and foes of Anwar to solicit their opinion. And we ploughed through works on

Malaysian political history. Finally, we produced what we called 'Unthinkables' – six scenarios that the old man could use to undermine Anwar.

It was no good accusing Anwar of corruption; his integrity was unimpeachable. There was little point in accusing him of having an affair; it was not an uncommon practice among Malay politicians. It had to be something that the Malays, especially the rural brand, find particularly reprehensible. The scenario labelled 'Unthinkable 3' anticipated that Anwar would be accused of homosexuality, perhaps involving coercion. It turned out to be prescience.

5.

After a stormy cabinet meeting, Anwar was unceremoniously dismissed by Mahathir on 2 September 1998. Masked and heavily armed men broke into his house, and arrested him at gunpoint. He was savagely beaten up. One of our friends and colleagues, an advisor to Anwar, Munawar Ahmad Anees, was also arrested. Other advisors, friends and colleagues of Anwar were being rounded up. I was following the tragedy as it unfolded from London. Hysterical calls to Merryl were made, begging her to come back to London. She refused.

A few days later, the phone rang in the middle of the night. 'Prof Zia?', asked the voice at the other end of the phone. I recognised it. It was Nasaruddin Jalil, Anwar's political secretary. 'Nasar' as he was known, was a short, slim man, with a perpetual grin on his face. He was always planning and making a deal. His political instincts as sharp as his mind. 'Get Merryl out! NOW!', the voice said, and terminated the call. I knew I had to act immediately.

But it was no point ringing Merryl.

I rang a mutual friend. 'Dr Beverage', as Merryl used to call him, taught information technology at the Mara Institute of Technology. A member of the St David's Society and a frequent visitor to Merryl's film weekends, he regularly organised lavish soirees for the expat community. Whatever the event, he took full charge of the drinks (I am told, he used to make a killer Martini). Would you, I asked, kidnap Merryl and get her out of Malaysia? He admired Merryl; and was aware of the dangerous nature of the situation. 'Leave it to me', he replied without hesitation. From Merryl's own accounts, I learned later that he had to 'manhandle' her as she was unwilling to leave. 'If I have to be manhandled', she said, 'than I would choose Dr Beverage for the assignment'. He stuffed the boot of his car with some of Merryl's belonging and drove her, past the plain clothed security men who were watching the villa, to Singapore.

Merryl stayed in Singapore for two weeks campaigning on behalf of Anwar. Then, on the advice of some of our more knowledgeable Malaysian friends, moved to Batam, an Indonesian island located twenty kilometres off Singapore's south coast. She had no funds to keep her going, but fortunately she took the Diner's Club card I kept in KL for emergency use with her. It came in handy as she checked into a hotel with a grand view of the Strait of Singapore. She called it 'Paradise Cove'. From her new base she wrote hundreds of letters, countless press releases, and tried to get in touch with anyone and everyone she could to solicit support for Anwar's campaign. She tried also to secure her belongings back in KL. She engaged a lawyer and hired a packing company. But with no result. Eventually, our kitty dried up. She had to return to London. But that was tantamount to admitting defeat – something she was not used to. Anwar was in prison. Most of his advisors and supporters were in exile. Nasaruddin Jalil had escaped to Jakarta. One of our closest friends, and advisor and companion of Anwar, journalist and businessman, Ahmad Nazri Abdullah, had his businesses confiscated or closed; he was forced to move to London with his family. There was no hope that Merryl could return to KL. Justice had evaded us. She sent a CompuServe email:

To: The Denizens of Plumpley
Subject: Arrival imminent of She who Must be Obeyed
Batteries needed. There be no Giblets.

So, after twelve years in Malaysia, and fifteen months on Batam, at the end of 1999, Merryl said goodbye to 'Paradise Cove', and flew to London.

I could not contain myself when I saw her. She had gained considerable weight. Her face was disfigured. Stress and anxiety had led her to endlessly grind her teeth and clench her jaws. Most of her teeth had fallen out, or were loose. Her finger nails were all chewed. We hugged each other and cried. 'I look like an *hantu*', (Malay ghost), she joked. But she could not hide her pain. Her world had collapsed. She had lost everything – her treasured *objets*, her carefully curated library, her cherished video collection. She was penniless. 'Chappu', she said, 'what is to be done?'

After a few days in London, she went to Merthyr and became a seclude. She would not answer my calls; and, when she did, she wouldn't (or couldn't) speak. I dealt with my angst in my own way by putting Anwar's story and my relationship with KL on paper. The result: *The Consumption of Kuala Lumpur*, which was published in 2000. But what I could not do was to let Merryl stay in Merthyr and wallow in her sorrow. Eventually, I manged to lure her to London with a promise of a job: an appointment as the Media Officer for the Muslim Council of Britain (MCB). She stayed with my daughter, Maha. They had an extraordinary attachment to each other. Merryl first met Maha when she was only two years old; over the years, godmother and goddaughter forged themselves into a combined entity. As an infant, whenever Maha saw Merryl, she would yell 'Meeraal' and jump onto her lap. The practice continued ever since; the fact that Maha was in now her twenties made no difference. They had their own mode of receptive speech and frequently engaged in long, convoluted conversations, accompanied with relentless giggles. Merryl was not keen on working for MCB. 'Too many *heavyyoon*' – folks with too much piety and narrow outlook, she complained. But spending a year with Maha was tremendous therapy. I could see that her trauma was easing.

She left the MCB, and returned to Merthyr. For a while, she did odd jobs, such as writing the booklet, *Islam UK*, that accompanied the BBC 2001 Islam Season; and a short treatise on *Darwin and Fundamentalism*. But she had no real income. I was also in rather reduced circumstances. Merryl thought about going on *Who Wants to Be a Millionaire?* She was convinced that she could win – all the way to a million. Her encyclopaedic knowledge of relevant and irrelevant facts notwithstanding, I was not convinced. She asked me to do some 'dry runs' with her, after which I had no option but to agree. We put her name forward; and waited for the phone to ring. We tried week after week to get her on the show. But she was never called. Then, the 9/11 attacks happened.

I was at home watching the events unfold on television. A shell-shocked woman emerged from the debris and dust cloud swirling around the Twin Towers. She looked at a waiting television reporter, and asked a direct, distressed question: 'why do they hate us'? I immediately rang Merryl, who was also glued to her television. Even before I could say anything, she said, 'I heard her. Loud and clear'. And after a pause: 'we know how to answer the question, don't we?'. Within a couple of days, I had secured a contract, with a decent advance, for *Why Do People Hate America?* The publishers wanted the manuscript within three months. I suggested we should treat the question as an inquiry. Merryl suggested we use Hollywood output to frame the book, rolled out a number of titles for me to secure: *The West Wing*, *Rules of Engagement*, *The Siege*, *Delta Force*, and *Shane*. 'I always, always wanted to write about *Shane*', she said. I suggested the television series *Alias* (motto: 'sometimes the truth hurts'), which I was following. She complained: 'Chappu, stop lowering my standards with all these terrible American action films'. But I insisted; and she eventually agreed.

We sat to work; and completed the task in designated time. The book came out in April 2002; and was an international bestseller.

Success and a modicum of financial security brought her mojo back. She wanted to write a follow up to *Why Do People Hate America?* The publishers were keen on the idea. But I was working on another project – *Desperately Seeking Paradise* – and suggested that she take a break. It came in the form of a tour of Nigeria, courtesy of the British Council. She arrived in Kano in the middle of the controversial Amina Lawal case, which was on the front page of every newspaper. On 22 March 2002, an Islamic Sharia court in Funtua, Nigeria, sentenced Lawal, a beautiful young woman, to death by stoning for conceiving a child out of wedlock. Merryl wasted no time in seeing the Head of the Sharia Council of Nigeria. 'A very personable medical doctor', she said. 'As Muslims we are united in agreeing Islam means peace', she told him,

> that we are not a religion or people dedicated to lopping off hands and stoning women to death. We say Sharia defines our culture and the future for our society. But when Sharia is instituted lo and behold the first thing that happens is a woman tried for adultery. The nefarious activities of men go unchecked. Do you think a just God would approve of such an unjust deed?

He assured her that he will convey her message to the Sharia Council and do his utmost to ensure that the judgement of the lower court would be thrown out. And it was. By the time, Merryl sat down to write our second book on America, *American Dream, Global Nightmare,* Lawal's sentence was

overturned by Katsina State Sharia Court of Appeal on 25 September 2003.
By now, we were working together like a finely tuned machine. We talked
every morning, wrote for most the day, and gave progress reports to each
other in the evening. Apart from finishing *American Dream, Global Nightmare*,
we also wrote *The No-Nonsense Guide to Islam*. We were going to move on to

other projects. But Merryl's mother, Maisey, slipped on ice just outside her
home, and broke her leg. Merryl acquired caring responsibilities.

At about the same time, Anwar came out of prison. Our attentions
reverted towards him. There was a tear-jerking reunion at Nazri's London
house, near Queensway. Anwar became Visiting Fellow at St Anthony's
College, Oxford; and Nazri hosted many more meetings at his house. Nazri
was also a regular visitor to my house, and Merryl travelled from Merthyr
to see him. Nazri is an exceptionally jovial individual, always smiling and
chortling – even in times of adversity. He is half-a-hafiz: someone who has

memorised half of the Qur'an; and he recites the Qur'an beautifully. Apart from his glasses and a fine insignia moustache, Nazri's facial furniture also includes a distinguished scar. It does not announce its presence effortlessly; one has to look closely to note its charisma. I asked him: how did you manage to get that scar? 'According to my mum', Nazri related, 'I was caught by fire at the age of four at a wedding gathering in our village. In those days, there was no electricity in the village and we used gasoline lamps during festivals. One of the lamps had run out of gasoline and needed refuelling. The person refuelling the lamp was ignorant. Instead of waiting for the burner to cool down, he poured the spirit and lit it with matches. The lamp blew up. I was playing close by and got caught in the ensuing fire. They took me to the hospital. I vaguely remember my head was wrapped for quite some time and I could not play with other kids'. But the scar did not dampen Nazri's indefatigable spirit. 'The scar gave me aspiration to struggle and work hard. Never looked back. *Alhamdulillah*. I was the first boy from my kampung to enter University of Malaya in 1972. I still remember my family and relatives congregating at Alor Star Railway Station to send me off to KL.' He went on to become an illustrious journalist, becoming editor of the Malay newspaper, *Barita Harian*; his career brought to an abrupt end with the arrest of Anwar in September 1998.

We dubbed the meetings with Nazri 'what is to be done?' gatherings, devoted, as they were, to discussion of political strategy, the progress of the National Justice Party (KEADILAN), which Anwar established while in prison, and the overall direction of 'Reformasi', the reform movement in Malaysia. Anwar could not return to politics until his disqualification – a product of imprisonment – expired in 2008. He used the time to establish his credentials as a global statesman, and gained appointments at Johns Hopkins and Georgetown Universities. He joined his friend Al Gore, the former US Vice President, to work on the climate emergency, promote democracy in the Middle East, and shape more just and humane futures.

Meanwhile, Merryl wanted to write a third book; but I had enough of America. 'Chappu', she said, 'it should be trilogy'. I had signed up to work on an experimental blog for the *Guardian*, and wanted to devote all my time to 'Blogging the Qur'an'. She insisted; and we agreed on a compromise. She would help with the blog: 'I will make sure you don't commit calumnious follies', she declared. I insisted that the analysis in the third book, *Will America Change*, should be based on history and politics rather than film. I would write the blog, send it to her to check for accuracy and 'follies', before submitting to the *Guardian*. She would send drafts of the chapters, with gaps clearly marked for my additions, which would be returned for editing and polishing. She kept adding film analysis, I kept deleting them; and it went on like this for a whole year as we simultaneously worked on the two projects.

By the time *Will America Change* came out, Anwar was back in Malaysia campaigning in the 2008 General Election. However, the election was held a month before his disqualification from politics had expired, to deliberately exclude him from contesting a seat. A few months later, he contested in a by-election and returned to Parliament. His party, Keadilan, had done well but did not secure a majority; and his attempts to form a majority coalition did not succeed. There were other concerns. The growing support for his party was seen as a direct threat by his detractors. They resorted to the tried and tested tactic: fabricated accusations of 'sodomy' began to surface yet again. In July 2008, he was arrested once more; there was a long, drawn court case, and Anwar was finally acquitted in 2012.

Merryl followed the events in Malaysia very closely. As her mobility went the way of the Dodo, Merryl adapted to keep herself in the know. This began with constantly having one news outlet or the other on in the background, an ambience of information. When the UK stations went to sleep, the US networks kept the pace until dawn. When she wasn't judging the flaws of each broadcast, she was analysing how the events will unfold. She also had a preternatural ability to connect with people and extract the gossip and opinions on a variety of matters. Her network was strongest amongst those who remained in Malaysia, particularly the expat community, who regularly reported to her developments left out by the largely state controlled Malaysia news outlets. But there were also concerns close to home

Her mother was in and out of the hospital, and required close, full time attention. Then, in February 2009, Maisey died. At her funeral, Merryl described her mother as 'a lady who took the trouble to listen, to read and to reflect about her way of faith and mine'. She contributed her zest for life and enthusiasm to her job as Director to the Merthyr Tydfil Institute for the Blind, the volunteer organisation Soroptimists, and to a fellowship at Christ Church and many other local organisations. Her portrait has pride of place in the Institute's office in Merthyr.

Distraught at the loss of her mother, and confined to Merthyr for a number of years, Merryl wanted to 'go somewhere completely different'. I was going to Pakistan to work on an issue of the left-wing international magazine, *New Internationalist*. She decided to accompany me.

In July 2010, Pakistan suffered 'the worst flood in living memory'. Heavy monsoon rains devested the country. Around one-fifth of Pakistan's land was underwater. When we arrived in Karachi in March 2011, the north-west frontier state of Khyber Pakhtunhwa, which had suffered the brunt of damage and casualties, had still not fully recovered. The first questions she raised were utterly typical: what affect did the flood have on Pakistan's historic site Mohenjodaro, the city built around the twenty-sixth century BC and the cradle of Indus Valley civilisation, and the historic site of Taxila, the largest continually occupied urban settlement in the world? And did previous floods lead to the end of the Indus Valley civilisation? She wanted to travel to Mohenjodaro. But then changed her mind and decided to visit a remote village in Khyber Pakhtunhwa: Pir Sabaq, which was under water for seventeen days. It was going to be a hazardous journey, and I was not too keen. But, as usual, she had her own way.

At Pir Sabaq she found the echoes of her own life. 'The sudden deluge sent its 6,000 inhabitants running for their lives', she wrote. 'They left behind everything they owned. From the barren mountains where they took refuge, they viewed the total devastation of the lives they had known', she wrote.

> As I walked around the village there was total absence of the normal agricul-
> tural sounds and smells of livestock. For a farming village it is multiple loss: a
> source of transport, power to plough and work machines, milk as well as meat
> – it all has to be replaced or substituted from outside for money, which is in as
> short supply as the beasts of the fields...I (saw) just one, scrawny ox hitched
> to a cart. When Noah began again, he at least had two!

She was interested in how the women rebuilt their lives; and she lived with them for a number of days. Being stripped bare of everything is unimaginable, incomprehensible, she said. There are no more savings, no nest eggs to rely on, no family members from whom to borrow, no credit rating, few jobs to be had and everyone is in the same boat, or rather without a boat to float.

She returned from Pir Sabaq much disturbed. The plight of the village clearly affected her. But she was also thinking about her own deprivations. The loss of her mother. Everything she left behind in KL. And her concerns for Anwar, who was, once again, being politically dispossessed. Her own history had come back to hound her. She became every ill. We had to stay in Pakistan till she had somewhat recovered.

Some time after our return from Pakistan, Merryl rang. 'Chappu, don't panic!', she said. 'I am having a heart attack. The ambulance is on its way'. Before I could reply, the ambulance had arrived, and she put the phone down. I spent a couple of hours pacing my attic room. The phone rang again. 'I am on my way to the operating theatre. Don't bother coming to Merthyr. I will call you when it's all over'. After a week, she was back home. She acquired a measure of cheerfulness; and continued in her role as Director of the newly relaunched Muslim Institute in London, a learned society of Fellows. The Fellows of the Institute had come to adore her as she regaled them with her wit and banter year after year, at the Institute's annual Winter Gatherings. She was also now regularly writing for the Institute's quarterly *Critical Muslim*, which was started in 2012. But Malaysia was always on her mind.

In the 2013 Malaysian General Election, Anwar led a coalition as the Leader of the Opposition. The coalition won 50.9 per cent of the popular vote but this was not enough for him to dethrone the incumbents. There were allegations of jerrymandering; Anwar also alleged that extensive electoral fraud had taken place. There was little doubt in our mind: once again, Anwar presented a clear and present danger to the ruling elite. Within a year of the election, the incumbent government started conspiring against him. The sequel to his 'sodomy' case, Sodomy II as the legal aficionados in Malaysia had dubbed it, had not quite found its conclusion.

We met Anwar at a London hotel on a bitterly cold morning in February 2014. By now the plot against him was in full swing. There was to be a hearing at the Court of Appeal. The government was going to contest his acquittal on the second sodomy charge. We pleaded with him not to go back to Malaysia. 'Stay in London', Merryl said. 'We can carry on the fight from here'. But Anwar brushed our concerns aside. It was, he said, a matter of principle for him to return to Malaysia. 'Don't worry', he said with his customary grin, 'I will be alright. Their appeal will be rejected'. But under government pressure, the Court of Appeal suddenly decided that the early High Court acquittal did not critically evaluate the evidence against him. The acquittal was overturned; and Anwar was back, for the third time in his life, in prison.

History was repeating itself. First time it was a farce. Now? Well, we were forced, after Hal Foster, to ask, *What Comes After Farce?* Foster was concerned about left wing cultural politics; we were anxious about Malaysian politics and Anwar's future. Merryl immediately launched into campaign mode. Meetings were held with Nazri and members of Anwar's party. Letters were written. Western politicians and journalists were contacted. Articles were published. But our efforts were futile.

We were broken like a shattered pot. Merryl found it difficult to write. She was constantly ill. The skin on her left leg became blistered. Then tumid. After a few months, the right leg also got infected. Both her legs were now swollen and painful. She was diagnosed with cellulitis and given antibiotics, and cream to rub on her legs. It did not work. More antibiotics followed to no avail. She found it difficult to walk. She could not continue her work as the Director of the Muslim Institute. She was asked to write an introductory text on anthropology. Something that she would have taken in her stride was now a daunting task. She struggled for months.

A perpetual air of melancholy shrouded her.

Scars can be worn as a badge of pride, as Nazri showed. Broken pots can be restored to become more beautiful and stronger than ever.

6.

Nazri rang. I was in Istanbul, in a car, on my way to a workshop in a rural part of Turkey. 'We are on our way to win the election', he announced. It was May 2018. A few days later, Pakatan Harapan, the coalition that Anwar formed as a leader in absentia, became the new government. Within a week, Anwar was granted a royal pardon and released from prison. There was a problem. The new Prime Minister was none other than Anwar's old adversary, Mahathir Muhammad. The leaders of Pakatan Harapan had decided that in the absence of Anwar, the 'old man' would be interim Prime Minister. His wife, Wan Azizah Wan Ismail, who had stood by Anwar and courageously faced all the tribulations visited on her, her husband, and her Party, by the 'old man' as well as those who succeeded him, would be Deputy Prime Minister.

Anwar asked Merryl to return to KL. A 'spacious and luxurious' room in his office building was prepared for her. She arrived to find herself in a sparsely furnished large room, with an attached bathroom. 'More like spartan than luxurious', she said. By now, cellulitis had taken a permanent hold on her legs. But she was back in her element, holding court in her room, drafting speeches, providing bountiful advice, and engaging in long, convoluting arguments – always with a cigarette in hand, flask of coffee by her side. The television in her room would be permanently on as she would be half-listening to BBC World or CNN. Anwar would drop in for an involved conversation (sometimes of political nature, sometimes of literary bent), and will be criticised frankly but lovingly while being handed a list of references to consult. Sometime she would sneak out to share a cigarette and gossip with Nazri. Even though she had difficulty walking, she loved going out for 'food and beverage'. She had developed an affectionate connection with our young colleague, Scott Jordan. Long lectures on the history of Malaya, Wales, the evils of the British Empire, the subtle art of objet curation, and, of course, the Indian Ocean World, were visited on the poor chap. Scott, who took her out on regular shopping expeditions, had picked up our lingo and engaged with Merryl in our trade mark repartee. That, no doubt, brought them even closer. The best place for 'food and beverage' was undoubtedly Nazri's (late and lamented) restaurant, Symphony. We would gather there frequently for lavish dinners, accompanied by generous amounts of Sharia-compliant wine, heated arguments, latest political gossip, and scintillating conversations, till closing time. For a while, it looked like the happy times of 1980s and 1990s had returned.

Merryl saw her work as repairing what was done to Anwar and Malaysia, a process of restoration that transforms loss to recovery, tragedy to triumph. A bit like *kintsugi*, the Japanese technique of repairing broken pots. The pots are repaired with lacquer and gold. While the cracks are all too visible, the pots are restored to their original function but now, with the added beauty of gold, they become works of art. They tell stories. There was much to do to take Anwar's story forward; as she obsessed over making a trilogy out of the America books, she took to seeing Anwar's trilogy not as one of Sodomy show trials, but as the proper rise, fall, and transcendence of the hero's journey more attuned to the old films they bonded over. She devoted all her energies to the required work.

We worked on delineating Anwar's vision for Malaysia. We turned his vision into a policy framework based on sustainability, care and compassion, mutual respect, innovation and the Malay notion of prosperity that seeks to balance material growth with spiritual fulfilment. We developed plans and future scenarios. But there was a nagging doubt. Will Mahathir hand over power to Anwar? Anwar had publicly forgiven Mahathir; and was convinced that he had changed. We were not persuaded. Mahathir was dillydallying. 'Do scorpions act against their nature?', Merryl asked pointedly. As the famous Sufi parable of a frog and a scorpion illustrates – they don't.

During Christmas of 2018, Merryl went to South Africa to attend a wedding and spend time with her niece. On the return Qatar Airways flight to KL, she fell seriously ill, was removed from the plane at Doha, and taken to hospital. She woke up in an intensive care unit.

Several days had passed and she was now in a different year than the one she was last conscious in. For a couple of days, we had no idea where she was. Frantic phone calls were made before she was traced. A week later she was cleared to depart from Doha. When she eventually got back to Kl, she was a different woman. Her legs were badly swollen because of lymph fluid build-up. Bandages on her legs had to be changed on a daily basis. A nurse, Grace, was appointed, to perform the task. Drying agents were applied to tame the swelling, followed by lotions to soothe the dead skin, and reduce the swelling. Wan Azizah, the one force on this earth Merryl would instantly give in to (at mere mention of Wan Azizah's impending arrival, she would put out the cigarette she was in the middle of and hide any remaining stragglers), had enlisted friends and professionals to completely rewrite her diet. She was put on a cocktail of medicine – Western and non-Western! It was an indication that her body was battered beyond endurance.

The relationship between Anwar and Mahathir was also in intensive care. Towards the end of 2019, we developed a set of political scenarios. The worse scenario, entitled 'Full Metal Jacket', suggested that Mahathir will – once again – declare war on Anwar; and use all in his means to prevent him from ascending to power. When the scenario was presented to Anwar, he refused to think about, or engage with, it. He was still convinced that Mahathir will keep his word; and move out of the PM's office so he could move in.

Yet again, history was moving in cycles. And no one was more concerned than Merryl. But it wasn't just Malaysian politics that were repeating the mistakes of the past; the world itself was also treading the same course. The most problematic thing we inherit from the past, Merryl said, is how we think about our problems. 'We cannot resolve our problems with more of the same, simply using the same old ideas that helped produce our present problems. We have to understand how we came to think about our economy, politics, the world system, nature and the environment, as we do. We have to trace the roots of our way of thinking to realise there are other possibilities, different ways to understand the problems, and think about their solution'. We need to learn to ask new questions, she emphasised.

The question regarding Mahathir was settled. He declared full scale assault on Anwar, just as our scenario suggested. The carefully restored pot began to fall apart. In a series of political manoeuvres, in which Mahathir and Anwar's former allies played a sinister role, Pakatan Harapan lost power. Anwar was the Leader of Opposition, *de novo*. The psychological impact on Merryl is difficult to judge. But she was clearly shattered. She confined herself to her room; and refused all my and Scott's invitations to go out for dinner or to socialise with others.

Her legs were now weeping profusely. She had to be taken to hospital. The solution was standard, a course of antibiotics. But Merryl was beyond the usual antibiotics, she required the 'nuclear bomb' of antibiotics, full course. Each run truly took it out of her. While being treated for her legs, she had a setback and was moved to an intensive care unit. Her condition deteriorated rapidly. Doctors told us to prepare for the worst. It appeared that the new team of specialists now seeing to her were running out of options. There was fear that the bugs we were dealing with were resistant to the available antibiotics. Also, the toll on the body was beginning to push an already weakened heart. They were engaged in a balancing act of applying enough antibiotics to take on the multiple bacterial infections in her system while also using blood pressure regulators at the right dosage to keep her heart functional. We waited and prayed.

For several days the less news was for the better. In prior hospitalisations she would jest about how the placard could be changed outside her spacious and luxurious room like the one changed at the gates of Buckingham Palace informing the public of the condition of the Royal

Family. Now we would get daily updates in the form of WhatsApp messages from Nurse Grace and her attending physicians. Due to the complications of the Covid-19 pandemic, visitation was highly limited. Scott managed to see her and review her condition. He found her between spouts of consciousness but this did not deter his mission to report the multipage list of the headlines that he knew she'd be without in her ICU room. He also managed to play Mike Oldfield's Tubular Bells for her on my request. My constant playing of the song in our various residences drove Merryl to develop disdain for the tune. The logic was that with hearing only a few notes of the song, she would have to return to consciousness, if only to give the coldest death stare to the perpetrator of the artistic crime. Slowly her moments of consciousness improved to interactions and vocal communication. She was recovering. We had a video chat. She looked warped. 'Hello!', she said. 'I am here. I am still with you. You are not going to get rid of me yet'. Doctors instructed her to stop smoking. 'Let me think about it', she replied.

A few days later, doctors announced that she was well on her way to recovery. Her 'spacious and luxurious' room was now restructured, turned into a two-bedroom flat, furnished according to her taste, with extra facilities to help her mobility. Anwar even managed to stop by and see her. She was conscious and awake when he arrived, in the middle of one of the twice-a-day sessions with the doctors. Anwar was amazed, he had only seen pictures that indicated the worst during this stay, the last thing he expected was to see Merryl in her element, witty as ever, expecting updates on the political situation, while also critiquing the comfort of the numerous hospital beds she had been in, none of them qualifying as comfortable. Anwar was happy to see her joking and smiling, but when she gave him time to speak, he had important words for her. 'Merryl, things are going to have to change. We need you healthy. Your diet and lifestyle. No more smoking!' Anwar waited for the expected retort. The 'No, no, no, no' followed by an Excuzzee!' But instead, she smiled, closed her eyes, and put her hand on her heart. 'Yes Mr. Prime Minister. Alhamdulillah!' The room was colonised by silence as the army of medical professionals taking readings and changing tubes were frozen. Merryl would slip back to sleep after the utterance. Anwar was dumbfounded. These would be the last words she would say to him.

On 1 February 2021, she returned to her base, Nurse Grace in attendance. She had a video chat with Maha and I. She was lying in bed, appeared calm, albeit a little confused. 'Get some rest', we said. 'Talk to you tomorrow, be be!', she replied. Immediately afterwards, she asked Grace to help her move over to the other side of the bed. She took her final breath as she was being moved.

She shined wherever she went. She enriched my life; and every life she touched. She leaves us faded by her terrestrial absence. But she will be a constant intellectual and spiritual presence on the rest of my days. Her intellectual legacy will, to use her favourite word, endure.

In moments of solitude, I imagine she is having a pleasant but protracted argument with God. I murmur: '*Ye, ye, Meraal. Said Qi?*'. She replies: '*Ye, ye, Chappu! Systi Ok*'. Why should a mere thing like death separate us?

THE PUZZLING MEMOIR OF HANNA DIYAB

Robert Irwin

'The reader familiar with tales of people now dead, with the feats of those plunged in the cavern of extinction never to emerge, with the lore of those who scaled the heights of power, and with the virtues of those whom Providence delivered from the stranglehold of adversity, feels that he has known such men in their own time. He seems to join them on their pillowed thrones and lean companionably with them on cushioned couches ... It is as if all that company were of his own age and time; as if those who grieve him were his enemies, and those who give him pleasure, his friends. But they have ridden in the vanguard long before him, while he walks in the rear-guard far behind.'

> *Al-Wafi bi al-wafayat* (Abundant Book on Dates of Death) a biographical dictionary compiled by the fourteenth-century scholar and government official, al-Safadi.

Hanna Diyab's *The Book of Travels* is a travel narrative which doubles as a memoir of youth. In *For Love and Money* (1987) the travel writer Jonathan Raban wrote as follows: 'Life, as the most ancient of all metaphors insists, is a journey; and the travel book in its deceptive simulation of the journey's fits and starts, rehearses life's own fragmentation. More even than the novel, it embraces the contingency of things'. Though this is fluently persuasive, the novelist Vladimir Nabokov took the trouble to refute it in advance; and in his novel *The Gift* (1938) he created an imaginary philosopher, Delalande, in order to deliver the contrary message. According to Delalande 'the unfortunate image of a "road" to which the human mind has become attached (life as a kind of journey) is a stupid illusion; we are not going anywhere. The other world surrounds us always and is not at the end of some kind of pilgrimage'. I believe that a reading of Diyab's strange narrative gives support to Nabokov and his mouthpiece, Delalande.

Hanna Diyab was born in Ottoman Aleppo circa 1688. His Maronite Christian family were traders who had close links with the French expatriate community in the city. However, Diyab seems to have taken an early decision that commerce was not for him and in 1706 he began a novitiate in a Maronite monastery in the Lebanese mountains, but it did not take him long before he realised that the monastic vocation was also not for him and the abbot happily concurred. Shortly afterwards Diyab teamed up with Paul Lucas, an antiquarian adventurer and charlatan, whom he served as translator and general factotum, and he accompanied Lucas in his travels from Syria to Cyprus, then Egypt, North African Tripoli, Tunis, Corsica, Livorno, Genoa, Marseille, Paris, and Versailles. In Paris he met Antoine Galland, a distinguished classical scholar who was already becoming famous as a result of his ongoing translation of *The Arabian Nights*. In October 1708, Diyab and some caged jerboas were presented by Lucas before Louis XIV and his court in Versailles. The animals and the Christian Arab were regarded as objects of considerable curiosity. A little later Diyab broke with Lucas and slowly made a perilous journey back to Aleppo via Istanbul and Anatolia. Back in Aleppo he was welcomed by his brothers and set up as a trader in broadcloth. He married and became a solid citizen. Many years later he wrote a narrative of his adventurous anabasis. The manuscript of his adventures ended up in the Vatican library where his authorship was only identified in the 1990s.

The discovery of the identity of the author created a sensation in the world of *Arabian Nights* studies. How much do some of the most famous stories in Galland's version of the *Nights* owe to Diyab? Was he perhaps the real author of 'Aladdin', 'Ali Baba', and 'Prince Ahmed and the Fairy Peri Banou'? But Diyab's story raises quite a number of other puzzles. First why did he write this memoir? It is possible that he set out his aims in the opening pages, but unfortunately the first eight pages of the manuscript are lost. Then why does his narrative end so abruptly? There is a brief account of a reencounter with Lucas in Aleppo and how he witnessed Lucas's anticlimactic exploration of a remote cave and then the words, 'Climbing up to the vineyard known as al-Qul'ayah, we had lunch and spent the rest of the day there. When evening came, each went on his way. This is the end of my story and my wanderings. I ask God's forgiveness for any undue additions. Completed on the third of March in the year 1764 of the Christian era.' Why did he wait so long to tell the story of his youth? What, if any, were its literary models? How can the narrative be so very precise in so many of its details and yet sometimes obviously confused in its chronology? Did he keep a diary?

Accounts of retrospective narratives of youthful adventures which crucially shaped the mature man are common enough in Western literature. Goethe's fictional, but heavily autobiographical and rather baggy *Wilhelm Meister's Wanderjahre* (1821) is an early example of a gap-year narrative. Twentieth-century examples include Laurie Lee's *As I Walked Out One Midsummer Morning* published in 1969, but chronicling his time in Spain in the 1930s; and there is also Patrick Leigh Fermor's *A Time of Gifts* (1977), an elegiacally moving account of a journey on foot from the Hook of Holland to the Middle Danube, also set in the 1930s. Then there is *Blood Knots: Of Fathers, Friendship and Fishing* by Luke Jennings (2010), a more recent and compulsively readable memoir about childhood innocence, fishing, and the boy's mentoring by an army intelligence officer.

But in the eighteenth-century Middle East there were no such precedents in Arabic. Come to that there was very little indeed in the way of an autobiographical tradition in the pre-modern Arab world and works which look like autobiographies are not so really. Thus Usama Ibn Munqidh's twelfth-century *Kitab al-i'tibar*, Book of Examples, is just that – a series of examples drawn from his own experience, to demonstrate such things as the role of luck in warfare, the courage of women, and the craziness of the Franks. It is not a straightforward narrative of his political and military career. Then again the fifteenth-century religious scholar al-Suyuti has been credited with an 'autobiography', but on closer examination the work in question is hardly more than an extended curriculum vitae setting out al-Suyuti's credentials to be the top scholar in Egypt and indeed in the world at large. In pre-modern Maronite literature, there are even fewer candidates to be considered as memoirs. The most interesting one was written in the seventeenth century by Ilyas al-Mawsuli which gives details of his journey to America and what he saw there. Diyab owned a manuscript of al-Mawsuli's work, but it is more a travelogue than a personal memoir. The first Arabic autobiography, in the full sense, was the Egypto-Syrian novelist Jurji Zaydan's *Sirat hayati* (The Story of My Life) which was published in 1908.

As noted, what has really excited scholars is the meeting with Galland and what Diyab took with him to that meeting. This happened while he was with Lucas in Paris. Lucas and Galland shared antiquarian interests and were friends. *The Arabian Nights* is an amorphous collection and over the centuries it lacked proper policing by editors. It contains all sorts of stories which feature in some manuscripts or printed texts but not in others. Thus, for example the *Sinbad* stories were not part of the oldest substantially surviving *Nights* manuscript dating from the late fifteenth century. Moreover, it has long been known that Galland, who had translated that manuscript as well as the *Sinbad* stories, was running out of material to pad out his multi-volume *Les mille et une nuits* and he was therefore pleased to take notes on the sixteen stories that Diyab told him over a matter of weeks. (Galland did not choose to use all the stories that he was told.) These stories, most of which do not *seem* to have any close Arabic originals, include some of the most famous: 'Aladdin', 'Ali Baba' and 'Prince Ahmed and the Fairy Peri Banou'. In the past there has been much scholarly debate about the degree to which Galland Frenchified the stories he was told by Diyab. Was it even possible that he composed the stories himself? Now, with the publication of Diyab's memoir, the scholarly debate has moved on and intensified.

Diyab does actually not say much about what may have been his own contribution to these stories, most of which have since been labelled 'orphan stories'. He was in Paris with Lucas. 'During that time, I became discouraged and discontent with life in those parts. An old man who was assigned to oversee the Arabic library [of the King] and could read Arabic well and translate texts into French, would visit us often. At the time, he was translating into French, among other works, the Arabic book *The Story of the Thousand and One Nights*. He would ask me to help him with things he didn't understand, and I'd explain them to him. The book was missing some "Nights", so I told him a few stories I knew and he used them to round out his work. He was very appreciative, and promised that I ever needed anything, he would do his utmost to grant it.'

Galland did not keep that promise and so Diyab, who had hoped to be appointed keeper of the Arabic books in the Bibliothèque Royale, eventually decided to return to Aleppo. Now the survival of the narrative of his *Wanderjahre* has allowed scholars to question the real origins of the

stories and the detail within them. Paulo Lemos Horta has led the charge
here. His recent book *Marvellous Thieves: Secret Authors of the Arabian Nights*
argues, among other things, that in his telling of the three most famous of
the orphan stories, Diyab drew on his adventurous association with Paul
Lucas, as well as on his introduction to what were for him the exotic
marvels of Paris and Versailles.

It is time to turn to the man who with fair promises had brought Diyab
to France. Paul Lucas (1664-1737) was employed by Louis XIV to travel
through the Middle East in search of antiquities and rare plants. He
published several narratives of his travels, which included accounts of
some places he had not actually visited and his books were further padded
out by scholarly ghost writers. Out in the East he was an antiquarian
conman who masqueraded as a doctor and he used crushed pearls in
concoctions and semi-precious stones hung as pendants as vaunted cures
for every ailment under the sun. (The ailments were confidently diagnosed
according to the humoral system.) He gave it out that he preferred to
receive payment in the form of ancient coins or medals or precious stones.
The coins and medals he received were customarily pronounced by him to
be near worthless rubbish (though in private they often scrubbed up rather
well). His most spectacular acquisition which he succeeded in smuggling
out of Egypt was a complete mummy. He also directed several
explorations of remote caves, though nothing much came of those
explorations. Despite Diyab's manifold services to Lucas, he is never
mentioned in that charlatan's books.

Diyab's presentation of Lucas is subtly ambivalent. Though he was
aware that Lucas was not a real doctor and the 'cures' had no other aim
than to get hold of antiquities on the cheap, again and again Diyab reported
the success of the fraudulent medications provided by Lucas. When Diyab
in Egypt was mercilessly harried by lice, Lucas was even able to produce
a lice-repellent stone. Curiouser and curiouser, when Diyab travelled
through Turkey, on his way back to Aleppo, he took on the guise of a
French physician. His French was excellent and his vaunted status as both
a Frenchman and a doctor made his travelling much easier and gave him
all sorts of exemptions from tolls and other obstacles. Inevitably he was
besieged by people seeking treatment for a whole range of ailments, for
which Diyab, following the example of Lucas, would provide some kind

of randomly concocted medication and yet not once were his treatments reported to have failed.

Diyab recorded the frequent resort of Lucas to cheating, lying, and smuggling and yet he does not denounce his master's stratagems. Perhaps he tacitly admired that way of conducting business. So now, was Lucas the real-life precursor of the wicked sorcerer in 'Aladdin'? Possibly. It will be remembered that in that story the sorcerer inveigles the youthful Aladdin to enter a perilous cave in order to fetch out a magic lamp. But when Aladdin takes fright that the sorcerer is going to abandon him in the cave after the lamp has been handed over, he refuses to cooperate any further and thereupon the sorcerer does indeed close up the cave and abandon him. Aladdin will eventually escape through use of a magic ring and he returns home with a lamp which he and his mother discover is the home of a powerful jinni who will become Aladdin's wonder-working slave. As several scholars have spotted, there may have been a precedent for the opening part of the story of 'Aladdin' in an incident that occurred very early on in the partnership of Lucas and Diyab. On the way from Aleppo to the coast, Lucas, called *khawajah*, or excellency, by the Arabs, came across a cave tomb protected by a boulder. At first nobody could be persuaded to enter the tomb which might have become the lair of a wild beast, but eventually Lucas was successful in paying a goatherd to venture in. The goatherd descended into the tomb and first handed out a skull. Then the goatherd found another skull. Then Lucas 'threw a piece of sturdy cloth down to the goatherd. "Collect everything you find on the floor of the tomb and hand it to me." The goatherd gathered what he found and handed it all over. Among the objects was a large plain ring. The *khawajah* studied it and saw that it was rusty. There wasn't an inscription that he could see, nor could he tell whether it was made of gold, silver, or some other metal. He kept it.

"Feel around along the walls of the tomb," he called out to the goatherd, who did as he was instructed, and found a niche. Inside the niche was a lamp, similar to those used by butter merchants. He didn't know what kind of metal it was made of, but he took it anyway. There was nothing left to find, so the goatherd climbed out and went on his way, and we all returned safely to the village.'

The coincidence of a searcher in a cave (which was thought to be dangerous) being directed from outside and discovering first a ring and then a lamp is indeed striking, but these objects do not appear to have been valuable, still less magical, and we never hear of them again. But, in any case, the business in the cave is only a small part of the story of 'Aladdin' and the way the story subsequently develops owes much more to an Arabic pre-Galland story, 'The Lover of Alexandria and His Magic Lamp' and it also has striking affinities with an Afghan story 'The Sultan's Lamp Served by Jinn', and to 'The Fisherman and His Son', which is found in the Wortley Montagu manuscript of the *Nights*. At best, Diayab, can be credited, not with creative genius, but rather with a good knowledge of traditional Arab storytelling.

Even so, there may be influence of a different kind upon the story of 'Aladdin'.

For Diyab, France was an exotic realm, a place of wonders and marvellous stories. One of the earliest of the wonders he encountered in France was the revelation of western military discipline. 'After the companies passed in inspection, they lined up in formation, one after the other. They marched in unison, without a single foot out of place!' And so on at length. He had difficulty in describing the mysterious manoeuvres that he had witnessed. 'Alas, words don't do justice to this display: I simply can't give an accurate account of the manoeuvres I saw during that drill! Nothing like it exists in the East: it's simply unheard of.' But that is by the way. Other marvels he witnessed in France may well have coloured his narration of the orphan stories.

In the story of 'Aladdin', Aladdin gives instructions to the *jinni* regarding the conjuring up of a palace that will be fit for the princess that he is to marry. The palace will be of marble and precious materials. Aladdin continues, 'I want you to build a great room, surmounted by a great dome and with four equal sides, made up of alternating layers of gold and silver. There should be twenty-four windows, six on each side with the latticed screens of all but one – which I want left unfinished – embellished, skilfully and symmetrically, with diamonds, rubies, and emeralds, so that nothing like this will have ever been seen in the world. I also want the palace to have a forecourt, a main court, and a garden. But, above all, there must be in a spot you decide, a treasure house, full of gold and silver coins. And I also want this palace to have kitchens, pantries, storehouses, furniture stores for precious furniture for all seasons, and, in keeping with the magnificence of the palace, stables filled with the most beautiful horses complete with their riders and grooms, not to forget hunting equipment'. Well, the architectural detail is rather bling. But the palace placed on order by Aladdin sounds a lot more like Versailles than it does the Aleppo Citadel.

Here is Diyab's account of his own first impression of the real palace: 'As we approached Versailles, I perceived something glittering in the distance, so bright it dazzled the eye. "What's that I see?" I asked my master. "The king's stables", he replied. As we drew near, I saw that it was a splendid imposing building, roofed with those black stones that people write on. The chimneys had gilded funnels, and when the sun shone it was impossible to fix your gaze upon them, as they gleamed so brightly. We spent half an hour driving by those stables before arriving at Versailles. As we approached the king's palace, I could see that there was a vast open space before it, surrounded by an iron fence as tall as a man with his arm outstretched, and topped with points as sharp as spears. At the centre was a gate that opened onto the space, flanked by tall soldiers carrying battle-axes and spears, and snarling like panthers ...' A little later in his narrative, Diyab wrote that the king had 'initiated the construction of Versailles, building a palace unequalled in any part of the world. He decorated it with all sorts of indescribable gardens, parks, and promenades'. And all this without the assistance of any Jinni! It was certainly one of the exotic marvels of the Occident. Then, shortly before his meeting with Galland, he witnessed another marvel at the Paris Opéra. It is not clear which opera he saw, but in the course of the performance there was a quasi-magical transformation. After an hour or so of singing and dancing everything 'that had been on stage flew up ... and vanished in the blink of an eye! In its place appeared a palace as splendid as the palace of the king of France, complete with towering columns, pavilions, salons, crystal windows, and other beautiful features. The palace had an arched entryway made of black and white marble'. Later, in the action-packed and confusing plot, the palace in its turn was magicked away.

It is perhaps a little surprising that Diyab shows no awareness of the subsequent renown of Galland's translation of the *Nights* or of the quests of European scholars and travellers to find more manuscripts of the *Nights* in the Middle East. Alexander Russell was with the Levant Company in Aleppo in the 1740s and 1750s and he and his brother Patrick, who followed him to Aleppo, were very interested in the professional storytellers who worked Aleppo's cafés and markets and the Russells hunted with limited success for more manuscripts of the *Nights*.

More could be said about the possible ways that details of Diyab's travels influenced his retelling of marvellous stories and Paulo Horta's book thoroughly explores those possibilities. But there are other things which puzzle me. There is no indication that Diyab kept a diary or even a summary record of his journeying and sometimes he gets the chronology wrong. Even so, the precision of his recall in other respects is astounding. He remembered exactly what was provided for lunch in that Maronite monastery all those years ago: 'There were three sorts of food on the table: a soup with lentils, wheat berries, grains, and other similar vegetables and pulses; some curd cheese; and figs preserved in molasses'. (More understandably he remembered that the shelves of the refectory were crowded with the skulls of deceased monks and that put him off his food.) To take another example he remembered the price of wine in Limassol. It was five piasters for a *qintar*. The price of fried fish in Lower Egypt also stayed in his memory. A portion cost one *fils* (a copper coin).

Diyab's Arabic prose is unpretentiously plain and there is no poetry in his vision of the world. Though he frequently digresses from the narrative of his travels to tell stories about remarkable adventures that befell other people, those stories mostly concern European Christians. He shows little or no interest in the jinn or Islamic magic and his digressions do not include retellings of Islamic folk tales. He chronicles his adventures in facing pirates, brigands, shipwreck, starvation, threats of murder, thuggish janissaries, and violent mobs, and yet he does not present himself as the hero of his adventures. Rather he reveals himself to be a complete coward. *Khawf* (fear), *faz'* (fright) and *tawahhum* (apprehension) feature prominently in his vocabulary. If there was a hint of danger he was invariably scared and, faced with the imminent danger of shipwreck, he fainted.

The Aleppo that Diyab grew up in was a prosperous centre of commerce. But his narrative bears frequent witness to the desolate state of much of the Mediterranean coastline. Nicosia was a large city, but most of its buildings were in ruins. Paphos was similarly in ruins. Over-taxation was driving people out of Cyprus. In North Africa, the first harbour their ship can find to anchor is an abandoned harbour with a ruined quay. Then Djerba's chief monuments were towers of skulls. Sfax was in ruins. On the way from Sfax to Tunis a muleteer explained that the region had once been prosperous and well-populated. 'Then one day God grew angry with people, and kicked up a great storm that levelled the town and buried it in sand'. So the eventual contrast with Genoa and its magnificent buildings, lofty palaces, and splendid churches was striking.

Diyab was at first shocked when he encountered unveiled women in Livorno. That took getting used to, though later he tried to help an Arab husband resident in France persuade his wife to cease wearing the veil. In Cyprus he soon came to hate the Greek Orthodox Christians and in Egypt he similarly took against the Coptic Christians. He also transmitted several anti-Semitic stories about French Jews. He was more at home among Muslims and Catholics. As a Maronite he was happy to worship in Roman Catholic churches, and in Tunis he attended church services at which a Jesuit preached at length about the creation, hellfire, and heaven. These sermons left Diyab 'feeling giddy, dazed and disoriented, as if in a trance.' Finally, while contemplating all that he had heard from that preacher, he did fall into a trance and was discovered after mass kneeling but unconscious. He was fanatically devoted to the Virgin Mary. His prayers to the Virgin never failed him and he had quite a few stories about people in trouble who similarly prayed to the Virgin and consequently were saved from execution or ruin.

Why did he take so long to set down the tale of his wandering youth and who did he anticipate would read it? After his audience with the 'Sultan of France' Louis XIV, he wrote that 'I have faithfully recounted everything that took place, without any additions or omissions. But I've also been brief about it, so the reader won't suspect that I dreamt all this up. After all, I witnessed many things on my journey that I haven't set down in writing, and that haven't remained in my memory these past fifty-four years. As I now write this account of my voyage, it is the year 1763. I visited Paris in 1709. Is it possible I could have retained everything I saw and heard in perfect detail? Surely not.' On his way back through Turkey he wrote that 'I wasn't aware of the importance of learning new things. I was a vagabond under the sway of youthful and foolish passions'. Looking back on how his hopes of becoming a librarian of the king of France had been dashed, he wrote that nevertheless 'as it would turn out, this was all for my good, and part of God's plan'. Are we to take it that God planned that Diyab should get the wanderlust out of his system before settling down in Aleppo and becoming a prosperous and well-respected trader in broadcloth? And whom did he imagine his reader would be?

Why did Diyab bother to write his book so long after the events it records? Somewhat hesitantly, I draw upon my own experience here. In the late 1960s I made several visits to an Algerian *zawiya* (a kind of Sufi monastery) and stayed there to study Islam. During my travels to the *zawiya* I slept in gutters, ditches, and caves. I was threatened by an Egyptian with a knife and an Algerian hotelier with a double-barrelled shotgun. In the *zawiya* I experienced many strange and inexplicable things. My visits to the *zawiya* were regarded as suspicious and I was interrogated by the police as a suspected CIA spy. Strange things would continue to happen on my returns to London. Then quite suddenly in the early 1970s in short order I acquired a job, a wife, a mortgage, and a daughter. My days of sleeping in ditches en route to some mystical goal were firmly in the past. Then, in 2010, I felt mysteriously impelled to write an account of my *Wanderjahre*, *Memoirs of a Dervish*. The point here is that, when I had finished writing that book, I immediately felt much lighter. It was as if I had been carrying those past years about with me as one who was heavily pregnant and now at last, I had been delivered of the baby, no matter how weird and ugly that offspring may have been.

By the way, the title of Patrick Leigh Fermor's magnificent *A Time of Gifts* is taken from a line in Louis MacNeice's no less magnificent poem, 'Twelfth Night', 'For now the time of gifts is gone'. The next two lines of the final verse are 'O boys that grow, O snows that melt/ O bathos that the years must fill'. It may be that, as Diyab wrote the story of his youthful travels, he sensed that he was approaching his own Twelfth Night.

MUHAMMAD ASAD, THE NEGLECTED THINKER

Josef Linnhoff

Born to Jewish parents in 1900 in the Austro-Hungarian Empire, Leopold Weiss converted to Islam in 1926, changed his name to Muhammad Asad, and became a famous Muslim of the twentieth century. Asad is best known for his iconic autobiography, *The Road to Mecca*, which tells the remarkable story of how a young Jew from central Europe left the religion of his birth for Islam before proceeding to live for several years in the deserts of central Arabia. In later years Asad moved to British India, witnessed first-hand the creation of Pakistan, and represented the country at the inaugural United Nations Assembly. By the time of his death in southern Spain in 1992, Asad had lived in almost a dozen countries, East and West. But Asad was no mere wanderer or convert; he was first and foremost an intellectual. His long career stretches almost the entire twentieth century and offers a window into the many social, political, and intellectual currents of modern Islam. Asad's writings traverse many fields of the modern Islamic tradition, including Qur'an and hadith sciences, political theory, and Islamic legal theory. A small but significant trend of Western converts, including Murad Hoffman, Muhammad Knut Berstrom, Maryam Jameela, and Jonathan Brown, have spoken of the role that Asad played in their journeys to the faith.

Yet, Asad remains a somewhat marginal figure. We still have yet to see a major study of Asad in English. Nor do we hear his name when we talk of some of the major Muslim thinkers of the last century. Few are aware of his second biography, *Homecoming of the Heart*, covering his post-Arabia years from 1932. Indeed, our main source for Asad's life remains Asad himself, even if this is – slowly – starting to change. In Muslim circles, the neglect is even greater. We struggle to find Muslim PhD students or academics engaging his ideas, or Islamic institutes founded in his name. One hardly, if ever, hears Asad's name in a Friday *khutbah*.

Muhammad Asad is a richer, more creative, and far more complex Muslim thinker than is commonly recognised. He has a great deal to teach us today, almost three decades after his death. While the broad contours of Asad's life are known, there remains much that we still do not know. Much of what we *think* we know about Asad, meanwhile, does not stand up to scrutiny. But above all, Asad is *relevant*. Asad's life and thought raises themes of identity, belonging, reform, and the future of Islam that speak no less to our time than his own.

Let us begin by correcting a common misrepresentation. Where Asad does feature in scholarship, he is widely seen as a bridge or mediator between Islam and the West. Popularly known as 'Europe's Gift to Islam', the entrance square to the United Nations building in Vienna has been named 'Muhammad Asad Platz'. But the truth is far more complex. Asad framed his conversion to Islam as a revolt against the relativism, consumerism, and confusion of postwar Europe. He soon left Europe, moved to Arabia, and devoted his life to the cause of Muslim renewal and reform. In so doing, he drew on diverse trends of the Islamic intellectual tradition, including the modernist reformism of Muhammad 'Abduh, the revivalist anti-Sufism of Ibn Taymiyyah and the legal theory of Ibn Hazm. Asad was also a harsh critic of European secularism throughout his career. In an early work, *Islam at the Crossroads* (1934), Asad warned Muslims on the verge of independence from colonial rule against following Europe's secular path. He argues in this and later works that secular modernity is an era of crisis and decay; the exclusion of religious truth from the political sphere, he writes, lay at the root of the many crises of the modern world. Social, political, and military conflicts were but a symptom of this deeper turmoil. It should not surprise us, then, that upon moving to British India in the 1930s and with the establishment of Pakistan in 1947, Asad called for the creation of a true Islamic State that implemented the Sharia:

> Islam does not content itself with merely demanding a certain 'spiritual attitude'... but insists on the believer's accepting its own scheme of practical life as well. Within the framework of this scheme, called Sharia, Islam has its

own views on progress, its own definition of social good and its own pattern of social relations…Islam stands and falls with its ability to shape our society.

Asad's conversion to Islam drew on many prevailing tropes of early Zionist discourse; a yearning for rootedness and community, disenchantment with Europe; the romanticisation of the Orient as a site of purity and authenticity. But Asad found his resolution in Islam, not Israel. Such affinity for Zionist themes belies his anti-Zionist politics. His first work, *Unromantisches Morgenland (Unromantic Orient*, 1924), expresses sympathy for the Arab inhabitants of Palestine and introduces the theme of 'Zionist colonialism' decades before it became popular in progressive circles. Nor does Christianity fare better. Asad derides it as a 'spent force' content with providing spiritual 'mood music' rather than taking an active role in shaping the political sphere. He also foreshadows the later post-colonial critique of Eurocentrism, accusing Europeans of conflating their rejection of Christianity with that of religion as such. In an article from 1947, we read:

> Because Christianity was the Occident's only religious experience for so many centuries, the Occidentals have grown accustomed to identify it with 'religion' in general; and their modern, obvious disappointment with Christianity has assumed the colour of disappointment with the religious principle as such. In reality, however, they have become disappointed with the only form of religion they had ever known.

It is hard to square this with the popular image of Asad as an ecumenical bridge between East and West. Asad was, in fact, a Muslim thinker whose conversion to Islam was rooted in no small measure by his rejection of much of the Europe of his day. That the popular image persists is a lesson to Muslims: this is what happens if we neglect our scholars. The meaning of their life, thought, and legacy is shaped by others.

Yet Asad's relations with his fellow Muslims were not straightforward. A sense of distance and disconnect followed Asad throughout his career. He never joined a mass movement or organisation like the Muslim Brotherhood or Jamaat Islami that would have further spread his ideas. He was also an independent thinker who drew on diverse trends. His emphasis on the role of reason in Islam, for example, evoked the Mu'tazili theological tradition. But Asad also shared considerable common ground with the Islamists. Both Sayyid Qutb and Abu Ala Mawdudi praised Asad's acerbic critique of secularism. That Asad offered an insider's critique, as a European convert, only increased his prestige in Islamist circles of the 1940s and 1950s. In true idiosyncratic form, however, what Asad meant by 'Sharia' was unique. A close reading of Asad's ideas on Islamic law show him to be a disciple of the Ibn Ḥazm and the Ẓahiri legal school, the hitherto extinct *madhhab* which has been, since at least the fourteenth century, excluded from Sunni legal consensus:

> The reader should not propose that the views propounded by me are an unheard-of innovation in Islamic thought...(T)hey were held by the Prophet's Companions themselves as well as by their immediate successors and, after them, by some of the greatest scholars of Islam - and particularly by the man who is justly regarded as one of the three or four most brilliant minds which the Muslim world has ever produced: Abu Muhammad ibn Hazm of Cordoba.

Asad was also liberal on social matters and mocked the social conservatism of 'the mullahs'. In a short work, *Principles of State and Governance in Islam* (1961), he sketched his vision of a true Islamic state, based on Zahiri principles. The resemblance to a liberal Western democracy in terms of universal suffrage, freedom of conscience, and gender equality is clear.

The point is that Asad is not easy to place. He defies neat classification and our tendency to sharply categorise and define scholars. Is he liberal or Islamist? Progressive or reactionary? Heretical or mainstream? In Asad we see a commitment to social liberalism alongside strident anti-secularism; Mu'tazili-esque theology alongside Zahiri legal theory. The result is that no school of modern Islamic thought fully claims him as their own. The fault lies not with Asad but with our urge to reduce a rich and complex Islamic tradition to such simplistic binaries. Asad challenges these boundaries, forcing us to question what it means to be 'liberal', 'Islamist' or indeed any other kind of Muslim thinker.

There are perhaps deeper reasons for the disconnect between Asad and his fellow Muslims. Throughout Islamic history, converts have brought many pre-existing beliefs and practices with them into Islam. No one is a *tabula rasa*. Asad was the convert who left Europe and found spiritual sustenance in Islam. But it was an Islam that Asad understood on *his* terms, and it would seem that his conception of 'religion', 'reason', and 'reform' was heavily shaped by his formative influences and upbringing in Europe.

Consider his denial of miracle stories in the Qur'an. Such stories, he explains, are parabolic myths that serve a solely didactic purpose; they do not refer to actual historical events. The story of Jesus speaking in the cradle (Q3:46, 19) is a 'metaphorical allusion to the prophetic wisdom which was to inspire Jesus from a very early age.' On Jesus creating birds out of clay (Q3:49), Asad draws on his Arabic prowess. The pre-Islamic Arabic word for 'bird' (*tayr*) in poetry also meant 'fortune' or 'destiny':

> Thus, in the parabolic manner so beloved by him, Jesus intimated to the children of Israel that out of humble clay of their lives he would fashion for them the vision of a soaring destiny, and that this vision, brought to life by his God-given inspiration, would became their real destiny by God's leave and by the strength of their faith.

Asad here reveals an Enlightenment conception of 'reason' that aims to harmonise religion and scripture with the empirical sciences - an issue that had so decisively shaped Jewish and Christian discourse in the twentieth century, far more so than it has occupied Muslim thinkers. Indeed, scepticism of miracles goes against much of traditional Muslim piety. As the Ottoman Shaykh al-Islam Mustafa Sabri would insist, the Islamic tradition saw miracles as proof of Muhammad's prophecy. It is thus unsurprising that Asad was controversial in some Muslim circles. The initial sponsor for his Qur'anic translation, the Saudi-based Muslim World League, withdrew its support for the project in 1964 and later banned the work outright in 1974, even before publication. For Asad, this rejection stung. He bitterly complained in a private letter in February 1969:

> If you knew on what minor, almost insignificant ground, various of their 'experts' objected to some of my interpretations, you would be astounded to know to what depths intellectual activities have fallen among some of our so-called scholars, who are afraid of every bit of fresh air. Apparently, they regard Islam as extremely brittle to use his own mind!

Asad later claimed in an interview in his final years that had Islam been in the 1920s like it was today, he would likely have never converted. Asad promoted a 'rational Islam', then, that stood against the beliefs of many of its indigenous followers. In short, an Islam emptied of Muslims. He knew of this disconnect and in a sobering note in *The Road to Mecca*, he asks:

Why is it that, even after finding my place among the people who believe in the things that I myself have come to believe, I have struck no root?

The answer is that Asad's conception of Islam, reason, and reform can only be fully understood in terms of the intellectual culture that he had ostensibly left behind. It was easy for Asad to leave Europe. It was harder for Europe to leave him.

Asad thus reflects the 'authenticity deficit' that continues to plague the Western intellectual. Does he serve or betray the tradition? Is he replenishing and indigenising the faith in a new Western frontier, or rather intellectually colonising Islam, playing the unwitting role of the 'white saviour' who teaches the natives their religion? Had Asad lived a decade or so more, the sense is that he would have ultimately made a far more direct and explicit appeal for Western Muslims to lead the revival of Islam. For this seems the direction in which he was travelling in his later years. It is a nascent theme in Asad's final major work, his Qur'anic translation and commentary, *The Message of the Qur'an*.

Written between 1958 and 1980, this work includes a detailed introduction, four appendices, and no less than 5,371 footnotes. In his introduction, Asad speaks of seeking to bring the Qur'an nearer to the hearts and minds of people in the West. He dedicates the work to 'People who think' (*li-qawmmin yatafakkarun*). This is no doubt a sign of his modernist reformism, but Asad is surely aware that such a call to 'reason' will appeal to Western audiences. Asad also makes a series of lexical choices that seem designed to resonate with Western readers familiar with the Bible and Christian teachings. He chooses 'God' over 'Allah', for example, foreshadowing later translators like Abd al-Haleem. He uses the pronouns 'Thee', 'Thy' and 'Thou' and verbs 'shalt' or 'dost' in a style reminiscent of the King James Bible. Asad translates the terms *rasul* and *nabi* not as 'Prophet' or 'Messenger' but instead 'Apostle', a term with strong Biblical overtones. The Quranic term *khalifa*, often translated as 'vicegerent' or 'successor', is translated as 'one who shall inherit' the Earth, in a nod to Mathew 5:5. This may indicate Asad's own background; we see here the residual influence of Asad's upbringing in Europe. Or it may be a deliberate attempt to present the Qur'an in a way amenable to Westerners. It could of course be both.

This would further explain Asad's take on miracles; he knows miracle stories are being challenged in his age and are unlikely to appeal to a Western audience. It would also account for the frequency with which Asad's invokes Islam's rejection of key Christian doctrines such as Original Sin and vicarious atonement. Asad brings this into his footnotes at every turn, even when commenting upon Qur'anic verses that seem to have no relation to these doctrines. Consider his take on 35:18:

> And no bearer or burdens shall be made to bear another's burden, and if one weighted down by his load calls upon [another] to help him carry it, nothing thereof may be carried [by that other], even if it be one's near kind.

Asad says the first half of the verse is a rejection of the idea of Original Sin and that the second denies the vicarious atonement. No other English translator, from Yusuf Ali, Pickthall, Arberry to *The Study Qur'an*, refers to these Christian doctrines. Asad knows these doctrines have lost much of their purchase to Westerners. His aim, then, is to demonstrate what he sees as the true rationality, cogency, and egalitarianism of Islamic teachings. Implicit in this is the idea that Islam and Westerners are the perfect fit for the other. Islam can win over a West that has grown tired of Christianity. Western audiences, meanwhile, are a more fertile soil from which to plant the revival of Islam.

If our reading is correct, it is possible to catch glimpses in Asad's final work of an argument that has since gained traction; that Western Muslims are the hope for the future of the *ummah*; that only Western Muslims possess the freedoms and critical inquiry necessary to bring about a renaissance of Islam. It is a claim that we hear today from the likes of Khaled Abou El Fadl and Murad Hoffman. It would also mean that Asad returned, in some way, to his European roots. The causes that first led him to embrace Islam and leave Europe ultimately brought him back, albeit in a way that Asad could never have imagined and had yet to fully express.

We are currently passing through an important cultural moment in which themes of race and identity are under the spotlight as never before. Notions of 'systematic racism' or 'white privilege' have moved from academic and activist circles to the mainstream. Asad lived and died long before this. As a prominent and early white convert to Islam, however, his experiences may still contribute to contemporary debates.

On the one hand, Asad was certainly the beneficiary of 'white privilege' throughout his career. We cannot fail to notice the ease with which he accessed elite circles wherever he went; Mustafa Maraghi in Egypt, Ibn Saud in Arabia, and Muhammad Iqbal in India. No doubt his intellect played a role. But European converts were a true novelty at the time and Asad used this to great effect. Nor do we see any trace of sheepishness in his works at the privilege he was afforded by Muslims of colour. But on the other hand, a closer look at Asad's life also strengthens the sense that whiteness somehow invalidates Islam, that white Muslims and converts cannot be 'truly' Muslim. In *Homecoming of the Heart*, Asad speaks of the discrimination he faced while working for the Pakistani government between 1947 and 1951 on account of his not being *desi*. More troubling are the anti-Semitic tropes that followed Asad throughout his career in the Muslim world. It is little known, for example, that while working on *The Road to Mecca* in New York in the 1950s, Asad faced a character assassination campaign in the Pakistani press. He had to repeatedly deny claims that he was an Israeli spy or had reverted to Judaism. The following is an extract from a private letter from Asad to then-Pakistani Foreign Minister Zafarullah Khan, dated 6 July 1953:

Dear Chaudhri Sahib,

I am sorry that every time I write to you it is about something unpleasant, but I really see no way out of a difficult situation without placing before you the facts of the libel and slander to which I am now exposed. Since my resignation from the Foreign Service, a spate of malicious rumours, both oral and in the press, has been put into circulation to the effect that:

1) I have forsaken my allegiance to Islam and have reverted to Judaism;

2) I have exerted my influence in the Pakistan Foreign Ministry in favour of the Jews and have been advocating Arab rapprochement to Israel;

3) In the course of my recent tours of the Middle East I have surreptitiously visited Israel;

4) I have married in the United States a Jewess...

We can feel the pain and hurt of Asad as he continues:

> (T)he few points which I have quoted above do undermine the reputation which I have built up for myself in the course of my twenty-five years' work for Islam and the idea of Pakistan. You can well imagine how it hurts to be accused of disloyalty by the community to which one's whole life has been devoted....

The ostensible trigger for this was Asad's decision to divorce his second Arabian wife for an American Catholic convert to Islam. It is indeed a sad irony that Asad was forced to defend his commitment to Islam at the time of writing a book that sought to explain to a Western audience all what he found beautiful about his faith. Seen from another angle, however, much of this is not unique to Asad. Until today, white Muslims and converts continue to speak to a sense of alienation from wider Muslim spaces. Alongside the celebration of (white) converts sits a more sombre reality, one in which they are interrogated upon entering mosques, isolated during religious festivals or even accused of spying on the community. White Muslims remain either fetishised or marginalised, but seldom treated as equal. The career of Muhammad Asad speaks to this reality. It is instructive to think that upon his death in 1992, Asad had been Muslim for sixty-six of his ninety-two years. Yet he was, and will always, be seen first and foremost as a convert.

This smear campaign is one of many largely unknown aspects of *The Road to Mecca*. Published to wide acclaim in 1954, the book purports to tell the story of how Asad left his European-Jewish heritage and embraced Islam, immersing himself between 1926–32 with the Bedouins of central Arabia and becoming a close confident of the Saudi founder, Ibn Saud. Part travelogue and part memoir, it is today considered one of the great spiritual biographies of the twentieth century, rivalled perhaps only by that of Malcolm X.

The work's iconic status is yet to be fully reflected in critical scholarship. But what we do have is telling. *The Road to Mecca* can no longer be read as a reliable and historically accurate account of the life of its author. The one major critical study of the text by Gunter Windhager (in German) does much to separate historical fact from narrative fiction; Asad's Bedouin travelling companion in the opening chapters, Zayd, for example, is shown to be a purely literary figure. Consider, too, the notable omissions in the text. In an early critical review, Judd Teller accused Asad of wilfully downplaying the Jewish element of his story:

> It is remarkable that he does not discuss European anti-Semitism, as though this had no effect on him. Yet he was born in Galicia, where the Jews were caught up as scapegoats in the power struggles of the anti-Semitic Ukrainians and Poles and the dubiously tolerant Austrian government. He was brought up in Vienna, when it was the capital of European anti-Semitism...Did all this leave him untouched?

Asad also provides no details of any formal study throughout these Arabian years. To this day we do not know what texts he studied, with whom, or what impacted his ideas about the Islamic intellectual tradition – a notable lacuna for someone who will seek to reform that very tradition. Most telling is the failure to disclose the true reasons for his eventual departure from Arabia in 1932. A curt reference to a restlessness of spirit and desire to explore other Muslim lands hardly convinces; one suspects far more has been left unsaid. Asad's private letters also lead us to question his avowed intention in writing the text. In the Introduction, Asad claims to be motivated by a desire to communicate the beauty of Islam to a Western audience. His private letters from the period point to something more mundane: financial hardship and a lucrative contract offer from Simon & Schuster.

Asad is hardly unique in this. No autobiographer can be purely objective in telling their story. And perhaps a focus on historical 'fact' blinds us from the deeper 'truths' that Asad sought to convey. But the task for future scholars is to explore the full extent of Asad's editorial enterprise. This must include a cross-reading of the four different editions of *The Road to Mecca*, published between 1954 and 1980. It is too little known that Asad made a series of editorial changes across each edition. Even a cursory comparison of the texts is revealing. Consider the criticism of Ibn Saud in the first 1954 edition of *The Road to Mecca*.

> His (Ibn Saud's) unprecedented rise to power at a time when most of the Middle East had succumbed to Western penetration filled the Arab world with the hope that here at last was the leader who would lift the entire Arab nation out of its bondage; and many other Muslim groups besides the Arabs looked to

him to bring about a revival of the Islamic idea in its fullest sense by establishing a state in which the spirit of the Koran would reign supreme. But these hopes remained unfulfilled. As his power increased and was consolidated, it became evident that Ibn Saud was no more than a king – a king aiming no higher than so many other autocratic Eastern rulers before him.

A good and just man in his personal affairs, loyal to his friends and supporters, generous towards his enemies, graced by intellectual gifts far above the level of most of his followers, Ibn Saud has, nevertheless, not displayed that breadth of vision and inspired leadership which was expected of him. True, he has established a condition of public security in his vast domains unequalled in Arab lands since the time of the early Caliphate a thousand years ago; but, unlike those early Caliphs, he accomplished this by means of harsh laws and punitive measures and not be inculcating in his people a sense of civic responsibility. He has sent a handful of young men abroad to study medicine and wireless telegraphy; but he has done nothing to imbue his people as a whole with a desire for education and thus to lift them out of the ignorance in which they have been steeped for many centuries. He always speaks – with every outward sign of conviction – of the grandeur of the Islamic way of life; but he has done nothing to build up an equitable, progressive society in which that way of life could find its cultural expression.

Now compare this with the exultant praise seen in the same passage from the 1973 edition:

His unprecedented rise to power at a time when most of the Middle East had succumbed to Western penetration filled the Arab world with the hope that here at last was the leader who would lift the entire Arab nation out of its bondage; and many other Muslim groups besides the Arabs looked to him to bring about a revival of the Islamic idea in its fullest sense by establishing a state in which the spirit of the Koran would reign supreme.

A good and just man in his personal affairs, loyal to his friends and supporters, generous towards his enemies and implacable towards hypocrites, graced by intellectual gifts far above the level of most of his followers. Ibn Saud has established a condition of public security in his vast domains equally in Arab lands since the time of the early Caliphate a thousand years ago. His personal authority is tremendous, but it does not rest so much on actual power as on the suggestive strength of his character. He is utterly unassuming in words and demeanour. His truly democratic spirit enables him to converse with the beduins who come to him in dirty, tattered garments as if he were one of them.

Perhaps the passing of two decades led Asad, by 1973, to reflect more fondly on Ibn Saud. But this seems unlikely. The sense remains that the first edition of 1954 is closest to Asad's true feelings. This would explain Asad's departure from Arabia in 1932 after his growing disillusion with the leadership of Ibn Saud. Yet this in turn raises the question: why the hagiographic shift in 1973? Several scholars point to the controversy around his Qur'anic translation and commentary during this same period; these edits are, perhaps, an attempt to restore Saudi sponsorship of the project. If so, the 1973 edition of *The Road to Mecca* – the same year as the oil boom – could be read as an early witness to the growing reach and influence of Saudi financial and publishing clout in the modern Muslim world.

These editorial strategies show us that *The Road to Mecca* is not a static text. It is, rather, a dynamic account of the life of its author, which Asad re-shaped at different times and in light of changing circumstances. An exhaustive comparative study of each edition would surely reveal the full depth and breadth of this strategy. It would also give a rich insight into the many ways in which Asad's positions changed over the course of his long career.

Why, then, do we still await a comprehensive study of this formidable Muslim thinker in English? Perhaps it is the sheer size of the task. A proper study of Asad requires competency in at least four languages (English, German, Arabic, and Urdu). The researcher must tackle an intellectual output that includes seven published works (plus, for *Islam at the Crossroads* and *Road to Mecca*, different editions thereof), six edited issues of the journal *Islamic Culture* (January 1937-1938), ten issues of his journal '*Arafat* (1946-47), numerous radio talks, articles and public speeches, private letters, and interviews with surviving friends and family. Such a study would require extensive research to illuminate the backdrop to various stages of Asad's life; from early-twentieth century European Jewry to the formative years at the dawn of the Saudi and Pakistani states. Asad's own account would have to be cross read against competing voices. It is, in short, a daunting task.

Yet there is another facet to consider. The answer may also lie in the intellectual dryness of modern Islam and the failure of Muslims to claim

Asad as one of their own. To the modern Muslim's need for easy answers and quick certainties, for example, Asad only provokes questions. To our tribalised 'Sufi-or-Salafi' milieu, Asad defies neat classification. To those who prefer to memorise, Asad calls for critical thinking. The disconnect that followed Asad in his life, then, has continued long after his death. The sense remains that had Asad served Zionism or Christianity like he served Islam, there would be numerous studies venerating his life, thought, and contribution. It is perhaps telling that the best scholarship on Asad today is found in the academic field of Jewish Studies. Muslims, meanwhile, scholarly and popular, are largely absent. A formidable intellect of the twentieth century thus converts to Islam and devotes his life to the faith, producing much by way of thought and argument. Upon his death, however, he recedes into the background. There is little effort to preserve, spread, engage, or develop his ideas by the community of which he was a part. Where Asad does feature today, it is an airbrushed version, a ecumenical 'bridge' cleansed of much of his actual thought.

The result is that we are left with half-truth, simplification, and ignorance. Asad is neglected and misrepresented in equal measure. If known at all, he is shaped and defined by others. The far more complex and interesting story of who Muhammad Asad was and what he can teach us remains largely unexplored. Whatever we are to make of Asad, a deeper appreciation of his life, thought, and legacy is both required and overdue.

LOOKING FOR TRANSCENDENCE

Shabana Mir

Let me tell you a woman's story of how the sun of Sufism rose in the diasporic West, and how that was supposed to change something.

Once upon a time, Islamists held Sufis in a grappling chokehold. Modernists, liberals, fundamentalists, and Salafis had been smacking Sufism around as ignorant, irrational, inauthentic, and heterodox. Men were presidents and women were secretaries in organisations; men were principals and women were teachers at the Islamic schools. When the masculinity-centric Islamists were dislodged and the Sufis returned, it should have been a triumph, right?

I'm a former Islamist. But I won't build a state-funded career across the Atlantic on that notoriety. After all, in the 1980s and 1990s, who wasn't an Islamist? I worked at a university that was then on a list for allegedly having militants on the premises. But when the US was engaged in its proxy war via Pakistan, who *wasn't* cheering along those mujahideen – excuse me, militants? When the Iranian Revolution took place, who wasn't celebrating an Islamic republic that told a superpower where to stick their CIA?

For part of my new-found Islamic life, I was an Islamist engaged in *jihad* against the heresy of Sufism. For the remainder of my life, I was the Sufi punchbag. I was Chishti-Sabri – but before the big post-9/11 Sufi wave hit the US. Until that shift, I was a mostly undercover Sufi, in three continents. In North America and the UK, whether Muslim Students Association (MSA) or Federation of Student's Islamic Societies (FOSIS), the Cambridge mosque or the Bloomington Islamic Center, Sufi was not the thing to be in the 1990s. To be engaged in mainstream Muslim causes you buried your angular edges and performed as a good, sober, Qur'an-and-Sunnah Islamist. In an American mosque, even an excess of tearful humility during prayers could be seen as immoderate. You certainly made no references to *pirs* – Sufi guide – and shrines. Forget Sufism: technically, in that period, music, democracy, and feminism were all officially outlawed for Muslims. How were we to live our Muslim ethics together in diverse Muslim communities? And were Muslim women part of 'us'?

After the Sufi wave hit the American diaspora, and achieved an initial high, it settled into the same old story. Men performing in passion plays of power.

I have spent far too much of my life holding back, hoping that the Muslim establishment(s) would listen to the voices of scholarly and sexual minorities, women, and critical Muslims. I looked towards choosing and making new homes, creating new free spaces, instead of seeking a foothold in boys' clubs, old or new. Where I once found comfort in tradition, I have lost patience with the male *ummah* of Traditionalists, imbued with their middle-class historical nostalgia disconnected from the real lives of ordinary Muslims. I am comfortable in tiny nests of emotional, ideological, and activist communities – tiny groups of progressive anti-imperialist Sufis and Muslim feminist academics.

Like many of you, I am on an island, whence I frequently – but briefly – visit the surrounding archipelago of my heart.

Growing up in Lahore, I aspired to be religious. Perhaps too religious, because religiosity was calibrated by gender. If you mastered religiosity *too* much, you weren't moldable enough to be feminine. No prospective spouse (or his mother) wanted you to be *that* smart or *that* religious.

If there was limited Muslim scholarly engagement in 1970s and 1980s Lahore, it was worse for women. We had access to the usual lay texts - pious descriptions of death and stories of the saints - but not to mosques, madrassahs, or the rarefied air of Muslim movements. In my teens, when girls were secretly calling up boys, I called the Jamia Ashrafia, Lahore, to discuss Islam with a resident scholar. I wrote an article the Jamia published in their magazine; but under the title, they published my initials: *sheen-meem,* a discreet veil drawn over the femininity of my name. '*Acha nahin lagta* (it doesn't look nice),' the scholar said.

Four decades later, through three continents, in most Muslim public settings, where invisibility, erasure, and tokenism persist, I still don't look nice.

For me, as a teen, an immediate source of religious authority was my cousin, Shahida Apa. An officer of Islami Jamiat-e-Talibat (IJT), the women's student organisation of Jamaat-e-Islami (JI), Shahida supervised my religious training via family visits and letters. A Catholic school educated girl with Western cultural expertise but yearning for a home, I idealised her religiously conservative petit bourgeoisie family. I wanted to study Islam. Anyone can do that, they said, you need to master Western culture. I must be an ambassador to English-speaking Westernised elites, colonial heirs of cultural and economic power, who were the enemy, the agenda, and the goal for Islamists.

With its bureaucratic organisational structure and cheap, accessible publications, the JI was an easy source of pseudo-rational Islamist authority. I never made it past the level of *hami* (supporter) in the IJT. You earned membership stripes through self-evaluation surveys, submitted by mail every fifteen days. The surveys collected data about our *namaz* and reading of Qur'an (specifically *Tafheemul-Qur'an*, Abu Ala Maududi's Quranic exegesis, my primary religious diet for a decade), and JI-approved Hadith collections and Islamic literature. How many prayers were missed; how much reading was logged? The officer's feedback, sometimes stern, followed report submission, with reminders to hear and obey.

Salafi-inspired JI spirituality in the days of Gulf-Islam money actively resisted 'excessive' reverence (reverence for the Prophet and the saints, but not so much for Maududi). I could not deny, though, that my most powerful early experience was during the standing *salam* for *Ya Nabi Salam Alayka* (O Prophet, peace with you) at a *milad* celebrating the Prophet's birthday. I did not know, then, that the *milad* and the standing-salam were considered *bid'ah* – undesirable innovations. I only felt like the earth below me was quaking, and I was aflame with love. That world was closed to me after being properly initiated into the JI curriculum.

Character reform was a largely behavioural, technical performance. I don't recall hearing much about *love, heart,* or even humility in my JI days. I didn't see quite enough of 'personal piety initially unaided by structural reform' observed by Ziauddin Sardar in *Desperately Seeking Paradise*. Since it was never clear when we were *done* with personal piety and must proceed to structural reform, it seemed reasonable to focus on the latter anyway, to embark upon a lifetime of that overemphasised Islamist virtue

- the enjoining of good and the forbidding of wrong. Regarding *nawafil* (supererogatory prayers), JI people reminded us that these were optional, but *iqamat-e-deen,* the public establishment of religion in life, was an obligation. The only IJT curricular offering a more spiritual focus was a solicited collection of women's essays, *My feelings about Allah, Most High* — largely shallow musings of sincere seekers with no profundity of knowledge regarding spiritual excellence or gnosis.

The development of personal piety was unaided. You managed on your own, a rugged individualist, intellectually, wilfully engaging in behaviours that you read or heard about, with no inspiration, little collective devotions, nothing like *muraqaba* (meditation) or *qawwali* of the Sufi circles. You could engage in reflection and contemplate nature, but mediation on spiritual presence would be wrong, as God was Transcendent, Ibn Taymiyah, the thirteenth century literalist theologian was king, and why focus on things that didn't lead to the establishment of religion in public life? If you ran on empty, that was your personal shame. Having done all the technical dos and don'ts, I plateaued, burned out, and asked, was this *it?* The JI diet sufficed for many, but maddeningly, everyone was exhorted to adhere to that basic diet.

The utopian vision of political Islam Sardar became disillusioned by centred on structural reform via the acquisition of political power. True Muslims, who exercised Divine rule should have earthly power. We foot-soldiers must invest with complete power the strongman/men responsible for establishing Islam in all affairs of the state. The Islamisation narrative of General and President Zia-ul-Haq dovetailed nicely with the Islamist agenda. With his tokenistic usage of Islamic symbolism, he offered the sop of discursive representation to lovers of Islam-anything. State representatives repeated Islamist mottos of 'Islam is the solution' and stated 'Islam Is a Panacea For All Social Ills' at public events – ad nauseam. It is a testament of the resilience of Pakistani people that they retained any love for the faith after Zia.

Maududi's Islamic 'systems' of life eclipsed our spiritual lives and certainly the lives of the marginalised. The easiest system to manage, with greatest visual impact, was gender. With *purdah* and *hudood* punishments, sex segregation would ensue. Islam would navigate the complexities of the modern world primarily by shutting them down. After the Islamic systems had been established in society (by men of faith), true faith would blossom in our lives. True faith was demonstrated by our investment in promoting Islam in all political and social spheres, rather than personal faith or interpersonal ethics, was the Pakistani Islamist agenda of the 1980s. Systemic oppression would end and/or our problems will become inconsequential once we had true faith. Earthquakes and rampant corruption were Divine retribution for our irreligious behaviour (and, I thought guiltily, my failure to submit my Islamic surveys!).

What were my ideological choices? Bewildered by my mastery of Western discourse, fearful of my Islamism, feminist elites – the ones I was supposed to convert – were alternately disgusted and fascinated by me and my unfashionable fundamentalism. Pakistani liberals did not engage in dialogue because of their long-standing contempt for Islam and religious Muslims. I fangirled over Maryam Jameelah, the American convert to Islam who became the female voice of JI, closest I came to Islamic critique in a woman's voice and interviewed her for the Kinnaird College magazine at her old Krishan Nagar house. Her *Islam and Modernism* had already inoculated me against Muslim modernism by the time I encountered it at college.

With my ravenous appetite for religious scholarship, I created a world of my own from books and tapes. When I called Tanzeem-e-Islami, an offshoot of JI founded by the Pakistani theologian and scholar, Israr Ahmed, with questions, they sent me free-of-charge content that described perfect *purdah* in excruciating detail. At sixteen, I put the strictest version of *purdah* into practice. Face-veiling from unrelated males was not enough: Israr Ahmad roared, 'even the father should not look closely at his daughter'. I proceeded to alienate peers and family with my gender politics and downwardly mobile Islamism. Always suspicious of the professional religious classes, my father hated me socialising with them. Because we didn't socialise with JI families, I did not observe their everyday religious compromises, slippages between strident rhetoric and actual practice. They remained a utopian idea, though I was puzzled that none of my JI friends actually put the purdah ideal into practice like I did.

Lonely, perpetually fighting, exhausted, and depressed, I had a crisis of faith at age seventeen. Was I a believer? I wasn't sure. My mind was certain in faith; my heart was hollow. Assailed by doubt, in a state of cognitive dissonance, I wrote to my JI advisors, laying out my malaise.

They read the letter, but I never heard back. They had nothing for my soul. My mind was a flurry of doubt and questions, like houseflies at a picnic, like tumbleweed – rootless, rolling through the desert of my heart.

That year we had a family visit from another set of religious relatives: an aunt and uncle active in Islamic Society of North America (ISNA) circles, with the keen, newly religious, partially-Arabised spirit of many Muslim Americans. My aunt wore Arab-style hijab and, refusing to wear shalwar kameez, she preferred dresses because 'they disguise the shape of the body'. She, too, had no answers for my angst, which she found not unhealthy but almost inspiring. Apparently, my thirst was transnational. Plenty of foot soldiers in both homelands and diaspora were suffering from ideological malnutrition. But for the first time I looked to North America as an Islamic hope.

After a few months of this crisis, I decided to get over myself. Since my heart was not in accord with my intellectual certainty, I would wage ideological warfare even if I was dead inside. I would hang up my spiritual angst and show up for the work of joyless piety. And, I reflected pragmatically, in the absence of a thriving spiritual life, perhaps I could marry the right person and build an outwardly Islamic family life. Perhaps a truly believing man would solve my problems. In my twenties, educated in Westernised institutions, I hadn't properly witnessed the nature of patriarchal 'Islamic' marriage, nor did I understand that my eccentric family lived religious acceptance and gender values I had not yet explicated for myself. I thought I only wanted the company of truly religious people.

Leaving the social world of the college where I was an anomaly, I decided to attend Punjab University for my MA and plugged into IJT circles. Initially warmed by the presence of burqas and beards, I was disillusioned by their religious shallowness and lack of ethics. My sister's marriage into Shahida's JI family – the one I idealised – demolished any remaining illusions I had. Beaten black and blue, she fled the family that I had looked up to for over a decade. The patriarchal oppression during the marriage and the ensuing divorce case may have precipitated my eventual immigration. There was no way I was going to get into a marriage that might end up remotely like this one. The idea of marriage and men nauseated me.

My JI networks had previously referred me for employment with the International Islamic University, Islamabad. Farhat Hashmi, then Women's Campus principal, later director of the organisation Al-Huda, hired me as faculty. I was going to an Islamic university! At last! An ideological home! No more *dawah* to the barbarians! An adventure awaited me, as I became friends with devout Muslim students from Indonesia, Afghanistan, Sudan, Egypt, Somalia, China, Kazakhstan, and many other nations. But through this adventure, my Pakistani Islamist religious-cultural certainties were dislodged. It seemed that dancing, music, and courting were not universally prohibited, not all religious Muslims embraced the burqa, nor did they universally outlaw Sufi practices, and the Islamic state was not everybody's goal. Had I been lied to?

Yet, there were limits to women's scholarly adventures. I discovered that the men's campus comprised the *main* campus. Male faculty visited the women's campus to teach. Women students visited the main library only on specific days and times. And, the vice president, an Ikhwan stalwart, would sometimes appear, clad in angelic white robes, shrieking a stern, nasal 'get out of here' to drive burqa-clad women students away from the main campus. A custom-built campus was later constructed, where the two campuses were in the same area, but ultimately the message remained the same, that women's scholarly pursuits were inessential, canceled by the far greater importance of hiding their female bodies.

Though the Saudi-funded International Islamic University was a bastion of Salafism, ironically, I met Sufis there. Like me, my new roommate had plateaued after Islamism and found Sufism. I suppose we were part of a new trend. My first halaqa-e-zikr was like being struck by lightning. In my JI life, I'd never seen anything like Sufi devotions. When I encountered Abdul Qadir Jilani's *Futuh al-Ghaib* and Ali Hajweiri's *Kashful Mahjub*. I was insatiable. I read as if for the first time, 'But recite the name of your Lord withdrawing yourself from everything, devoting yourself exclusively to Him' (The Qur'an, 73: 8), and pleaded, in the quiet night, 'I don't know You. Let me know You'.

Though my spiritual state was appalling, I didn't want to hand over my soul to anyone again. 'I won't give allegiance to anyone', I told Wahid Baksh Rabbani, a Sufi of the Chishti order and translator of Ali Hajweiri's

Kashful Mahjub, 'but I will do the zikr, because I'm desperate'. As a part-time Sufi, the very first night that I woke up for night prayer, and terrified, I completed *zikr* and felt a great change palpably enter my heart – and settle there. Those days, I wandered the streets of Islamabad, riding public buses in my burqa, with a pocket Qur'an, reciting the Names of God, filled with a sense of Presence like never before. I wrote to my *pir* anguished letters about my spiritual state, and he replied to my adolescent questions with grace, patience, and Sufi stories. If I wrote him a seven page letter, he replied with an eight-page letter, because, he said, that was the requisite etiquette. He was a Pakistani man like few I had ever met, traditional yet urbane, always reminding me of my endless potential as a lover of God, and never recognising any limits for me as a woman. I am sure my order has flaws, and I am sure there are many where women have better experiences, but it was exactly what I needed then. I never found anything like that again.

Like my mother, my roommate's mother was concerned about our marriage prospects. My roommate was sent to attend the ISNA Convention in hopes of finding a religious Muslim spouse – who, importantly, wasn't lower middle class, like religious Pakistanis were then. Though my roommate enjoyed her experience, she returned unattached. Diasporic Muslims were growing religious *and* wealthy, but the homeland was running behind, so ISNA was a transnational beacon of marital hope.

Sufis were still on the defensive. In his books, my *pir* responds to Salafi, Orientalist, and missionary allegations that Sufism is heretical and not organic to Islam. Hashmi, holding these anti-Sufi beliefs, eyed the changes in me with growing outrage. She invited my Sufi friend, a sweet older woman, to speak about Sufism at the newly-found al-Huda centre, but launched into a tirade against Sufi ignorance immediately afterward. I had attempted, but there was to be no intra-faith alliance. It was a parting of the ways. My Sufi practices became a matter of gossip at the university and I was approached with warnings.

I had been teaching for three years and, frustrated with Pakistan's educational practices, I was keen to pursue a higher degree in educational improvement. But when I applied for study leave, I was turned down, unlike far less qualified male faculty. I called the President of the

University, an Islamic economist who had supported Farhat Hashmi at the Women's Campus.

'You can pursue this degree,' he said, '*if* you can get approved for study leave'.

'Okay,' I said, sensing the edge in his tone, 'will you approve my leave?'

'No.' His swift response was crisp with enjoyment; he had been waiting to say it. The vision of my potential futures there - in a horrific marriage like my sister's, or a dead-end job without professional advancement, working for authoritarian supervisors – filled me with despair. My father was devastated. He knew that if I didn't get leave, I would have no professional ties in Pakistan. This would drive me away from the country.

And he was right. At 3 am one morning in Islamabad, with an impractical floppy suitcase belching clothes on the floor, I gave up on study leave, and scribbled my resignation. Pakistan was never to be home again. I had never before considered moving abroad. I hadn't even owned a passport. But now, I was being driven away.

I have no triumphant immigrant story to relate. It just happened around me. Today, when Pakistani men in positions of power taunt me for immigrating, claiming credit for staying in Pakistan and serving the nation, I have nothing to say to them.

The daughter of Kamal Helbawy, the now UK-based leader of Muslim Brotherhood, had been a student of mine at the International Islamic University. When the Pakistani government expelled the Arabs under US pressure, Helbawy left for London, the same year I left for Cambridge. The Helbawy family welcomed me on my arrival. At Cambridge University, where women were segregated, I offered my services to teach Qur'an and Hadith. Two male Islamic Society officers (there were no women officers), several years younger than myself, vetted and approved me to teach Qur'an. It was a popular group, radiant with sisterhood and vibrant with spiritual thirst. But I realised that Sufism must remain veiled. Islamist networks were the main gatekeepers in Muslim organisations, and Islamist, often Gulf, funding and networks were the main source of support. I trod a careful route, emphasising intention, sincerity, and God-awareness, establishing irreproachable scholarly credentials, never suggesting anything that might detract from correct form. At the Abu Bakr Siddique mosque, the epicentre of Salafi-Sufi battles, Sufis chafed at the bit. A group of non-Salafi *desi* women, tired of Salafi ideology, asked me to lead a second study circle in Urdu. I discovered later that my new study circle was founded as a rival to the Salafi women's circle. In the words of an Islamic Society officer, I became an unwitting pawn in Sufi-Salafi wars, while Salafis called me a tool of disunity. But it was a wonderful group.

As my first term ended, I drove with friends to attend the Young Muslims Bosnian-themed winter camp at the Islamic Foundation, Leicester in 1994. Judging by their literature and authors' names, they were obviously connected with JI networks. The director, Khurshid Ahmed, would later invite me to serve as resident scholar. I declined, unwilling to tie my future with an organisation whose ideological underpinnings were no longer home. At a lecture for young women, a male Islamic Society of Britain leader discussed life in the Islamic movement, pointing out how annoying it was when his wife complained, 'Ah, I have a headache; *you* change the baby's diaper'. The young girls giggled obediently, but when I gave him a public earful during Q&A, I heard sibilant whispers from the young British-Pakistani women: 'She's from Pakistan'. To this day, I am that liminal person, an expatriate in the West and in Pakistan, always surprised by how little I belong anywhere.

One Spring morning, I opened a letter and read that my pir had died. I felt inexpressibly empty. Where he had been my home, I now had to find or create a home.

After graduating with an MPhil., I moved to London and worked as translator and editor for Helbawy's Muslim Brotherhood Information Center. I also did clerical work at FOSIS and directed the FOSIS women's hostel. I always felt out of place in British Muslim spaces. Pakistani Islam had never pretended to offer equality - but shouldn't diasporic Muslims be different? They certainly imagined themselves to be different, despite the male speakers and the segregation. Helbawy tried, but we didn't get along. 'She talks to me like a teacher,' he grumbled to his colleague. 'She *is* a teacher!' his Pakistani colleague chuckled.

It seemed appropriate, as I concluded my employment, that Helbawy asked me to work together on an English translation of Abu Hamid al-Ghazali's *My Dear Beloved Son*. 'Ghazali is with us in spirit as we work on this,' he said exuberantly. Clearly, the more perceptive Islamists saw a Sufi future looming ahead.

In London, I personally knew only one Sufi – a disciple of one Shaikh Nazim. 'I'll take you to meet him,' she said. As he concluded his discourses, Shaikh Nazim suddenly started to take an impromptu allegiance with some followers, hands over his hand. Not for me, I thought, I have a *pir*. He looked at me. What? Did he hold out a hand with an imperceptible invitation or just invite me with his mind? Partaking must be okay. After all, I had not met my *pir* in a long while, and now he had left this world. There was no home, no nest, no hometown, no community. I grasped the cluster of hands and words rose up around me.

My friend, his disciple, told Shaikh Nazim tactfully, 'But she *has* a shaikh.' I didn't need to take allegiance with a new *pir*. 'I have renewed her *baiat*,' he said. 'Now she is free to go.' I never saw him again.

The British Muslim community was a weird place, and in its tight-knit, almost tribal corners, there was little space for a family-less single woman without full-time employment, waiting on PhD funding. I lived for some months in a rooming house owned by Yusuf Islam, the singer formally known as Cat Stevens, with a motley assortment of people - Bosnian refugees, Islamia School teachers, and a pregnant young convert fleeing her family. This convert's Pakistani boyfriend, who was not terribly religious, had been persuaded by his Islamist brother that juristically the couple could not marry until the baby was born. Pro-women assumptions were even less normative in communities then than they are now. Feeling protective toward this trusting young woman, I visited Mrs Helbawy, and got a ruling written in Arabic on a scrap of paper. I brought this to the young woman, and within a day, her boyfriend had picked her up, taken her home, and married her. That little escapade, one among many, still warms my heart. We women had a whole underground life, behind the public Islamic scenes, where we figured out ways to support each other and to engage in everyday interpretive work, whatever the statements issued by official all-male panels.

When I moved to the US for a PhD, I discovered for myself the exciting, unwieldy world of ISNA, and the Muslim Brotherhood and Jamaat-e-Islami gatekeepers that today are gender activists and interfaith speakers. The rising star of ISNA conventions, Hamza Yusuf 1.0, ranting about the evils of the West, performed a Sufism Lite, one that trickled down via Sufi-ish networks like Zaytuna, Taleef, and Deen Intensive. Even Sufism

Lite was pretty dangerous at that time. At the Saudi-dominated Bloomington mosque, Salafism was the only available discourse. Avoiding being branded a heretic, as one Arab-American student cautioned me, I remained underground as Sufi.

That year, a new player emerged on the Muslim American scene - not new in terms of existing, but in terms of breaking into mainstream organisations. A young couple, diehard, second-generation MSA/ISNA activists, ventured to attend the Islamic Unity conference in 1996, wondering if these Sufis could offer anything of value. Her lip curled as she described turbaned Naqshbandis scurrying to kiss Shaikh Nazim's hand. How much emotive space their chanting and devotional songs occupied! The young ISNA member didn't like the Naqshbandis. And yet there she was – either looking for love or scoping out the competition.

Weirded out by segregation and overwhelming Gulf-maleness, the second-generation Muslim American students had, for the most part, made themselves scarce from the Indiana University, Bloomington MSA in the mid-1990s. Stepping into the mosque, you felt like you were on a different planet, with total sex segregation and sermons about hijab and End of Days. People rolled their eyes, prayed, and left. One year, I invited Bloomington's interfaith religious leaders to the mosque. The Salafis first raised a furore about how I had invited Jews and Christians to the mosque, then sidelined me, appropriated the event, and appointed a panel of three men to speak. This cycle of erasure and domination would continue until I abandoned the religious community for the non-Muslim workplace.

Several students complained about how the entire MSA executive committee (EC), except for a Sisters' Representative, was male. Mosque gatekeepers said women were not permitted to be on a mosque EC. Many Muslim students simply faded from the mosque. Why even bother to struggle to remain part of a community that didn't even recognise us as full persons? A Great Debate was held at the Bloomington mosque to discuss whether women could contest the MSA EC election. People lobbed textual evidence at each other, a hadith regarding 'women rulers' and the evils of social mixing among men and women. Today, they said, men and women will be on the EC together; tomorrow, there will be fornication in the mosque!

Frustrated with Islamophobic secular dogmatism in academia and misogyny and ignorance in the mosque, I started getting out to speak on the MSA lecture circuit. At one conference, a wildly popular Islamist youth speaker railed about women attending co-educational universities. His sister, an engineering student had asked him, 'But what if I work on group projects with, say, three male students, and I'm not alone with a man?' 'In that case,' he had replied sagely, 'there is not one *khilwah* (privacy with an unrelated member of the opposite sex), but *three* khilwahs.' In the next lecture, I attacked toxic Muslim masculinity in MSAs and mosques.

My invitations suddenly dried up.

Grasping at hope, I thought, all I needed were some Sufi friends. Muslim Americans needed Sufism. Then, suddenly, the Sufis became popular.

After 11 September 2001, pundits branded Islamists *en masse* as true or embryonic terrorists, and Sufis as good Muslims. Politicians wanted to fund Sufis and build their organisations. The last thing the unpopular kid wants is to be a teacher's favourite. Feelgood Rumi quotations were bandied about as Sufis were re-presented as apolitical pacifists. The West could embrace *these* Muslims. The West could promote them! The West could *use* them. And everyone needs a job.

As Shaikh Hisham Kabbani, the deputy and heir of Shaikh Nazim, capitalised on this coopting of Sufism, numerous Muslim American religious leaders and academics mouthed Sufi-ish language and demonised other Muslims. But, at least in Muslim spaces, critical voices became bolder and louder than before. Sufi language was now somewhat acceptable.

Political Islam didn't die out from our lives; it became part of the furniture. But I learned to avoid the groups that had historically marginalised Sufis, Shias, and other non-Islamist Muslims. I now avoid Muslims who raise the Sufi banner and buy into state projects against 'radicalisation'. I am not with Muslims keen to be accepted by White liberals. It is a complicated time. The notion of 'ummah' is not a simple one. I did not experience the post-9/11 rise of Sufism as an unadulterated triumph, nor did I fall in love with the new progressive or liberal Muslims.

I really tried to find a Sufi home in the US, and I know it takes all kinds, but little worked for me, and what did work, didn't work for long. The discursive practices of North American *tariqahs* were, for the most part, not my style. My *pir* wrote in clear Urdu and straightforward English, peppered with Farsi poetry and Qur'anic verses, and spoke the sweet Saraiki of his native Bahawalpur. He did not drop mysterious hints, nor did he wear foreign regalia. A humble man who signed his letters 'the most humble of God's servants', and wore earth-coloured plain shalwar kameez, *dhoti,* and shawls, he gave more respect than he received. The Sufism I encountered in the West was often marketed as a *priestly* consumer brand. I was far too used to having down-to-earth conversations about ordinary things with my *pir* to be drawn to charisma and spectacle.

Sure, it was nice not to have to hide anymore in mainstream Muslim organisations. There were a lot of radiant devotional experiences. But masculinity-centric *tariqahs*, where women were submissively 'feminine' – these were no home for me. Filled with hope and yearning, I'd attend a meeting, only to find the brothers centring a maleness barely tempered with chivalry – the goofy Sufis and the hidebound *fiqh*-boys, the Sufis in enclaves and the Sufis in corridors of power. I hear news of Sufis who have found ways to work through gender, and I hope to find and visit these groups and communities and bring their stories to others. I'm still looking. From Islamist to Sufi, I am now a lone Sufi modernist Muslim feminist, sometimes traditional, sometimes not, shopping for true hearts where I can find them, and looking for love in all the right and wrong places.

Once they emerged from the woodwork, I wondered, why were many Sufi and pro-Sufi leaders buying heavily into authority and status, silencing criticism and debate, attacking critics of racial hierarchies, and failing to hold leaders accountable for unethical behaviour and sexual exploitation? As an epidemic of secret marriages and spiritual abuse sweeps the Muslim diaspora, there is too little concern for their victims, and offenders often return quickly to their pulpits. Boys being boys again, whether with rosaries and chants or books and lectures.

The theoretically anti-modern, nerdy, Traditionalist Sufis were happy to deploy and to consume modernity for social mobility. These, unlike the 'Classical' Sufis, were dogmatic not on hijab or ritual, but on gender roles and hierarchy, reading Divine mystery into vanilla masculine domination. And why were the 'Classical' Sufis' obsessed with foreign, old texts? So contaminated were the present time and diasporic reality, that we must be beamed out far away and long ago. More pietistic and more judgmental than the Salafis, they relied on the rulings of persons who had never known the contemporary reality, and their primary bad guys were modernists. Detractors of egalitarian Muslim politics called them un-Islamic and foreign. Ugly economic ties developed between Gulf dictatorships and some of these Sufis: accept the status quo, they preached, obey your *amir,* avoid rebellions, and be not envious of those who have more. Same old, same old.

This story of exile was difficult to write because I wonder if I will ever feel really at home in any Muslim community. Our stories have been stuck in our throats for too long. I clear my throat, trying to reclaim my words, but I don't have the requisite permission and contacts. I speak, but claims have already been made, terms defined, authorities crowned, and saints canonised. So when I read and loved Ziauddin Sardar's *Desperately Seeking Paradise,* I recognised names, places, and groups in it, but I did not see myself in it. As with everything else in religious content and collectives, it is a story of men who wander the world and walk the streets without being told they should stay indoors. Men who meet important personages and aren't told their presence is a source of disorder because of their bodies rather than their ideas. Men who visit important cities and have profound experiences without even being aware that their *bodies* are present, the way I am always hyper-aware among Muslims. Men who are never told 'Get out of here' by elevated personages because a place is too *Muslim* for women's bodies. Men who dream up new worlds and create them, without being told their main job is creating babies. Men who are never asked to justify their presence and men who shift ideological alliances overnight without consequence. Islamist today, Sufi tomorrow. Obscurantist today, moderate tomorrow. Sexist today, gender activist tomorrow. Sexual offender today, reformer tomorrow.

Perhaps this is a story about re-enchantment. Perhaps the problem was that political Islam sought to become a staple for everyone. Even Sufism – of whatever variety – won't be enough for everyone. Sufism never was a thing for all people. Nothing is meant for everyone. But whatever we read into the Word surely must be life-giving for everyone. Otherwise, it is already dead, awaiting another swing of the pendulum.

MUNSHI ABDULLAH

Hilman Fikri Azman

Malay history is full of mythological characters, with historical fact shrouded in fable and legends. But none is more mysterious and controversial than Abdullah bin Abdul Kadir, the nineteenth-century literati, writer, innovator, translator, and teacher of mixed Arab and Indian ancestry. He left an autobiography, *Hikayat Abdullah*, as well as a string of other notable books, which have had a profound impact on Malay thought and literature. His works not only transformed Malay language but also serve as important sources of historical, political, and literary study of the Malays during the British colonial period.

Abdullah was born in Melaka to a well-respected family who valued education. His parents and forefathers were all well-educated, and he received a proper education too, particularly in languages and religious studies. The value placed on a good education paid off well for his family, gaining them economic and social prominence in society. The precocious Abdullah himself began exercising his scholastic abilities in his early youth, helping his uncle with teaching the Qur'an to soldiers of the British Indian Army (Sepoy) in Melaka. Later, Abdullah started working as a scribe and translator for the British, a talent he inherited from his father, notable for his work with British officers in their correspondence with the Malay rulers. He went on to teach the Malay language to British missionaries, officers, businessmen, and traders for a total span of thirty years. Among students included notable British administrators and missionaries. The Sepoys adored him; taking to calling him 'Munshi', an Urdu term for teacher, educator, and scribe. The moniker stuck!

The Munshi married his first wife at the age of 25. They had five children; the younger daughter died aged eight; two years later, his wife died too as a result of complications following the birth of a son. Abdullah then moved to Singapore, and although he fails to mention this in his autobiography, we came to know from the discovery of his last testament that he remarried – and had three more children. In February 1854, Abdullah boarded the *Sublassalam* at a port in Singapore, a ship taking pilgrims to Mecca. He reached Jeddah on 30 April 1854; and set about writing an account of his thoughts and religious experience on separate parchments that were later collected as *Kisah Pelayaran Abdullah ke Mekah* (The Story of Abdullah's Voyage to Mecca). The cause of Abdullah's death remains unknown, but we know he died on 27 October 1854 in Mecca. Eleven days before his death, Munshi Abdullah penned a last testament and will, dividing his assets among his family of six sons, a daughter and a wife.

John Turnbull Thomson, a British surveyor and contemporary of Abdullah, who translated *Hikayat Abdullah* into English, describes the Munshi as follows: 'in physiognomy he was a Tamilian of southern Hindustan: slightly bent forward, spare, energetic, bronze in complexion, oval-faced, high-nosed, one eye squinting outwards a little. He dressed in the usual style of Melaka Tamils. Acheen *seluar*, checkered *sarong*, printed *baju*, square skull cap and sandals. He had the vigour and pride of the Arab, the perseverance and subtlety of the Hindoo – in language and national sympathy only was he a Malay'.

Just how Malay was Munshi Abdullah has been debated endlessly. We know that he never explicitly described himself as a Malay but he identified himself as such. He devoted his life to Malay language and culture. For Abdullah, the Malay identity is rooted in one's culture and practices, not in one's biology. He was Malay even by the accepted definition of a Malay as enshrined in the Federal Constitution in Malaysia today – 'a person who professes Islam, habitually speaks in Malay, conforms to Malay custom, and was before independence born in the Federation or in Singapore or born of parents one of whom was born in the Federation or in Singapore, or is on that day domiciled in the Federation or in Singapore, or is the issue of such a person'! The debate of his Malay-ness, alongside the verbose language of the constitutional definition of a Malay, speaks to the fastidious issue of identity in contemporary Malaysia. It had little importance during colonial rule as such definitions were unnecessary prior to independence from the British.

But can Munshi Abdullah be described as 'the Father of Modern Malay Literature' - an epithet that many modern scholars have applied to him?

Certainly, on the basis of his prodigious output the Munshi is aptly ascribed. His literary output includes two masterpieces: his famous autobiography, *Hikayat Abdullah* (The Chronicle of Abdullah), and his account of his travels to the east coast of the peninsula, *Kisah Pelayaran Abdullah* (The Story of Abdullah's Voyage), published in 1838 and 1849 respectively. His other works include *Kisah Pelayaran ke Mekah* (The Story of Voyage to Mecca), *Ceretera Kapal Asap* (An Account of Steamship), and *Ceretera Darihal Haji Sabar Ali* (An Account of Haji Sabar Ali). He published two volumes of poetry: *Syair Singapura Terbakar* (Singapore Ablaze) and *Syair Kampong Gelam Terbakar* (Kampong Gelam Ablaze). He translated the *Panchatantra*, the ancient Sanskrit text from Tamil into Malay. He edited *Sejarah Melayu* (The Malay Annals) and *Kitab Adat Segala Raja-Raja Melayu dalam Segala Negeri* (The Customs of the Malay Rulers in Every States), besides contributed to, and helped produce *Bustan Arifin*, the first ever Malay language magazine. And co-authored the first Malay dictionary, *A Vocabulary of the English and Malay Languages, Containing Upwards of 2000 Words*, published in Melaka in 1820. So, the Munshi's achievements are surprisingly substantial.

We also know that Abdullah played a major part in introducing printing to the Malay Archipelago. Of course, printing was well established since Johannes Gutenberg introduced it in Germany in 1440. But during Abdullah's days, scholarly and literary works were still being produced by manual copywriters and distributed as old-fashioned manuscripts. The printing press was brought to Melaka from Bengal in 1816. It transformed publications in the Malay language. The Munshi learned the art of printing from Walter Henry Madhurst who worked with the missionaries of the London Missionary Society (LMS) in Melaka. The LMS helped produce the 1820 English-Malay dictionary. When the LMS was taken over by the American Board of Commissioners for Foreign Missions (ABCFM) in 1834, Abdullah continued to work alongside their missionaries in helping with the translation and editing of several works. Abdullah and Alfred North, who was appointed as assistant missionary in 1835 and learned Malay from Abdullah, worked together to produce an edition of *Sejarah Melayu*. During this period Munshi also translated and published several English school's textbooks on such subjects as astronomy, geography, and natural history.

The printing press was the key to the advancement of education and literature in the Malay Archipelago. Indeed, some scholars have even argued that it played a crucial part in revolutionising the Malay literature from its traditional typology characterised by feudalism, collectivism, and regionalism to a new and modern one, characterised by anti-feudalism, individualism, and inclusiveness. Without a doubt, Munshi Abdullah's role in the emergence of the printing press is paramount; and it played just as an important part in the spread of his own works.

It was his friend and collaborator, Alfred North, who encouraged Abdullah to write something different than the existing Malay classics. The result was *Hikayat Abdullah*, which covers not only some of the most vital aspects of his life – his origins, childhood, family, teaching profession, his associations with the Europeans in Melaka and Singapore – but also his observation and critique on local societies, the Malays, Chinese, and Indians, the affairs of the rulers, and his experiences during various travels. In other words, the *Hikayat* provides contemporary sociologists, historians, and scholars a crucial description of the social and political setting of the Malay society in the nineteenth century – something that is plainly lacking in existing historical records.

But Munshi's autobiography has faced some serious criticism. For example, Yusof A. Talib, a historian based at National University of Singapore, has shown that some claims made by Abdullah are not historically accurate. Abdullah could not have studied under the scholar Sayyid Shaykh bin Alwi Bafaqih, as he claims, as the latter was born very much earlier than the former. On Abdullah's claim of his ostensibly miraculous birth after being predicted and graced by the prominent Arab saint, Habib Abdullah al-Haddad, Talib suggests that this is impossible as the renowned Habib Abdullah had died in Hadramawt in 1719, some seventy-six years before Abdullah was born. In both instances, Yusof claimed Abdullah's resort to these figures was to surround the events of his life with an 'aura of distinction'. This is interesting given that Abdullah himself condemns the contents of old literary chronicles as mostly '*bohong*' (lies, or simply fiction). However, he regarded them as valuable in terms of their intrinsic value, as a source of inspiration for one to produce more realistic and beneficial writings. The Munshi also mentions the importance of being critical and truthful in one's words, consistently advocating for an inquisitive attitude against hearsay and lies.

What is important and innovative about the *Hikayat* is its literary shift from the traditional Malay works which focussed on the courts of the Malay rulers. Abdullah repositions the spotlight on to himself, writes in the first person, makes himself the protagonist, and writes about his own life and journeys. This was not a Malay custom! Malay political vocabularies are replete with words like *taat* (loyal), *setia* (devoted), *patuh* (obey), *perintah* (order), *sanjung* (praise), *derhaka* (treasonous) and *kerajaan* (royal institution or government), which are noticeably absent in Abdullah's writings. In the pre-modern period, there were no clear boundaries and political frontiers, so the sense of loyalty was directed to the ruler, who was the centre of power and the embodiment of the proto-state, whereby the demise of a strong ruler often spelled the end of a particular polity. By downplaying their significance, by writing his autobiography, Abdullah made a major departure from the conventional Malay style of writing.

This does not mean that he overlooks the Malay rulers of his time. Indeed, he devotes three chapters to events directly related to Tengku Long, Sultan Hussein Shah and Tengku Temenggong. However, the royals do not take the centre stage anymore as Abdullah also adds affairs related to the British rulers. Moreover, the royals are not mentioned in a positive manner, the way a traditional court authors would do. He criticises their thinking styles, decision-making, and physical attributes. For example, he associates Sultan Hussein Shah with 'compounded ignorance', an Arabic expression to denote a state of utter idiocy for turning down the offer made by Stamford Raffles to send his son together with the sons of the Temenggong and Ministers to Benggala to study. He makes lengthy remarks on Sultan Hussein's physical appearance upon assuming power, as an indication of an unhealthy lifestyle and unpleasant attitude. Through his departure from court-centric proclivity and his emphasis on independent thinking, Abdullah situated himself beyond the perimeter of his society in a realm between the East and West. We could say that he was the first to embody what would come to be known as *Malaysian* – the twentieth century identity born of the unity in diversity shared between the people of Peninsular Malaysia and Malaysian Borneo. A man ahead of his time, he was the cultural embodiment of a Rosetta Stone, a celebration of the fusion of cultures, peoples, and ideas that coalesce in the Malay Archipelago.

The Malaysian intellectual and writer, Kassim Ahmad, reaffirms this view and suggests that a new concept of authorship emerges from Abdullah's writings. According to him, Abdullah deconstructed the traditional notion of an author who was expected to write in the interest of his master, and posited a high value to the independence of an author to express his or her views. There is no doubt regarding Abdullah's freedom from the shadows of the ruler's court, but was the Munshi a totally independent writer? Of course, he has his own biases and proclivity. But was he totally free from the bond of patronage? A closer reading of the Munshi's oeuvre suggests that he shifted his loyalty from the Malay rulers to the court of British administrators. While he harshly castigates the Malay rulers and the local people, he is rather kind to the British. Even where he seemingly criticises 'depraved Englishmen' for their detrimental actions, it is very subtle and friendly, hardly an admonishment.

It is for this reason that Munshi Abdullah is mocked as a lackey of the West, a British stooge. Several other instances may reinforce this negative perception. We know for a fact that Abdullah worked for a number of British companies throughout his life. To be fair, that was probably the only way to make a decent living in his days. Abdullah's father worked for the Dutch. Hence, working for the British was not an unusual thing to do for Abdullah. But in the *Hikayat*, he goes out of his way to defend the tarnished image of the British. He is willing to subject himself to condemnation and rejection by his relatives and friends by assisting the British to buy land for the construction of a chapel. On Britain's ability to win its war with China, Abdullah clearly declares his sense of loyalty with the British rulers. He also reveals information about the secret Tiendihui society, an ancestorial organisation like the Ming loyalist White Lotus Sect, to the British, even risking the life of his Chinese friend, who had helped him in retrieving the information in the first place, and who had also protected him from the Chinese community. Abdullah also explicitly favours colonialism to self-government or independence. He demonstrated his fondness for the British in *pantuns*, Malay poetic form written in quatrains; the longest pantun he ever wrote was in praise of Governor William John Butterworth, in which he praises him for being a gentleman and a successful governor of the Straits Settlements. So, it is obvious that Munshi Abdullah's criticism was only limited to the Malays; the British were uncritically adored.

Apart from the British, Abdullah is quite objective when it comes to describing events and phenomenon of his times. He dismisses magical elements, miracles, and superstitions that were prevalent in most classical texts as 'irrational and a great deception' even though he himself is not immune from mystical tendency. He researches and investigates people and events to validate any information he has at hand. He interviews the Indian soldiers in Melaka and the people involved in the rumours about an English church in Singapore. He postpones his trip back home and spent some time in Singapore to witness the consequences of a fire that had taken place. He travelled for miles and spent some money to find out the secret art behind the capture of elephants. He spends time studying the modern inventions brought by the British, determining how they worked. His *An Account of the Steamship* demonstrates his attention to detail and the time he devoted to the understanding of science and technology. He advises Malays to embrace scientific thinking, writing in the magazine *Cermin Mata (Eyeglasses)* to explain the inner workings of helium gas balloons, the spherical nature of the planet, and modern ships! In the *Hikayat*, we are told that he tries his utmost to find truthful information.

It was due to this quality of rational inquiry, as well as the shift from the style of feudal court writing, that led Munshi Abdullah to be regarded as the 'Father of Modern Malay Literature'. But this is contentious not just for those who regard him as a stooge of the British, but also those who have a different perspective of the history of the Malay language. In this regard, Munshi Abdullah's main critic is the Malaysian Sufi scholar and historian, Syed Muhammad Naquib al-Attas.

In *Islam in the Malay History and Culture*, al-Attas argued that the title 'Father of Modern Malay Literature' given to Abdullah was unbefitting. Historically, the development of the Malay language was influenced by the intellectual activities of the scholars in the sixteenth and seventeenth centuries, the apex of Malay intellectual culture. This period witnessed the production of Islamic scholarship on Qur'anic exegesis, jurisprudence, Sufism, and other subjects which were written in Malay. This development led to two streams of the Malay language: The first emerged in Barus, in north Sumatra, before moving to the Pasai Sultanate, a place housing the oldest Islamic institutions of learning in the region, and finally established in Acheh. The second strand experienced decadence and slowly faded. The first stream, incorporating a plethora of Arabic vocabularies (before slightly transforming it to suit the Malay phonetics), has its own logical structure and arguments that display a strong influence of the Qur'an on its authors. According to al-Attas, the modern Malay language as it is today emerged from this Pasai-based stream. Abdullah's writing style, on the other hand, was based on the second stream of Malay language, the classical, feudal-imbued, which was far older than the Pasai-based Malay. It is in fact the language of *Sejarah Melayu*, the Malay classic which has a similar status as Shakespeare in the West, and is the prime text studied by Malay scholars. Indeed, there are striking similarities between some phrases used by Abdullah and the phrases found in *Sejarah Melayu*. Consider the following expression in *Sejarah Melayu*:

'... *jadi beratlah atas anggota fakir...*' (my limbs thus become heavy)

And Abdullah's expression:

'...*menjadi masjghullah aku serta beratlah rasanya anggotaku...*' (I become exhausted and my limbs become heavy)

It turns out that Abdullah's language style was not only confined within the old Malay style, but also copied word-by-word from *Sejarah Melayu*. Moreover, Munshi's Malay has been judged by several authors and scholars of the Malay language to be weak, unpleasing to the ear, whose main ingredients are an attempted imitation of the Malay classics - so far from the standards and mastery attained by his immediate predecessors and contemporary authors like Hamzah Fansuri, Raja Ali Haji and Raja Ahmad.

Al-Attas also argues that Munshi Abdullah's works are literary rather than intellectual. Indeed, many works of intellectual nature can be found written in Pasai-based Malay. The old Malay style also demonstrated remnants of animist, Hindu, and Buddhist concepts in its vocabularies as a result of extensive political and cultural Indianisation of Southeast Asia in the second and third centuries. Al-Attas suggests that far from being a pioneer of a modern literature, Abdullah was the last author of that old traditional language. The true 'Father of Modern Malay Literature', al-Attas argues is Hamzah Fansuri, the sixteenth century Sumatran Sufi writer who – supposedly – pioneered a new Malay style imbued with rationality and cogent arguments. A string of other, mainly Sufi, writers followed the style of Fansuri – all the way from the seventeenth century until the twentieth century. On the other hand, al-Attas argued, we can point to no one who followed Abdullah's writing style after his death because it was already on the verge of extinction.

Al-Attas may be correct in distinguishing the two streams of Malay language. But the suggestion that Hamzah Fansuri is the 'Father of Modern Malay Literature' is even more contentious. Like Abdullah, Fansuri was also a man of letters. He wrote poems and spiritual works elucidating the relationship between God and His creations. Despite forming rational arguments when expounding his ontological framework, Hamzah's works can hardly be described as scientific and modern. Moreover, as Malaysian politician and intellectual, Anwar Ibrahim, has also pointed out, Fansuri's works are mystically opaque and not accessible to ordinary mortals; indeed, there is no evidence that his works were read by anyone except the select few among the court elites – a sign that it is still within the epoch of Malay feudalism.

In contrast, Munshi's works were widely read; aided by the emergence of the printing press. And despite the perceived problems with his language, there is clarity and rigour in his style. While language style is important, it cannot be the only criteria for considering who and what shaped modern Malay language. It is clear that modern Malay was not totally influenced by Fansuri/Pasai-based Malay nor Abdullah/Peninsular-based Malay. Although Fansuri attempted to revamp most of the Malay vocabulary by replacing it with more nuanced Arabic words, it was not a successful attempt as the subsequent Malay language practised by the locals does not incorporate most of the words he introduced. However, Fansuri was instrumental in the development of a new, refined Malay literature. In contrast, while Abdullah adopted an old-fashioned Malay style in his works, he did integrate some Arabo-Malay words into his writings and left out words with pre-Islamic connotations, which means he does not entirely belong to the stream of old Malay language. I would argue that if a title of the Father of Modern Malay Literature is to be given, Abdullah deserved it more than anyone else.

We might ask: what made Abdullah fond of the language of *Sejarah Melayu* to the extent that he literally copied some part of it, albeit with slight changes, into his autobiography? Abdullah explains that the reason he studied *Sejarah Melayu* rigorously is because of its distinction among the Malays and the fine stature of the Malay language used in the work. *Sejarah*

Melayu was not just another classical work. The annals, which were attributed to Tun Seri Lanang, who belonged to the Royal Court of the Johor Sultanate and flourished between the sixteenth and seventeenth centuries, were accorded an almost sacred status and regarded veritably as holy scripture possessing supernatural powers, within royal Malay circles. A blend of ancient mythology and fables with authentic history, *Sejarah Melayu* relates the legendary history of the origin, transformation, and fall of the great Malay maritime empire, the Melaka Sultanate between the fifteenth and sixteenth centuries. It proudly suggests that the Malays are descendants of the great and just King Iskandar Zulkarnain, who is mentioned in the Qur'an (a disputed figure in history, mostly associated with either Alexander the Great from Macedonia, or Cyrus the Great from Persia). The iconic text of Malay feudalism was, indeed, *Sejarah Melayu.*

Before Abdullah took the trouble to edit *Sejarah Melayu* and get it printed, it was not known to most British. Abdullah produced the first printed text of *Sejarah Melayu* using Jawi scripts. It was published by the Singapore Institution in 1840 – not in the year 1831 as has been widely believed. Abdullah plucked it from the Malay courts, where it was kept wrapped in golden silk and read on ceremonial occasions to the accompaniment of cannon salutes, and made it accessible to a wider public. His edition became a primary source for the later editions of the text.

Munshi Abdullah was also one of the earliest scholars to think about Malay poverty and underdevelopment – and he lays the blame squarely on Malay rulers and his own people. The rulers, he suggested, were not interested in the plight of their own people, and frustrated all attempts at progress. The people, on the other hand, were oblivious to development and changes. Their conformist and conservative minds adamantly resisted any form of modernisation. Of course, the British colonial administration was also responsible in determining the limit and form of their progress. Nevertheless, the Munshi argued, due to the psychological and social regression, no creative and reformist Malay leadership can be expected to emerge from this malignant condition. Abdullah feared that if the Malays remain feudal and unchanging, they will be unprepared for the struggle for independence and self-government. This cogent criticism is much too much for many Malays. Munshi Abdullah is described as a British stooge and an anti-Malay writer. These anti-Abdullah sentiments began to proliferate, long after his death, during the rising Malay nationalism against colonial power, particularly after the British made more aggressive interference in the local administration in 1874.

Abdullah's critical attitude may be attributed partly to the fact that he only lived in Melaka and Singapore – states with no Malay rulers. The atmosphere there was definitely less feudal, with a little more freedom and some progress. I think Munshi Abdullah's works should be read not as the model of Malay literature, but rather for their remarkable social insight, for the historical light they throw on his times, and for his honest appraisal of the Malay condition. His writings and views awakened Malay writers of subsequent generations from a long acceptance of traditional themes and outlooks. The Munshi unleashed a chain of thought that continues to this day and hopefully will progress on into the future.

AAMER

Taha Kehar

Photo: Rehan Jamil

1.

At the age of sixteen, I came across a story about an Urdu romance writer who had lost her husband in the Second World War. Her name was Adiba. Disenchanted by her life in Delhi after Partition, she migrated to the leafy streets and illuminated bazaars of Lahore. In her new country, she was spurned by the literary intelligentsia for her outmoded tales of wonder. Undeterred, she continued to write and her words won the hearts of readers.

The story, titled 'Adiba: A Storyteller's Tale', sparked a creative flame. In those days, my attempts at writing fiction were viewed with suspicion and I had become insecure about ever being able to pursue writing as a career. Adiba's unflagging commitment to her craft erased my doubts and I discovered that no measure of harsh judgement could stifle the creative process.

Over time, I forgot the name of the writer whose story had brought me to this realisation. It came back to me at the age of twenty-eight when I found the story in Aamer Hussein's *Cactus Town* (2002). By then, I was the author of two novels and Aamer, my newest friend.

Our conversation began on 8 April 2019 – Aamer's sixty-fourth birthday. Two months before we became friends, I'd quit my job at a newspaper in Karachi and was writing my third novel. My second novel had been published in 2018 and I desperately wanted to take up a new creative project.

Aamer lived in Little Venice, West London, and was recovering from an accident in which he had injured his leg. He had to wear a surgical boot for a few weeks and was unable to walk. His Pakistani publisher had asked him to write stories about children in Urdu to keep himself creatively engaged while he recovered. I didn't know then that he had started writing in Urdu in 2012 and had published four short stories in the language in the literary journal *Dunyazad*. I later recalled that I'd read the English translations of some of these stories in Aamer's collection *The Swan's Wife*, but wasn't aware of the abiding influence of Urdu on his creative sensibilities.

We were spared the awkwardness of meeting as writers at a literary festival who had no prior knowledge of each other's work. Aamer had read my first novel about the troubled marriage between a Muslim lawyer and an Indian-born British heiress. I was surprised that Aamer liked the book as it seemed to be the antithesis to his own. His acclaimed novella *Another Gulmohar Tree* (2009), which explores a mixed-heritage marriage that resists cultural differences, was my literary lodestar through challenging times.

As our conversations shifted from Facebook to WhatsApp, I reread the novella and was eager to read more of his work. I was disappointed to learn that most of Aamer's previous collections were unavailable in Karachi. Driven by the thirst of an impatient reader, I asked him how I could find his earlier work. Within minutes, a soft copy of *Electric Shadows* landed in my inbox.

'It has a good selection of stories that were published in my first four collections,' Aamer told me.

As I excitedly immersed myself in Aamer's new and earlier work, I became conscious of how his creative life has evolved over the decades. Steeped in encounters with languages, places and people, Aamer's literary output mirrored his experiences, for example his great love for Java, which he visited twice, in 1992 and 2003. Whenever I would finish a story, I'd ask him questions about its genesis and his answers revealed that he was constantly negotiating the porous boundaries between fiction and autobiography. While he had initially written about people he'd known through thinly veiled fictional disguises, he had shifted toward the memoir in his sixties. 'How well do you read Urdu?' he asked me. I hadn't read the language since I studied Urdu literature at A-Levels. But I had no difficulty reading the stories he sent me. More stories arrived over the course of the year, which were later stitched together to produce his first collection of Urdu stories, *Zindagi Se Pehle* (Before Life). In exchange, I sent him chapters of the novel I was working on.

2.

In September 2019, Aamer visited Karachi, the city of his birth. He would have arrived sooner had it not been for his broken leg. For a week, we soaked in the familiar sights and flavours of the city with the tenacity of tourists. We went on long drives in Clifton and Sea View, visited the crowded gardens around Frere Hall, took pictures under a gold-orange gulmohar tree, and dined at cafes on E-Street and Tipu Sultan Road. At one of these cafes, he autographed a large stack of his own books for me. Later, he glanced at the contents page of one of his books and shared the inspiration for each story. I was told that 'Knotted Tongues-1', which was originally written in Urdu as 'Zohra', was the story of a young Pakistani poet he knew who had died in a car accident.

'Is it about Hima Raza?' I asked him. Aamer nodded. I instantly remembered a poem she'd written about evoking the 'ghost of a forgotten language'. It dawned on me that Aamer had brought those ghosts back to life.

One evening, we rode down a traffic-choked Shahrah-e-Faisal towards P.E.C.H.S to find Aamer's old house.

'We'll need to turn left,' Aamer told our driver as we waded through a sea of honking cars and wailing buses. 'I'll know how to get to Shah Abdul Latif Road from there.'

Darkness had stretched across the cloudless sky and the faint hum of the Maghrib *azan* could be heard in the distance. I feared that our quest for Aamer's childhood home would prove to be laborious, if not altogether futile. The streets of Block 6, P.E.C.H.S., though wide and orderly, bear a labyrinthine quality. But Aamer seemed to know his way around the neighbourhood.

'We have to turn right into that street,' Aamer declared, pointing towards an empty lane. 'That's 43/4/A!'

The car swerved into a dark street and reached an eerie cul-de-sac. As we parked and got out of the car, I caught sight of the smile on Aamer's face. We walked towards the gate of his childhood home and stopped at a safe distance.

'Here it is,' he said. 'The old house.'

With those words, Aamer conjured all those images that inhabit his stories and memoirs about Karachi. They momentarily became the measure of my imagination and I viewed my surroundings through Aamer's eyes. I could almost inhale the perfumed scent of fallen frangipani, hibiscus, and jasmine, which Aamer and his friends picked as children. I looked around for the terrace through which Aamer often saw Americans square dancing, wondering what sights could now be seen from it.

I wanted to ask Aamer to point out the house where the famous Pakistani actress Shamim Ara had moved to in 1967. But Aamer was lost in a dense grove of his own thoughts. Though we were standing outside, the old house had drawn him into its fold, ferried him into the realm of memories, a time before multiple migrations interfered with, and later enriched, his connection to Karachi. During the visit, Aamer told me stories of his childhood and family life in Karachi. 'Mum came to Karachi as a bride from Indore in 1948,' he said as we drove down Clifton. 'They lived in a house in Clifton. I was born there in 1955. When I was one, we went to live in Mohammad Ali Society. When I was two-and-a-half, we moved to P.E.C.H.S' (Pakistan Employees Cooperative Housing Society). I didn't ask him any other questions about his early life. Past conversations and his writings had already told me what I needed to know. Aamer's words provided written confirmations of details that he had mentioned and a window into things that he hadn't told me in too many words. In my mind, I alternate between these texts and conversations as they help me paint a complete picture of Aamer's life.

Karachi was the home Aamer's father Nawabzada Ahmed Husain had chosen for his family. The decision was not a conscious one. Though Ahmed Husain was also born in Karachi, he had never considered the city to be his home and lived instead in Delhi, Simla, Bahawalpur, London and Oxford. He belonged to a family from Shikarpur, Sindh, that had produced bureaucrats, parliamentarians, and ministers, and his father was a seasoned statesman who served as the prime minister of Bahawalpur. In the summer of 1947, he was based in Delhi and travelled to Kashmir on his aunt's request to escort his teenage cousins back to Karachi. When he was informed that his home in Delhi had been earmarked as evacuee property, he stoically accepted Karachi as his new home. Of all the houses he lived in during his years in Karachi, Aamer vividly remembers the time he spent between 1961 and 1966 in the house we visited in Block 6, P.E.C.H.S. Back then, Karachi functioned as Pakistan's capital. The city had a distinctly cosmopolitan vibe that catered to foreign diplomats and wealthy locals. Aamer belonged to this milieu of an English-speaking minority, though his mother was a lover of Urdu and encouraged him to speak the language. He attended art exhibitions and music recitals at the Arts Council, watched English and American movies screened at luxury cinemas and sat through plays by Shakespeare and Shaw at the Theosophical Hall, and heard concerts by Pakistan's leading singers. Aamer was also encouraged to read the works of Victor Hugo, Leo Tolstoy, and William Shakespeare.

Strong, independent women surrounded him while growing up in Karachi. Sabiha Ahmed Husain, his mother, studied classical vocal music with an *ustad* and Aamer owes his fondness for music to her. Mujeebunissa Akram, his aunt, published and edited the magazine *Woman's World*. His mother wrote for the publication and briefly ran it in the sixties and seventies.

Aamer attended Lady Jennings School and was subsequently admitted to the Convent of Jesus and Mary's co-educational junior school. The details of his schooling in Karachi have been compiled in a collage of memories titled 'Electric Shadows', which was the centrepiece of the book Aamer had emailed me. His classroom comprised Japanese, Canadian, French, and Norwegian students who were taught by Irish, Welsh, Goan, and Parsi teachers. As a Pakistani boy in a predominantly 'foreign' school, Aamer was in the minority.

'Electric Shadows' reveals how a private utopia was shattered by a public calamity: the 1965 war. Through the initial images, Aamer evokes his friendships with the children of diplomats and his life at home with his mother and three sisters, Yasmine, Shahrukh and Safinaz. The narrative also draws on the conflict brewing between India and Pakistan and shows how the euphoria of war intrudes on childhood games. His father was stuck in Bombay during the war and the family couldn't contact him for weeks. When he was allowed to leave India, he flew to Beirut and returned to Karachi soon after. But circumstances had changed after the 1965 war. For ten-year-old Aamer, this meant that Hollywood movies would no longer be screened at Rex, Bambino, and Scala now that the government had stopped buying them. For his father, the changes had deeper implications. Ahmed Husain decided against coming back permanently to Karachi after a holiday in Rome. He stayed on to carve out a new life for his family abroad as he feared that horizons were shrinking at home.

Still young, Aamer adapted to the absence of American films by turning to Pakistani movies starring Waheed Murad, Shamim Ara, Muhammad Ali and Zeba. The shift was a convenient one as he was bilingual by ear. Urdu had become akin to breathing for him, even though his exposure to the language at school was somewhat patchy. After the war, Aamer left the Convent of Jesus and Mary. He and his mother couldn't agree on a suitable secondary school for him so he spent several months studying Urdu and reading English novels at home. Meanwhile, his father's plan to move his family to a new city was delayed when he had two heart attacks, one in Rome and another in London. Ahmed returned to Karachi while his wife was in hospital recovering from meningitis. In September 1966, the family attended a cousin's wedding in Bombay and never returned to their house in P.E.C.H.S. They came back to Karachi in April 1967. By then, their landlady had died, the house had been reclaimed by her family and their belongings had been placed in storage at their aunt's house next door. Aamer's family remained at his aunt's house until December 1967. He was four months away from his thirteenth birthday when he left Karachi and wouldn't return to the city until he was forty-one.

3.

Not all aspects of the elite milieu of Aamer's childhood in Karachi have seeped into his stories. Instead, he uses his lived experiences in Karachi as conduits to a fictional moment. 'Little Tales', which came to him on a rainy afternoon in Rome, was the first story he wrote about Karachi. The story evokes a world battered by the 1965 conflict that bears similarities with Aamer's childhood. But Aamer writes about a family of modest means that confronts the knotty issues of ethnicity, migration, and nationalism. When 'Little Tales' was translated into Urdu by feminist poet Fahmida Riaz for the literary journal *Aaj*, it was incorrectly perceived as an autobiographical account. Even so, Aamer was thrilled that the story had found its home in Urdu and surrendered his rights on it. I read 'Karima' and 'Champion' at the same time - not by design, but because they appeared one after the other in *Cactus Town*. In these stories, Aamer also sheds his privilege and explores Karachi through the perspective of the underclass.

When I began reading *Cactus Town*, which was written after Aamer returned to Karachi, I assumed that Aamer had evoked his own world of the privileged elite. I was mistaken. The story is less about the wealthy Aunty Mehri and more about a scandal surrounding her orphaned niece that is complicated by the 1971 war. In addition, Karachi isn't mentioned once in the story and the eponymous 'cactus town' could very well be an invented realm where memory becomes a springboard for fiction. 'Two Old Friends on a Stormy Afternoon', which I came across in *The Swan's Wife*, presents a modern-day evocation of Karachi's elite. The story stems from a personal challenge to write a story in dialogue in the vein of celebrated Urdu novelist Qurratulain Hyder's story 'A Dialogue'. It depicts a meandering conversation between two men at a posh club in Karachi while a storm rages outside. In his spare, tightly wrought novel, *Another Gulmohar Tree*, Aamer backdates the social, literary, and artistic references from the fifties and sixties to reflect the stultifying impact of Field Marshal Ayub Khan's dictatorial rule.

I read *Gulmohar* when I returned to Karachi after completing a three-year law degree at the School of Oriental and African Studies (SOAS) in London. I channelled the courageous optimism of Lydia, the novel's London-born, European protagonist who leads a fulfilling life in Karachi. For the next five years, I wrote fiction in my spare time, and worked as a journalist at two newspapers in Karachi. Everything was going well until censorship cast a dark shadow on my career. Stifled by the fetters on press freedom, I had gone from showing Lydia's enthusiasm to displaying her husband Usman's diffidence. In *Gulmohar*, I found a story that was not just about creative freedom, but also the impact of its suppression.

When Aamer began experimenting with the boundaries between fiction and memoir, he drew on some aspects of his Karachi childhood. In 2017, Aamer reworked a transcript of his mother's diary into 'Lady of the Lotus'. The piece juxtaposes Sabiha Ahmed Husain's words from her diary with her children's perceptions on her passion for music, which she never actively pursued as a career. His new book, *Restless: Instead of an Autobiography*, contains an essay titled 'Words and Music'. The piece, written after Shamim Ara's death, documents his pre-teen fascination with Urdu films and music.

4.

I've never been to India, but have a strange relationship with the country as both my novels found a home there. After the Kashmir situation escalated in August 2019, strict import bans created complications for Pakistanis to publish in India. When I complained about how my recently completed third novel had elicited silence from publishers across the border, Aamer urged me to find a local publisher. In recent years, he had also found publishers in Pakistan. Aamer felt his work had become increasingly challenging for Western readers to accept. Even so, he had a thriving audience in the West. An interaction with one of his Western readers, a poet and publisher, had culminated in a short collection titled *Love and Its Seasons*. The advice gave me some hope and made me realise that my connection with India was, at best, superficial. Aamer's equation with India was different. He had not only been published in the country, but had also lived there. He often told me about his years in Ooty, a hill station in the Nilgiris district of Tamil Nadu; and his trips to Indore and Bombay as a child.

While they lived in Karachi, Aamer's family often visited relatives in India. During long weekends, the family boarded an almost hour-long flight from Karachi to Bombay. They lived at the house of Aamer's aunt in the Art Deco block that overlooked the sea. For Aamer, Bombay was the other city by the sea that was a pale reflection of Karachi, which he felt was cleaner and more orderly. Even so, the city was a portal to new experiences and creative possibilities. It was from Bombay's Santa Cruz that Aamer flew to London in May 1970 with an English translation of Mirza Hadi Ruswa's 1899 classic novel, *Umrao Jaan Ada*. On a sunny afternoon in Bombay in 1968, he met Qurratulain Hyder, the acclaimed Urdu writer, who almost two decades later sowed the seeds of inspiration by asking him if he wrote in Urdu. Five years after her death in 2007, Aamer began writing stories in Urdu.

His childhood perceptions of Bombay fuelled his literary imagination in unique ways. I realised this in October 2019 when I read Aamer's second novel, *The Cloud Messenger*, at the Margalla Hotel in Islamabad. We were attending a literary festival in the capital and Aamer had brought a copy of the book from London. In the novel, Mehran – who could very well be Aamer's alter ego – describes Bombay as a 'big, messy city' that 'grew upwards', which allowed him to see the Arabian Sea from every window. Mehran also considers the people of Bombay to be 'louder and freer' than the people he knew in Karachi. As a child, Aamer felt Bombay's allure was its glitzy film industry. He built upon this image of the metropolis in a story titled 'Last Companions', which weaves the tale about courtesans in Bombay's film world. The piece bears echoes of the Ruswa's *Umrao Jaan Ada* and the celebrated 1972 Indian film, Kamal Amrohi's *Pakeeza*.

Bombay was also a doorway to Indore, Aamer's maternal family home. His maternal grandfather was a feudal chieftain who belonged to the princely family of Darbargarh-Dasada in Kathiawar. He renounced his privilege to become a senior housemaster at the local boarding school, Daly

College. Aamer's maternal grandmother, who was well-versed in Persian and could recite classical poets such as Rumi and Amir Khusrau, took it upon herself to properly teach him to speak Urdu at the age of eleven. It was at their *haveli* on Manoramaganj that Aamer acquired even more of the courtly culture that was part of his history. His maternal family was his primary link to Rafi Ajmeri, his grandmother's brother who had died long before Aamer's birth. Rafi, who his mother referred to as 'Mamu Mian' (an affectionate term for uncle), wrote a volume of short stories that Aamer read as an adult. Rafi Ajmeri features prominently in Aamer's oeuvre. 'The Angelic Disposition' reimagines a different fate for 'Mamu Mian' in the era of the Progressive Writers Movement. Rafi Ajmeri also re-emerges as a strong presence in 'Skies' and *The Cloud Messenger*. Years later, Aamer wrote a memoir about him titled 'Uncle Rafi', which pays tribute to his great-uncle's influence on his writing after 1997.

By 1967, Aamer's father had initiated his plans to move the family to London. However, Aamer wanted to join his cousin at a theosophical school in the Blue Mountains of Ootacamund, South India where his uncle was vice-principal. In mid-1968, he arrived in Ooty and was greeted with loneliness and bleak weather. On the weekend, he'd watch foreign films at the local cinema or read in the school's dusty library where new books would arrive from Madras every few weeks. Aamer devoured biographies and books on British theatre. On a monthly basis, he'd received issues of *Imprint* and the *Illustrated Weekly of India* from Qurratulain Hyder.

In an autobiographical afterword to *Cactus Town*, Aamer states that Ooty was the first city whose topography he felt the compulsion to describe. He wrote three stories about his time in Ooty, which provide variations of the same event: the friendship of two boys at a boarding school. 'The Sound of Absence' in *Cactus Town*, has a more lyrical quality than the other two stories. It was originally published as 'Mirror to the Sun'. The second, titled 'The Blue Direction', is a novella-length story that I came across in *Electric Shadows*. 'Singapore Jay', the third story, was penned sixteen years later for an editor who had requested a shorter version of 'Mirror to the Sun'.

'I rewrote it as the truth,' Aamer told me when I asked about the origins of the final story. '"The Blue Direction" is similar and is the best out of the three. But "Singapore Jay" is the naked truth'.

Aamer reconnected with his Indian roots by visiting Delhi in 1981. On that trip, he also spent a few days in Bombay. In 1984, he returned to the country to hunt for locations for the Merchant Ivory film, *The Deceivers*.

5.

London is the only European metropolis where Aamer has lived for more than six months. It was once my home but I outgrew the city and abandoned it on a whim. After taking my final exams at law school, I realised that London couldn't inspire me creatively. On my twenty-third birthday, I boarded a flight back to Karachi and never returned to London. Aamer wasn't as impulsive as I had been. He stayed on and bridged the gap between the East and the West through his friendships and prose.

After spending eighteen months in south India, Aamer moved to London at the age of fifteen. At first, he had to readjust to living in a city after spending many months in the Blue Mountains. While he considered the city to be shabby, he enjoyed the liberty to wander through the streets. Public libraries were his haven and introduced him to a diverse spectrum of writers. Aamer read contemporary British and American writers, such as Muriel Spark, Iris Murdoch, Angela Carter, William Styron and Norman Mailer. He was most intrigued by James Baldwin's confessional style and his ability to portray complex relationships steered by race, class and sexual difference.

Even so, London exposed him to dry prose that was unmarked by the flavours of his mother tongue. To improve his reading skills in Urdu, he read the poems of Faiz Ahmed Faiz in a bilingual edition.

He was admitted to a college with students from various parts of the world. As he spoke English as a first language, he adapted easily. When he turned eighteen, he found himself without direction, and felt a deep sense of dislocation as he was detached from his roots while his peers at college always had homelands they could return to or places they could call their own. He tried to cultivate a place of his own through books and music, and even sang at folk clubs.

His father wanted him to follow in his footsteps and study law. Aamer applied to law schools on his father's insistence, but was rejected. He then decided to pursue his desire to study 'something Eastern', preferably languages, at SOAS. When his application was again declined, he took a gap year and sought comfort in literature and folk music. At the age of twenty, he recorded a music album of Indus songs that was never released. He travelled to Italy and Spain, learnt French, Spanish, and Italian, and read the works of Sartre and Natalia Ginzburg. Aamer's encounter with these languages allowed him to escape the stranglehold of English and the guilt of not being able to express himself in Urdu. A romantic relationship ended in heartbreak and disillusionment, and led him to write poetry. The experiences of his student years would later surface in 'The Girl from Seoul' and 'The Crane Girl'.

Since Aamer struggled with the Urdu script in his teenage years, his mother enrolled him in weekly evening classes with an Urdu teacher, Sayyad Moinuddin Shah, who was referred to as 'tall Shah Sahib'. After two semesters, Shah Sahib tutored him privately for an A-Level in Urdu. The text assigned for the exam was *Umrao Jan Ada* and Aamer scored the highest marks. In his sixties, Aamer would pay tribute to his Urdu teacher in a memoir titled 'The Tall Man'. Although it was too late for him to apply to universities, he got into a technical college in 1976 through the 'clearing' process and studied librarianship for a year. He soon shifted gears and worked as a junior officer at a bank before using his Urdu A-Level as a ticket to SOAS. He was admitted as a second-year student in South Asian Studies, with a special focus on Urdu, Persian, and History.

After graduating, Aamer divided his time between conducting research for films and television documentaries, and teaching language courses. Three years after he left SOAS, he studied psychoanalysis and philosophy, and began working on a dissertation on Sartre, Lacan, and Klein; and published his first story, 'The Colour of Loved Person's Eyes' at about the same time. He also dabbled in literary criticism but never saw himself as a critic, but a reader who worked arduously to interpret a text. In 1987, he interviewed Chinese-born author Han Suyin, who wrote novels in English and French set in modern China, for *South* magazine; and the two became friends. He began writing about Chinese literature in translation and was part of a project in the late 1980s called 'Asian Voices in English', which led to him attending a conference in Hong Kong.

6.

I escaped London to safeguard my creative voice from being stifled in a foreign land. As I revised my third novel, I realised that I was seeking validation from another foreign land to find an audience for that voice. During that period, I often reread 'Knotted Tongues 1 & 2', which tell stories of women who relinquish troubled homelands in search of a personal voice. In these stories, Aamer had chronicled the lives of two women he had known. His own search for a voice, though not laced with tragedy, was equally remarkable. Initially, he found it difficult to cultivate a literary voice for himself in English because, he says, its literature was monopolised by narratives of Empire. Aamer viewed himself as a writer from the 'Third World', which he perceived to be a far more inclusive category than 'Commonwealth Literature'. So, he sought out oppositional voices and read the works of writers from other countries who used English to reflect their own experiences. He felt a deep affinity with writers from Muslim countries, such as Naguib Mahfouz and Assia Djebar, who wrote in Arabic and French.

His encounters with Asia's writers were critical in helping him find his creative voice. His friendship with Han Suyin allowed him to look beyond restrictive literary labels such as 'colonial', 'postcolonial' and 'third world' and search for the 'inner music of your mother tongue'. Inspired by her words, Aamer spent two years writing a confessional novel about his childhood in Karachi. The novel, which he eventually discarded to write other stories, morphed into a three-tiered tale about his time in Karachi, Ooty and London. As a regular contributor of fiction to multi authored anthologies and a reviewer for *Times Literary Supplement*, he was taken up by London's literary circles, feeling both included and estranged. In 1992, he extracted thirty-three pages from his unfinished novel to produce the novella 'Mirror to the Sun'; and returned to that abandoned story and wrote *Electric Shadows* in 2000.

7.

Electric Shadows has a good selection of his earlier work that I often revisit to seek consolation in a distressed hour. Soon after I received the PDF, I printed it out and annotated it. On the title page, I scribbled down the names of each of his collections and the stories that were published in them. The notes that I'd clumsily scrawled became my map to Aamer's work. I struck out all the stories I'd read with a red pen.

As I read his stories, I found it ironic that Pakistani Anglophone readers knew Aamer because of his novella *Another Gulmohar Tree* when he had devoted his entire life to the short story. In one of his columns for *Dawn*, Aamer mentioned that publishing a large number of short story collections make it seem as though you are 'running some strange marathon in slow motion'. Aamer's literary career is undoubtedly a marathon, but I refuse to accept that he's been running in slow motion.

Although his second collection *This Other Salt* appeared six years after his first, the hiatus gave Aamer an opportunity to gestate. He believes that his voice began to emerge with this collection. Each story captures a self-contained reality and is enriched by his characteristic ability to weave techniques of Urdu fiction as well as fables and folklore into his work. 'The Lost Cantos of the Silken Tiger' engages the Qur'anic tale of Yusuf and Zulekha while 'Benedetta Amata' (which Aamer has blocked from being republished) is a tale of his own near-fatal depression. 'Painting on Glass' is about a painter's quest to reclaim his lost language and is welcome proof of the influence of Aamer's mother tongue on his creative sensibilities. 'Skies' was written in the spring after Aamer's father passed away and developed from his story 'Summer, Lake and Sad Garden'. Aamer felt he had left a lot unsaid and added two letters from London to two Karachi writers where he chronicles the realities of migrations witnessed by his parent's generation. 'Sweet Rice' builds on his study of Urdu novelist Muhammadi Begum and demonstrates how an expatriate woman from South Asia finds herself handicapped by limited opportunities in the West.

This story is an excellent preamble to Aamer's next collection, *Turquoise*, that provides insights into the lives of women. By then, Aamer was at home in his skin as a storyteller. He was about to complete the final story of *Turquoise* when the 11 September attacks took place. The event, which widened the divide between Islam and the West, made Aamer realise that his stories were about quieter times in Pakistan and his characters embodied the positive virtues of Islam. He did not churn out a '9/11 novel' or produce fiction that tackled aspects of radicalism or terrorism - though his story 'Your Children', written after the 1991 Iraq War, confirms that he was thinking about these issues for a long time.

Turquoise marked a turning point in Aamer's literary career. Two years after it was published, he was elected as a Fellow of the Royal Society of Literature in 2004. His next collection, *Insomnia*, is his favourite one. The stories in the collection deal with the 'grand narratives of our time', including the shrill rhetoric of Islam vs Christianity. In 'The Book of Maryam', a radical Pakistani poet who is searched at a New York airport, recites a translation of the Surah Mariam, which displays the similarity between both religions, a few days before Christmas. *Insomnia* also includes 'Hibiscus Days', which began its journey as a short novel that was never published. It took Aamer nineteen years to trim the story down; it explores an expatriate's relationship with his homeland during General Zia's regime.

After the publication of *Insomnia*, Aamer began teaching creative writing to MA students at the University of Southampton. The position came with tenure and a heavy teaching load but he managed to write three books during the nine years that he taught at Southampton.

Another Gulmohar Tree, released in 2009, received critical acclaim and was shortlisted for the Commonwealth Writers Prize in the Europe and Asia category in 2010. The same year, Aamer became a senior research fellow at the Institute of English Studies. In 2011, his first novel *The Cloud Messenger* was released, after which he was longing to return to the short story and desperately wanted to escape the confessional mode. He wrote 'Two Old Men on a Stormy Night'. The story appeared in the collection *The Swan's Wife* in 2014, which was published in Pakistan and an expanded edition of the book appeared in India as *37 Bridges*. Both books contained translations of his Urdu stories, two of which were done by his mother. Both *37 Bridges* and *The Swan's Wife* are seminal works where Aamer combines the creative output of Urdu with that of English, his workaday language. *37 Bridges*, which won the 2016 Karachi Literature Festival-Embassy of France Best Fiction Prize, has been viewed as an exploration of Muslim lives in the European context. It also builds on the conflict between faith and doubt, which is filtered through Muslim sensibilities. The collection is also fuelled by the encounters and exchanges that characters have rather than their own quest for self-examination.

Aamer retired as a professorial writing fellow from the University of Southampton in 2015. Over the last decade or so, Pakistani readers have started claiming him as their favoured writer. His most recent books include *Hermitage*, which contains stories, modern fables, faithful replicas of the stories told by mystics, and memoirs, and the Urdu collection *Zindagi se Pehle*. Weeks before the book came out, Aamer had translated the title story into English for Critical Muslim as 'What is Saved', which is a carbon copy of the original. This is noteworthy as in the past his attempt to translate his Urdu story *Maya aur Hans* resulted in an entirely new story. Translating *Zindagi se Pehle* was a difficult undertaking as many of his readers felt his vocabulary in the story was unusual. Aamer uses a mixture of literary and colloquial Urdu, and Hindi in his fiction, which can be difficult to put into standard English. However, the literal translation from Urdu to English reflects a new dimension in Aamer's quest to make a voyage between both languages.

8.

After our conversation about publishing prospects, I'd decided to take Aamer's advice and publish locally. I worked on co-editing a compilation of stories on the pandemic that found a Karachi-based publisher. I asked Aamer if he would agree to submit a story. He agreed; even though tragedy had cast a dark shadow on his life. In January 2020, Aamer lost his sister Safinaz to cancer. A few months later, when virus-related lockdowns were at their peak, his beloved mother also died. A few months later he was diagnosed with cancer.

Much to my delight, a story arrived in August 2020: 'The Garden Spy' is an elegiac tale that explores the value of friendship, loss, and mortality, and navigates the boundary between fiction and memoir. For his other readers, the story has all the ingredients that typify Aamer's quiet, poignant style. For me, it is the token of a literary friendship.

Despite a difficult period in his life, Aamer keeps writing. In addition to the story he had written for the compilation, he has produced an essay on Han Suyin's work and translated two stories by Italian author Lalla Kezich directly to Urdu. He travelled to Pakistan during a lull in lockdown in September 2020 where among other events the Karachi Arts Council held a celebration of his life and writing. He has since completed work on his forthcoming collection, *Restless: Instead of An Autobiography*, which includes new and uncollected fiction, memoirs, personal essays, and travelogues. It includes an account of his lifechanging visit to Palestine in 2013. His stories and essays would continue to land in my inbox. Our conversations about the written word are far from over.

DNA: A PERSONAL STORY

Jeremy Henzell-Thomas

I have long been very interested in my own family history, following in the footsteps of my father who was a keen amateur genealogist. By profession a chartered accountant, he was at heart a historian with a vast knowledge of heraldry, and even worked for a time as a volunteer guide in Canterbury Cathedral explaining to visitors which families were depicted on the plethora of coats of arms attached to the vaults of the cathedral. He schooled me from an early age in the history of the Henzell family, his mother's line, which he had meticulously researched to the extent of drawing up a family tree reaching back several centuries. Dwelling in the village of de Hennezel in Lorraine, France, the family were quite rare in being not only a 'noble' family with a coat of arms but also masters of the craft of glassmaking ('nobles verriers'). There is a museum in the village devoted to the family and their activities. As a Huguenot (French Protestant) family they were forced to flee persecution in France after the Massacre of St Bartholomew's Eve in 1572 when thousands of Huguenots were murdered through targeted assassinations and Catholic mob violence. Along with other Huguenot families, including the Tyzacks, with whom they had close familial ties, they migrated to various Protestant countries, taking up Queen Elizabeth 1's invitation to settle in England, where they were granted the use of the crypt of Canterbury Cathedral to hold services in French. These services are still held to this day at 3 pm every Sunday, and as a boy I accompanied my father to attend the occasional service. About one-fifth of the Huguenot population (estimated at 2 million in France in 1562) ended up in England, with a smaller portion moving to Ireland. The Huguenots are credited with bringing the word 'refugee' into the English language upon their arrival in Britain when it was first used to describe them.

Huguenot refugees were welcomed by their host countries for various reasons, and not merely the obvious one of being favoured by the

Protestant establishment often at war with Catholic enemies. They were valued for the importance they attached to education and literacy associated with their strongly intellectual Calvinist roots, from which they also inherited an active sense of opposition to religious oppression and privilege. They could not only read and write, but were often skilled craftsmen and entrepreneurs, especially prolific in the textile industry. The Henzells made a major contribution to the glassmaking industry in various parts of England, including Stourbridge, Newcastle upon Tyne, and Durham where they established glasshouses. In fact, it is well attested by historians that the contribution of immigrant Huguenot families to the development and modernisation of their host countries was out of all proportion to their numbers. In stark contrast, the departure of the Huguenots was a disaster for France, costing the nation much of its cultural and economic influence. In some French cities, the mass exodus meant losing half the working population.

My father was proud of his Huguenot ancestry, and often spoke to me of his admiration not only for the spirit of their opposition to Catholicism but also for their emphasis on skill, innovation, education, hard work, and ethical values. These were the qualities he strove to embody himself, and he was a hard taskmaster in his efforts to inculcate them into me and my siblings. I cannot of course claim to have lived up to such rigorous expectations, but I have always shared my father's rebellious spirit and opposition to privilege. He told me once how he had outraged the members of the Punjab Club in Lahore, of which he was a member during World War II as an officer in Hodson's Horse, part of the Armoured Corps of the Indian Army which had its beginnings as a cavalry regiment at the time of the Indian Mutiny in 1857. The Punjab Club was established as an Imperial social club in 1884 and was exclusively used by British and Europeans, its elected members consisting of high ranking civil and armed forces personnel, leading industrialists, entrepreneurs, and executives. It was transferred to Pakistan in 1962. My father's unforgiveable sin was to defy the rule excluding non-British and non-European members by letting a close Indian friend, one Ayoub Khan, accompany him as a guest into the club.

My father's anti-establishment inclinations may well have been one of the qualities that attracted my mother to him and led to their marriage in Lucknow in 1943. She herself was something of a rebel. Born in India in

1925, the daughter of a British engineer based in the hill station of Naini Tal, she was educated in a convent run by draconian German nuns who were quick to resort to the cane for every breach of discipline. She delighted in telling the story of how one day she locked a group of supervising nuns in the tuck shop and spent the day horseback riding in the foothills of the Himalayas. I told this story when I gave the eulogy at her funeral four years ago, as it seemed to reflect most vividly her independent spirit and love of freedom and adventure. I should add that the funeral service was held at the same Unitarian Church where my father's funeral had been held nearly thirty years previously. Why Unitarianism? Well, it was a dissenting Christian movement that rejected established church doctrines of Trinitarianism, original sin, predestination, the infallibility of the Bible, the vicarious atonement, and the Divinity of Christ (Jesus as an incarnation of God). The connection with the non-conformist and reforming ethos of the Huguenots is clear to see.

I have a real sense that my own non-conformist tendencies are somehow impregnated with the character of my parents. To what extent this is genetic or an outcome of upbringing (in other words Nature or Nurture) or a combination of both I cannot tell. I will return to this conundrum in due course.

I recall that my father always pretended to scold me for my school reports in religious studies, although I had a sense that he was secretly pleased. The religious studies teacher at the independent secondary boarding school I attended was the school chaplain, and to this day I have kept his reports dating back to 1964. Two out of the three in that year had only one terse comment: 'His comments depress me.' I have concluded that the reason for his grim assessment (for which he gave no accompanying explanation) was that I was vocal and insistent in questioning and challenging in class his doctrines and beliefs, to the extent, I guess, that I was seen as a thorn in the flesh, a bothersome iconoclast. I refused to attend Church of England confirmation classes and my grandmother was sorely disappointed because had I done so I would have been confirmed by no less than Michael Ramsey, the Archbishop of Canterbury, who was the presiding bishop in the diocese where my school was situated.

My non-conformity went much further too. The day I entered the school in 1961 at the age of thirteen, I was warned that only school prefects were allowed to unbutton their jackets, put their hands in their pockets, and walk across the grass of the school Close. So the first thing I did on hearing this was to unbutton my jacket, put my hands in my pockets, and walk proudly across the Close! I was accosted by a school prefect and told to meet him the following morning before breakfast when he would supervise me for a run of twenty laps around the Close. I duly completed the twenty laps and he said I could go, but I turned to him and said: 'If you don't mind, I'll just do one more lap.' Later, I often used to skip the weekly parades and training of the Officer Training Corps (OTC) even though attendance was compulsory in a school noted as a source of officers in the armed services. Instead, I walked brazenly past the lines of cadets to the music rooms, where I spent the afternoon playing the piano. But perhaps my greatest sin was when I was surprisingly made a house prefect in my final year (I guess it was hoped that by being given authority I would have to conform to the rules). I confounded all such hopes by refusing to follow the established regime of having what was known as a 'fag', a junior boy who would be at my beck and call as a kind of lackey, a tradition dating back to the founding of the school in Victorian times. It seemed to me to be high time for the rupture of an outmoded tradition and a determined step into a less stuffily hierarchical world.

At this point, it would be useful to reveal the findings of my DNA analysis, carried out about four years ago by MyHeritage. My profile turned out as follows: 31.1% North and West European, 29.5% Irish, Scottish, Welsh, 18.6% English, 11.2% Italian, 3.5% Iberian, 6.1% Central Asian (Kazakhstan, Uzbekistan). There is some controversy about how such profiles should be interpreted and some concerns that they are readily misinterpreted. But there are valid implications that can be immediately drawn from them. Sometimes too much critical scrutiny and the reservations they engender can cause us to miss the boat!

What emerges strongly from the profile is that over 60 per cent of my DNA is divided pretty well equally between North and West Europe and the Celtic lands (Irish, Scottish, Welsh). I can readily attribute a large slice of the European component to my French ancestors, the de Hennezels, from Lorraine. But how do I account for the strong Celtic connection? For this, I need to turn to my grandfather on my father's side, a man of the Thomas clan from the Welsh valleys. My father never knew him, having been told as a boy that he had died in a car accident soon after he married my grandmother in London in 1919. He had in fact been told this to cover up the shame the family felt that he had actually married my grandmother when he was already married, and had been sentenced to a 12-month term in Wandsworth prison for bigamy soon after their marriage and before the birth of my father in 1920. Withholding the truth from my father was also intended to protect him from the stigma he might well feel at being technically illegitimate, the bastard son of a convicted bigamist. At the time there was a full-page spread in that bastion of the gutter press, the *News of the World,* on the scandal, condemning Thomas as a 'villain of the first water', a rogue who cruelly deceived and seduced the innocent young woman my grandmother undoubtedly was. That deceit included lies exaggerating the professional and social standing of his family, when in fact his grandfather had been a colliery clerk and his father a tax collector.

I looked into his past and discovered that he had been a sergeant serving in the medical corps at the Battle of the Somme in 1916. He was a stretcher bearer and must have seen unimaginable horrors. He was also blown up and wounded by shrapnel and invalided out for 'shell shock' to the Maudsley Hospital in London where my grandmother was a nurse. I guess he must have had profound post-traumatic stress disorder, and this may also explain in part why cases in bigamy spiked well beyond the average at the end of the First World War, amplified of course by the large numbers of women who had been made 'available' to traumatised men by the deaths of so many married servicemen. My father eventually discovered that the story he had been told about his father's death was false and changed his surname from Henzell to Henzell-Thomas to bring him into the picture. He set out to find him if he was still alive, but sadly his father died in 1957 not long after he had come close to catching up with him.

Now, Tommy (as we came to call him) clearly had 'the gift of the gab' (I hesitate to say 'the Welsh gift of the gab' for fear of stereotyping the Welsh) although the biography I have so far told of him highlights the misuse of his eloquence to deceive and beguile. His early promise was in actual fact extraordinary. He was in great demand as a speaker on social and religious issues, and at the age of fifteen he was Deputy Chief Templar of a lodge connected with the Independent Order of Good Templars (the youngest member holding that office in the United Kingdom). The Order had been established in the nineteenth century to promote Temperance. He had great ambitions and aspirations but lived at a time of rigid social class which must have hampered him at every turn. When he was released from prison in 1921, he went on to become a Baptist Minister and became well known for his fiery sermons delivered in London churches. He also qualified as a Fellow of the Royal College of Organists.

Given this biography, it is not surprising that I, as a speaker and musician who has acted as parish organist myself, have come to feel a real sense of affinity with him and his Welsh heritage. In 2010, I gave a lecture at the British Academy in London entitled 'British and Muslim, a Personal Perspective' and in the following year I was asked to give the lecture in the Public Lecture Series organised by the Centre for the Study of Islam in the UK at Cardiff University in association with the Muslim Council of Wales and Muslim Youth Wales. I jumped at this chance to bring 'Welshness' into my own sense of multiple identity, entitling my lecture 'British and Muslim, or just Human…and what about Welshness? Some Reflections on Identity.' Referring to Chris Rojek's work on British identity, I noted his contention that in 'the high-water mark of empire' Britishness was regarded as 'the combination of the best and highest that nature and nurture could provide in the British Isles', with each nation within the Union providing 'crucial elements that the others lacked' – a composite identity representing a 'marriage between Scottish invention and discipline, Irish daring and imagination, Welsh decency and pluck, and English application and genius for compromise.'

The identification of Welshness with 'decency and pluck' reminded me of Shakespeare's characterisation of the Welshman Captain Fluellen in his play *Henry V*. The king himself describes Fluellen as a man of 'much care and valour', but 'out of fashion.' Fluellen embodies the unfashionable virtues of discipline, conscientiousness, rectitude, temperance and propriety over licence, licentiousness, dissoluteness, rudeness, and impiety. At heart he is a man of scrupulous integrity, honourable, honest, passionate and brave, open and true. He has some caprices and awkward peculiarities to be sure – I mean he can be a bit of a windbag (we may recall the politician Neil Kinnock being labelled the 'Welsh windbag') and in that he is true to what Hywel Davies said about the wordiness of the Welsh in a lecture in 1965: 'the one extravagance of the Welsh is words, and their abiding passion is literacy.' Fluellen's deep knowledge of the rules of warfare is firmly based on his vast book learning. And the love of literacy, expression, and learning has always informed Celtic culture in a way that has perhaps not been so evident amongst the English.

Our last two homes, currently in Glastonbury and before that on the Malvern Hills, have occupied elevated positions facing westwards towards Wales, and I feel a special affinity with that orientation. I cherish memories of inspiring hikes in the Brecon Beacons and of the 190-mile Pembrokeshire Coast Path which I trekked eight years ago to mark my sixty-fifth birthday. In Malvern, our view took in the hill where the British chieftain Caractacus, the epitome of Celtic British valour, made his last stand against the Romans. Taken as a prisoner to Rome, he avoided the execution usually suffered by defeated enemy leaders by making an eloquent and impassioned speech to the Roman Senate, a speech that so impressed the Emperor that he was pardoned and lived out the rest of his life in Rome.

I can see in Tommy, despite the misuse of his talents, the essence of this Celtic spirit. And I am reminded of the teachings of Aristotle, adopted by Al-Ghazali in his exposition of Islamic ethics, that vices are but the defect or excess of a virtue. Thus, in the same way as Al-Ghazali teaches that the vice of recklessness is the excess of the virtue of courage and cowardice its defect, so it is that lies and hyperbole in the cause of seduction might be seen as the excess of the virtue of eloquence, the misuse of the 'gift of the gab.' So instead of condemning Tommy for his misdeeds, I have tried to spend time in meditation to feel his presence and take him into my heart and love and forgive him. I do believe that our own biographies can heal the wounds we inherit from our ancestral history, and that this is a vital part of the way we conduct our own lives.

I have concentrated up to now on the Henzell and Thomas clans through my father's parents representing as they do the 60 per cent of my DNA that connects with North and West Europe and Celtic Britain and the affinity I feel with these roots. Adding in the share of English genes takes the total to almost 80 per cent. The English component might well be attributed partly to my mother's ancestors and to intermarriage between the immigrant Henzell clan and 'indigenous' English people over the last four hundred years (although there was also much intermarriage between the Henzells and other immigrant Huguenot families, notably the Tyzacks). My mother's great-great-grandfather was one James Liddell born in 1798 in Bodmin in Cornwall, a place closely associated with the Liddell clan since that time, although his parents hailed from Lancashire in England. James was a Commander in the Royal Navy, and many others in the line were Royal Navy officers or surgeons. In 1816 he was a midshipman aboard the 'Albion' and he sailed in her in the expedition to Algiers to release Christian prisoners held in bondage there. Even after retiring from the Royal Navy, he did not quit the sea, but was appointed Chief Officer of the 'Wellington', an East Indian free trader, making no less than eighteen voyages to Madras. He retired in 1845 and devoted the rest of his long life (he died in 1889 at the age of ninety-one) to public service to the Bodmin community, including being Mayor of Bodmin and a Borough Magistrate for a while. A paper read before the Royal Cornwall Polytechnic Society in 1928, celebrating his life, includes this appreciation of his character: 'Though imperious in manner, partly the result of his life as the monarch of his ship, the old "Captain" had a kind and generous heart, and there are those still alive who remember many acts of sympathy and kindness as well as the little incidents which revealed the spirit of the autocrat.'

If the Cornish connection is taken to have some degree of Celtic ancestry to add to the Welsh line, it may help explain my relatively high level (30 per cent) of Celtic DNA, but I cannot be sure of this, and the Cornish Liddells might have been more English than Celtic. Apart from these conjectures, I have very little knowledge of my English ancestry, although it does figure strongly in my own sense of identity. I have never lived in Wales, the 'land of my fathers' ('Hen Wlad Fy Nhadau', the unofficial Welsh national anthem), but was born, brought up, and educated in England (apart from a period as a toddler in Pakistan and a year of schooling in Bermuda). I do not speak Welsh, and am not stirred by Welsh choral singing at rugby matches, but am indeed profoundly moved by the singing of Parry's sublime setting (orchestrated by Elgar) of Blake's 'Jerusalem': 'And did those feet in ancient times walk upon England's mountains green...' I can see how the strand of 'Englishness', reinforced by immersion for so long in English culture, has been a vitally important element in my biography.

In *Henry V,* Shakespeare paints a picture of a united Britain which includes not only the Welshman, Captain Fluellen, but also his friend, the Englishman Captain Gower. Gower is very 'English' in thinking that the Welshman takes himself too seriously and is somewhat overwhelmed by his know-it-all-ness, although he respects him and often takes his advice, if only to keep him quiet. He is a man of great common sense who keeps the peace between the Welsh, Irish, and Scottish officers. In contrast to Fluellen's learning and eloquence, I am reminded of Stephen Fry's quip that a key marker of Englishness is 'joy in ignorance and anti-intellectualism', and Roger Scruton's more considered claim that 'silence' is the 'normal condition of the English in both public and private', and that silence and reserve is expressed in the way the English disapprove of what he calls 'the volatile humours of Mediterranean people and the fickle sentimentality of the Irish.' Andrew Marr seems to agree, saying that 'If God is still with the British (by which he must surely mean the English), He will be quiet, understated, embarrassed by enthusiasm...'. The 'stiff upper lip' and quiet reserve of the English sometimes seem, to my Celtic side, to be rather boring, but at other times I value very much the common sense, modesty, steady application, and genius for compromise that are amongst the recognised qualities of the English.

Reflecting on this has helped me to realise how we need to bring together the very best qualities of all the strands woven into our heritage. If we do not, we are in danger of falling into the negative brand of tribalism (*'asabiya*) condemned by the Prophet Muhammad as 'supporting your own people in an unjust cause.' We might justifiably associate tribal partisanship with nationalist populism and ethnocentrism and the bigotry and intolerance it can foment towards 'the other', although it is well to bear in mind that the fourteenth-century sociologist and historian, Ibn Khaldun also affirmed the positive aspect of *'asabiya* in promoting solidarity and social cohesion. He recognised that co-operation and community spirit are hard wired into humanity, and social organisation and community pride are necessary for an internally coherent civilisation to flourish. At the same time, the validity of one's own understanding and practice of universal values does not justify looking down on other ways in which such values may be realized in other communities. With that in mind, I find it valuable how each of the strands of my multiple identity

(Huguenot, Welsh, English) can contribute to a biography rooted in the search for harmony and balance. And I would of course add to that the pivotal influence of Islam, and especially Islamic Sufism, in my own ongoing search for integration and unity. I see that path, and the path of 'conversion', as a cumulative process of inner transformation, a continuing spiritual journey, a path of integration, not an identity crisis or a Road to Damascus experience. Neither is it a sudden rupture with the past, a wholesale abandonment of one culture for another, nor the embrace of some new and exotic tribal affiliation. Least of all is it the embrace of a clash of civilisations.

My encounter with Islam also raises the important question of how religion and culture can exert a massive influence in shaping our identity, even to the extent of superseding the genetic imprints of our ancestral history.

What of the remaining 20% of my DNA, the 11.2% Italian, 3.5% Iberian, and 6.1% Central Asian (Kazakhstan, Uzbekistan)? I was surprised to learn of this, as I know of no Italian, Spanish or Central Asian ancestors or relatives, and have never felt any strong affinity with these regions. It has occurred to me, however, that the four hundred years of Roman occupation of Britain (43–410), including intermarriage with the indigenous Celts, must have left a genetic imprint derived from Italy. On further reflection, I had to acknowledge that I did travel in Italy as a young man, working for a while in Piemonte and Rome as a teacher of English. But the memories that stand out for me are not the many visits to the vineyards owned by my adult pupils in Piemonte (and the inevitable bouts of wine-tasting to which I was treated), but visceral reactions to the barbarism of Rome that I sensed in a visit to the Colosseum and to the cruelty of religious persecution that I was well aware of in the Campo de' Fiori where I lived and where the Hermetic philosopher Giordano Bruno had been burnt at the stake upside down and with a clamp in his mouth by the Catholic authorities in 1600 for heresy, which included his heliocentric view of the solar system. Once again, my attention turned to the voices of 'dissenters' (including those Christians butchered in the Colosseum), so vividly associated with my own Huguenot ancestry.

Recent genetic evidence suggests that British Celts – our indigenous population – are descended from a tribe of Iberian fishermen who crossed the Bay of Biscay almost 6,000 years ago, probably landing in what is now South West Wales. And It may be surprising to learn that, in spite of later waves of settlers, including Romans, Anglo-Saxons, Vikings, and Normans, the genetic makeup of Britain and Ireland is overwhelmingly what it was in the Neolithic period: a mixture of the few thousand indigenous Mesolithic inhabitants with those Neolithic settlers who came by sea from Iberia and ultimately from the eastern Mediterranean. Research indicates that the Anglo-Saxon contribution to the genetic make-up of Britain was under 20 per cent of the total, even in southern England, and the Norman contribution was extremely small, perhaps only two per cent. There are only very sparse genetic traces of the Roman occupation, almost all in southern England. What is more, the settlement in Spain was only a staging post on an onward journey of migration. According to a very recent Leicester University study, most Britons, along with four out of five white Europeans, are descended from male farmers who left Mesopotamia (what is now Iraq and Syria) in the Fertile Crescent 10,000 years ago.

Several years ago, I went to Lascaux in the Dordogne to marvel at the 17,000-year-old cave art of earlier descendants of Cro-Magnon people who first came to Europe 40,000 years in their migration from East Africa. I was greatly moved by the very simple and striking realisation, inspired by that extraordinary art, of the common humanity I shared with these people, and, stretching back even further in time, to their ancestors who first moved out of Africa 70,000 years ago. I felt as never before that ultimate connection to a shared humanity. It was an authentically simple insight, at once emotional and intuitive, which might have completely transcended any analysis of all the complex factors supposedly involved in the makeup of my British identity, whether historical, genetic, or conceived of in terms of distinctive national character or values.

Yet, no matter how ultimately universal our worthy vision of shared humanity might be, it may be hard for us to identify in any deeply personal or emotive sense with a remote genetic inheritance. I do not feel like a Stone Age Syrian farmer or Iberian fisherman, let alone the first Cro-Magnon migrant out of Africa. It seems to me that the impact of a specific cultural or religious inheritance can dramatically trump whatever is in our genes. The contribution of the Normans to the gene pool of the British was extremely small, but their impact on our culture was clearly massive. After all, more than half of the English language comes from Latin through Old French, including (as one French wag suggested to me) all words of more than one syllable. And despite the modest size of my English DNA, at less than 20 per cent, I feel steeped in English history and culture.

At this point it is well to mention one major caveat concerning how DNA results are interpreted. In an article in *Scientific American* in 2018, the geneticist Adam Rutherford pointed out that 'when it comes to ancestry, DNA is very good at determining close family relations such as siblings or parents, and dozens of stories are emerging that reunite or identify lost close family members. For deeper family roots, these tests do not really tell you where your ancestors came from. They say where DNA like yours can be found on Earth today...We all have thousands of ancestors, and our family trees become matted webs as we go back in time, which means that before long, our ancestors become everyone's ancestors. Humankind is fascinatingly closely related.' Applying this caveat to my own DNA, the fact that I have 11 per cent Italian does not mean that I can infer that this strand is inherited from Roman invaders or settlers in Celtic Britain. It simply means that I have DNA that is also found in Italy, and gives no clue as to where that DNA originated.

In considering the final 10 per cent of my DNA, I was most intrigued by the Central Asian strand, and I think it is useful to consider it in relation to the Iberian strand, since it is entirely possible that both strands are the result of the ancient migration out of Mesopotamia I have mentioned. Having DNA labelled as 'Kazakhstan' does not mean that I have ancestors from that part of the world; it points rather to the likelihood that those living there today are descended from the same people who may have left Mesopotamia all those millennia ago, migrating both westwards eventually to Iberia and onwards to Britain, and also eastwards to Central Asia. In fact, this speculation accounts for both for my Central Asian and Iberian DNA.

The analysis of my DNA appears to strongly confirm the fact that, as a 'white Brit' I am deeply ensconced in Western Europe. I was rather disappointed not to be credited with any Scandinavian DNA from more northern climes. But as I have tried to show, our biography rests on much more than genes. In the words of the Qur'an, 'We will show them our Signs in the furthest horizons and in their own souls...'(41:53), and this encompasses both the endowment of our essential, primordial nature and the manifold influences from so many theatres of human experience that nurture our full development as human beings.

Our primordial nature is clearly indicated by the root of the word 'character'. Texts (and hence biographies) are composed of characters combined into words. But the word 'character' also refers to the qualities of mind and heart and the moral sense within an individual. In my Introduction *CM19: Nature*, I pointed out that the idea of human nature or 'character' as an innate endowment is embedded in the origin of the word 'character' itself. This comes from Greek *kharakter,* a derivative of the verb *kharassein,* 'to sharpen, engrave, cut'. Our essential 'Adamic' nature or primordial disposition (Arabic *fitra*), the Divine spark of our original pristine human character, is what is already 'stamped', 'etched', 'impressed' or 'imprinted' upon us in accordance with the Divine Prototype or pattern, or, as the Qur'an tells us, *fi 'ahsani taqwim* (95:4), which is variously translated as 'in the best confirmation' (Muhammad Asad), 'in the best of moulds' (Yusuf Ali), 'in the highest station' (Michael Sells) or 'in the fairest stature' (Arberry). It is that inner compass and natural orientation, the criterion (*furqan*) which enables us to perceive the truth and do what is right. In this way, the potential accorded to the human being as *khalifah* ('vicegerent') to fulfil the sacred trust (*amanah*) is already stamped or written within the full range of his or her God-given faculties, for 'He has endowed you with hearing, and sight, and hearts, so that you might have cause to be grateful' (Qur'an 16:78). Furthermore, the idea of human development as one of the unfolding of divinely endowed potential (rather than its more common sense of 'training', 'learning' or 'acquiring skills') is distilled in the origin of the word 'development' itself. This comes from Old French *des-voloper* which meant 'unwrap' or 'unveil', echoing the Latin *educere*, 'educe, lead forth, draw out'.

We might therefore conceive of the core of a biography as the extent to which it unfolds the Divine imprint within the original 'text' of human nature, or, in other words, the qualities or attributes of character which the human being has the potential to 'unwrap'. Such attributes can also be described as the Divine Names (*al-asma ul-husna*), of which there are traditionally ninety-nine in number. Granted, this may sound like a very lofty genre of biography, more like hagiography, but I contend that every human soul is striving, whether consciously or unconsciously, to embody the Names in whatever way and to whatever extent is afforded by his or her life. As Ibn 'Arabi said: 'It is He who is revealed in every face, sought in every sign, gazed upon by every eye, worshipped in every object of worship, and pursued in the unseen and the visible. Not a single one of His creatures can fail to find Him in its primordial and original nature.'

YASMINA KHADRA

Bina Shah

The Karachi Literature Festival is normally held at the Beach Luxury Hotel on the bank of the Chinna Creek in the tender February weather. Daytime temperatures hover around 25°C; shawls and jackets are needed in the evenings. The outdoor sessions are the loveliest: speakers and audiences sit under traditional *shamianas* (tents) by the tranquil waters of the creek and the old coconut trees dotted along its shore. Writers get to know each other over meals on a floating restaurant across from mangrove islands where egrets wade, fish, and roost. For atmosphere alone, in the South Asian literary festival circuit, the Karachi Literature Festival is one of its best-kept secrets.

The festival went fully digital in 2021 for its tenth edition while Pakistan battled a third wave of the Covid pandemic. This made it lose much of its charm but gain one advantage: writers who hesitated to come to Pakistan in person were able to participate virtually. As organisers rushed to become familiar with Streamyard and live broadcasting on Facebook, I was asked to interview the writer Yasmina Khadra in one of the sessions sponsored by the French Embassy in Pakistan.

One never knows what will set off angry religious sentiment in Pakistan; since November 2020, extremists had been pressuring the Pakistani government to expel the French ambassador over the issue of the caricatures of the Prophet Muhammed. But things had quietened down enough in March for the Embassy to participate virtually in the festival without too much fear of a backlash.

At first, I thought I would be speaking to the playwright Yasmina Reza, whose name had been floated in previous years, but she'd never made it to the Festival. My excitement turned to confusion when I realised that my interviewee was not Yasmina Reza but Yasmina Khadra. Another woman, I thought, but then a quick search on Google revealed that Yasmina Khadra is the pen name of a male writer: Mohammed Mousselhoul, born in Kendasa, Algeria, in 1955. As a high-ranking officer in the Algerian Army, Khadra had to adopt a pen name to avoid the censorship imposed upon writers by the military regime during the Algerian Civil War.

It was a scramble to prepare questions for Khadra, as his books are not available in Pakistan. Thank God for the Internet, through which I found out that his forty-plus novels encompass some of the most pressing issues facing the world today: war, the meeting of Islamic and Western cultures, extremism, fundamentalism and terrorism, and above all, how individuals, couples, families confront and transcend the emotional and physical pain caused by these circumstances.

This interested me immediately, as Pakistan has been struggling for the last twenty years with terrorism, religious extremism, and fundamentalism. Pakistan's alignment with the United States in the War on Terror, as well as its position as the staging ground for proxy wars between India, China, Russia, the United States, and Iran have caused more upheaval and damage to the country than its wars with India over Kashmir. Even though Algeria's Civil War and its struggles against colonialism and imperialism are unfamiliar to most Pakistanis, I thought there would be enough common ground to have a good conversation. We'd talk about Khadra's novels, of course, and what another part of the Muslim world looks like. We would even discuss what it means to be a Muslim living in France – the country having become a bogeyman for Pakistanis, amid the cartoon brouhaha.

English translations of Khadra's novels include *The Swallows of Kabul*, about life under the Taliban in Afghanistan; *The Attack*, about an Arab Israeli surgeon in Tel Aviv whose life is devastated by his wife's decision to become a suicide bomber; *The Sirens of Baghdad*, which takes place during the US invasion of Iraq; and *Khalil*, about a Belgian born man who is radicalised and becomes involved in a life of violent extremism. His latest novel, launched the week before our conversation, is *Pour L'Amour d'Elena*, a love story inspired by true events in Mexico during the cartel wars. Each novel portrayed atrocities, violence, extremism, human nature at its worst. Yet Khadra's writing testifies to the goodness of human nature, and its ability to contend with and defeat evil, if not physically, then philosophically and morally. When I later read *The Attack*, I realised that Khadra prefers honest endings to happy ones.

On the day of our conversation, it was a hot March afternoon for me in Karachi; I was speaking to Khadra in the book-lined study of his Paris home. He appeared on the screen, an older version of the photographs on the Internet: instantly recognisable as North African, with greying curly hair, warm skin, glasses, and a ready smile. I felt an immediate affinity with him, which isn't something that always happens in an online conversation. But something connected us all the same, beyond our mutual love of literature, and our background as Muslims.

Khadra was born in the Sahara to a deeply religious Bedouin tribe which 'revered both poetry and piety.' He loved to write in childhood – small stories, poems. Then, his father sent him at the age of nine to the Algerian army, for his education and later military training. 'But my time in the army only confirmed my thousand-year-old education, which was in my veins and in my blood. An almost religious veneration of poetry, of the word and of literature. I think this is why I retained my humanity.'

But why a female pen name? Who is the real Yasmina Khadra? The author explained to me that during his time in the army, he became a counterterrorism expert and wrote six books under his own name. Then the Algerian Army demanded he submit his writing for authorisation and censorship. He refused, used different pen names for eleven years, then settled upon his wife's name, Yasmina Khadra, as a tribute to her love and loyalty.

It was under this female pseudonym that he gained international fame. He did not reveal his true identity until he exiled himself to France in 2001. This shocked the French literary establishment, who had thought up until now they had 'found the authentic voice of the Arab woman,' as Stuart Jeffries wrote in the *Guardian* back in 2005, when *The Swallows of Kabul* was published in English.

I remarked how not many Muslim men could put aside their masculinity to assume a female identity. Khadra, who had been sitting relaxed in his chair, sat up straight and lit up with an inner fire. 'Those who do not like women are those who do not like life, and have nothing to do on this earth. They should just be dead right away.'

Most Muslim countries, including Pakistan, are hypermasculine. Where I live, it's considered an insult to be a female; 'wear bangles, then' is a common refrain with which rival Pakistani politicians taunt each other.

'Sister-fucker' is Pakistan's most popular insult, dripping with undisguised misogyny. I imagined all of these men who delight in male superiority dropping dead at once, and burst into laughter.

Khadra smiled at my reaction. I sensed he enjoyed startling people with his pro-women stance, as well as his gender reveal. 'A lot of Muslims are shocked that a Muslim, and one such as myself who has gone for the Hajj – a devout Muslim, and an ex-soldier, an Arab, a Berber, all these seemingly contradictory things. And still, for them it seems like a sacrilege (that I should have a female pen name).' But for Khadra, the female pseudonym is a source of pride. 'This is what makes man advance despite all the obstacles; the respect he has for women. If we can't respect women, we will never be able to get out of darkness.'

He related a story from the early 2000s, when he went to live in exile in France. Despite his renown as a writer, he was accused of being a war criminal by the French media. 'All the doors were shut in my face. This pained my wife a lot. I looked her in the eyes and told her, "for you, I will conquer this world!" And I did.' He credited his wife with the fact that his books have been published in fifty-seven countries and translated into fifty languages. Then he quoted from his novel *The Swallow of Kabul*: 'misfortune spreads wherever women are oppressed.' I thought of Pakistan, among the worst in the Gender Gap Index, as well as all the development tables – health, education, infant mortality – and shuddered.

Before Khadra revealed his identity publicly, there was plenty of suspicion about the gender of the writer; people did not believe that Yasmina Khadra could really be a woman, in itself a troubling assumption. Also, what about the issue of appropriation, of ventriloquising a woman's voice?

But this is a debate that wouldn't have happened back in the 1990's, long before Elena Ferrante, the Italian writer, became mega-famous in total anonymity. People were fighting different cultural battles back then, and it was not unthinkable to voice the idea that women were unable to write about 'hard subjects' like terrorism, war, or violence, or that a soldier could write about love – or write at all.

'But these are all cliches,' says Khadra. 'It's a matter of intelligence. I've been married for thirty-five years (sometimes it feels like thirty-five days). I could be sitting in the living room with my wife reading a novel or watching a Turkish serial on her tablet, while I'm watching a football match. But she knows exactly what I'm watching, what the kids are doing. This proves how much smarter and superior to man she is!' A silly measure of women's intelligence, but he was laughing again, and I couldn't help but laugh too. The battle of the sexes is sometimes won with reason and sometimes with wit and humour, and I had no doubt that Khadra and I were on the same side.

Then Khadra turned serious. Being a champion of women might make him 'a lot of enemies' in Pakistan and the wider Muslim world, but it didn't matter to him. Similarly, his defence of the Algerian Army made him plenty of enemies in the world of literature, especially in France, where those accusations of war crimes dogged him for years. But it's undeniable that he has been one of the most faithful chroniclers of the atrocities committed during the Algerian Civil War, on both sides. I recognise the dichotomy of assuming a position in society that appears to contradict the ethics and principles of one's personal creed. But Khadra made the choice to tell the truth through his writing, and eventually the writing won out. Courage, in life and in art, is one of his hallmarks.

Another is his philosophical view of life as 'a cosmic breath. It's nothing. It's a spark.' So Khadra prefers to spend his time with the things that fill him with wonder: art, music, literature, developing the mind, and dreaming, because life passes so quickly. Khadra's love of music, literature, cinema, dance is reflected in the many artistic forms in which his own work has been adapted: graphic novels and comic books, puppet shows, and even a forthcoming opera. In 2012, *What the Day Owes The Night* (Ce Qui Le Jour Doit A La Nuit), a love story between a young Algerian man and a French woman during the Algerian Revolution, was made into a successful feature film. The following year it was adapted into a dance performance by the Algerian-born choreographer Hervé Koubi.

Clips of the Koubi production are easily found on YouTube: Algerian music plays while eleven Algerian dancers (and one from Burkina Faso), clad in white, cartwheel and twirl in a dance reminiscent of the Sufi dervishes. Although I feared it would be overly sentimental or melodramatic, it seemed, from those brief glimpses, poetic and thoughtful, extracting from its source material a transcendence that often happens when art inspires more art. And the reference to Algeria's spiritual tradition is clear; Sufism, deeply tied to Algerian politics and society, played an important role in popular resistance against the French colonists.

For Khadra, literature is not just about writing words but about seeking out creativity and innovation which has no bounds. He was influenced by the Russian writers, he says, as well as Taha Hussain, whom Khadra considers the greatest Arab writer; Naguib Mahfouz, Jack London, Joseph Kessel, Antoine St-Exupery. His own work is often the result of a conundrum that Khadra is worried about or seeks to understand. 'I try to invent a story about a problem that I could not manage to decipher in real life. Through my texts, I understand the human factor and what happens elsewhere.'

Sometimes he does this so convincingly that his readers are completely persuaded, even fooled, in the best way: after he published *The Swallows of Kabul*, he was sought out by Afghan writers who wanted to know how long he had lived in Afghanistan. He had to confess that he had never been to Afghanistan. Despite the fact that many of his novels are set in turbulent places, encompassing conflict and violence, he likes to write about love, homelessness, hope, everything that encompasses the experience of being human. 'I always try to write books which are able to help people live better, understand their era better, and move ahead in life.'

Literature, says Khadra, allows him to travel to other countries, and through his books, he hopes to make his readers travel to places they haven't been before. In these pandemic times, where travel is restricted and the world is closed, the necessity of this kind of literature becomes even more obvious. Khadra adores it when readers see his books as a kind of 'flying carpet' – he uses the phrase without irony, not bothering to worry whether it's a kind of Orientalist metaphor – to different, foreign landscapes, characters and stories. Vastly preferable to those who see the backdrops – the Algerian Civil War, Islamic extremism, the invasions of Iraq and Afghanistan – and are dismayed by the violence, or who pigeonhole his books into the category of 'terrorist literature.'

Khadra said of the first group, 'It's preferable to experience violence in a book than in the street. Because in a book one can always understand it and control it, even neutralise it. In the street it's beyond our control.' He dismissed the second group as people who are unable to truly read his books, to go beyond the superficialities and dive deep into the text. 'There are even people who don't read my books because I'm Algerian. They think we have nothing to say.' He is proud of his five million-strong readership, as well as the success of the film adaptation of *Ce Qui Le Jour Doit La Nuit*, but in his mind, his writing is not a vehicle for fame and fortune. Instead, he sees it as his salvation. 'In my heart I am seeking wisdom. I want to be wise. This is the only way to attain true freedom and inner peace. My interior world is about my frenetic quest for peace.'

Khadra's experience as an Algerian writer in France intrigued me, since so much of his writing concerns the meetings, positive and negative, between European and Islamic culture. He considers himself lucky to have this multi-cultural background, a mix of Muslim, Arab, Berber, and Western. He insists that the clash of civilisations is a myth. Rather, it's the meeting of Roman, Greek, and Muslim civilisations that has given rise to today's society and culture, to its expression of humanity. 'The clash of civilisations does not exist. It's an insult to humanity. We are complementary to each other.' Khadra offers a rather poetic metaphor of human beings as bees in the garden that need to gather pollen from all the flowers to make honey. 'This is how I developed myself, by gathering from all the flowers in my garden.'

But is it tough to be an Algerian, a Muslim, living in France? The news filters back to Pakistan, about the French government's banning of niqab in public places, of French Muslim women not allowed to wear burkinis on the beach. The space for Muslims in France seems to be shrinking. 'There are many Muslims in France, and what I find honourable,' counters Khadra, 'is that they go about their business. They don't take seriously all these people who appear on television, all these charlatans and warmongers, these pitiful people who need to be seen by others.'

Muslims, he told me, live their lives as doctors, bus drivers, shopkeepers, engineers, scientists, and professors. Busy in their work, they see no need to react to the normalities of Western life as constant provocation; they simply let others talk. 'They do not fight everything they see in the Western world all the time.' Khadra has no problem being a practicing Muslim in France. 'I didn't wait for the arrival of the jihadists to start praying. I had been praying since I was nine years old. So that's nearly sixty years. But I think one must evolve with time; we must not let religion be a constraint.'

He related how he had appeared on an Arabic television channel – he wouldn't name it, except to say that it had become 'diabolical' now (I suspect he was talking about the Arabic-language channel of Al Jazeera, which differs a lot in tone and content from the English-language one) – and said that the world was witnessing the battle of two extremes: secularists who think freedom of speech is untouchable, and Muslims who think religion is untouchable.

This seemed to me a good explanation of what's happening in France today, as well as in Pakistan. In France, the extreme right and Islamophobia is on the rise, there are more strictures against practising Muslims. A female candidate from President Emmanuel Macron's party lost support because she wore a hijab on her campaign poster. And in Pakistan, people have exchanged private piety for a type of performative religiosity that can feel as oppressive as the hottest days of summer. The 'charlatans' abound on television, standing at fiery pulpits, issuing 'statements' and holding protests against everything they consider a provocation against them and Islam. It's as if they have *become* Islam itself, and every insult to it is an insult to themselves.

Despite Khadra's earlier assertion that the clash of civilisations does not exist, I still sense that Islamic and European cultures are far apart. With the ongoing protests in Pakistan against the blasphemous cartoons, and Emmanuel Macron's insistence that the cartoons will continue to be published as a matter of principle, especially after the hideous beheading of schoolteacher Samuel Paty, can there be common ground between the two poles?

Khadra narrowed his eyes, considering the question more seriously. 'We don't see eye to eye because we don't listen to each other,' he offered. 'Not all the French, but in the media and in politics, they have a simplistic view of Muslim issues. And on our side, it's the same thing: we do not know what secularism is.'

In Pakistan, I told him, we don't understand laïcité, or secularism: it's clumsily interpreted as atheism. What is the European urgency surrounding freedom of expression all about? To Khadra, secularism means to obey the institutions of the nation and practice his religion in the private sphere, not to mix everything together. Writers, said Khadra, as well as artists, and stand-up comedians, are the real prophets on earth today: the people who shed some light on the banality of our days. Politics lacks wisdom, concerning itself with conquest and domination, and power struggles, whereas poets enlighten and illuminate 'the transcendence of all these things.' Yet in the fervor of the Arab Spring, Khadra himself ran for the presidency of Algeria in 2013; why then would a writer want to get involved in politics?

Khadra gave me another smile, a toothy one this time. 'I didn't want to be president, but because I wanted to tell the regime to get out and go away, that's all. And to tell Algerians to take to the streets.' He wanted to attack the system, not limit himself to writing, like the newspaper writers who criticise the regime, but accomplish nothing. 'Let the youth build the country that they want. We are already gone. I'm sixty-six, I want to live my life as a man, love my wife more, travel, and know the world.'

Yet this same world, according to Khadra, belongs now to the youth. Students in the West, Latin America, Asia, are wonderful, Khadra told me. 'They have so many healthy dreams and they do what humanity has never done before. They live together. In a high school you'll find Asians, Blacks, Whites, Greys, Green, all together. This is tomorrow's humanity. I want this youth to succeed where we have failed in the past.'

I told Khadra I felt the same thing when teaching at university in Pakistan, and interacting with girls and young women insistent upon their rights to education and careers. 'Only yesterday there was a documentary on television about Pakistan,' enthused Khadra. 'I saw the work of women, the work of students. One must have faith in this youth and let them live their lives and not impose things on them.'

I ask him about Afghanistan, which is in the news every other day: the week our interview aired as part of the Karachi Literary Festival, sixty-four pro-government forces and twenty civilians were killed in attacks by the Taliban and other insurgents. Kabul, the setting of his novel *Les Hirondelles de Kaboul*, saw a gun attack on a Sikh gurdhwara where twenty-five people were killed.

'Ah, my God. The war must stop. There must be no more deaths. God created us to live, so let's live.' It was the first time in the conversation that I saw perplexity cross Khadra's face: the counterterrorism expert at odds with the writer within, knowing the impossibility of a situation contradicted his belief in the goodness of humanity. But he insisted that people had enough intelligence to find solutions that were self-created. 'People just need to realise that no profit is worth a human life, no profit is better than a human life, and that all lives are valuable.' I wasn't sure I believed this statement, a cross between a platitude and a plea. But that's how Khadra's optimism works: it persists, even in the face of uncertainty.

I ask him if there is hope for democracy in countries like ours, ruled by repressive dictators, traumatised by military regimes, still struggling for representation of and by the people. What about the lingering tensions in his own country, Algeria, and the other Arab and North African nations, where the people danced in the public squares, ecstatic that they had managed to overthrow repressive rulers, before the iron fist came down and made things, in some cases, worse than before?

'It's going to be difficult,' admits Khadra, 'because people are permanently frustrated. They cannot hang on to the Western train anymore. They have the feeling of lagging behind and being surpassed by events.' But he repeated his belief that the youth would be the solution to the counter-revolutionary waves that followed, and crushed, the Arab Spring. The Algerian youth have understood what people of his generation have failed to grasp: the need for a sense of responsibility and the confidence that they can build a 'superb' country on the Mediterranean Basin.

When the elders realise they have failed, they often turn to the idea of the young as salvation, a dynamic that can feel almost vampiric in the older generation's need to take succour from youthful energy and optimism. But as a writer, Khadra has given so much in his own life that in his case, it doesn't seem like an unfair expectation. He may not have succeeded in his run for the Presidency, but in his role as an artist, opposing repression, he is looked up to by readers who live in his native Algeria and across North Africa, and in France. They include a Maghrebi diaspora made up of migrants, refugees, and their children. Those children, especially, are now old enough to seek literature that represents and reflects the struggles of their parents and grandparents, as well as themselves, and to look for role models who portray and enact courageous dissent through art and literature.

I asked Khadra to comment on this, as he has been in the unique position of representing the Algerian establishment and giving up his plum position in exchange for a life of exile, encompassing artistic struggle and economic uncertainty. 'To oppose, the artist cannot oppose the regime,' says

Khadra. 'But [what counts] is the support given to the artist. One artist cannot do anything, but if everyone turns toward the artists and believes in them, the support will protect the artist and make the ideas advance.'

I think of the many writers and artists who joined the revolutionaries in the streets of Cairo, of Damascus, of Tripoli and beyond. Nawal el Saadawi, who went to Tahrir Square at the age of seventy-nine to raise her voice in protest against the government; Ahdaf Soueif, who went there too; Samar Yasbeck, who wrote *A Woman in the Crossfire: Diaries of the Syrian Revolution*; Syrian political cartoonist Ali Farzat whose arms were broken by the Syrian regime. Artists and writers, it seems, have always been at the forefront of revolution in the Middle East. And in Pakistan, where Faiz Ahmed Faiz wrote revolutionary poetry that became one of Pakistan's most famous resistance songs, where the dancer Sheema Kirmani had to hold performances in secret during the days of General Zia's pseudo-religious dictatorship.

But Yasmina Khadra was more interested in a concurrent revolution, not only the one on the streets: 'Art must enter schools. Literature must enter schools. There must be permanent debates on all that celebrates our intelligence.' According to Khadra, politics is not the arena where human intelligence is celebrated; that happens in art, music, theatre, cinema, literature. In countries like Algeria and Pakistan, schools are still struggling with the inclusion of the arts as part of the curriculum, and books can be banned for content that allegedly goes against Islamic values or establishment narratives. 'Now it's up to the people to defend those values. Our people have been so traumatised that sometimes we spend more time destroying our best images than preserving them, and that is a shame.'

Nevertheless, Khadra is convinced that change will come. 'I see progressive change coming, which is very thrilling. I am certain that we will finally understand that life is so precious that we should enjoy it to the maximum.' The formula, it seems, is not just that the people must go to the political revolution, but that the revolution of ideas must go to the people. And writers like Yasmina Khadra have spent a lifetime making sure it gets to them, one book at a time.

MY LIFE AS AN ANTI-RACIST

Hassan Mahamdallie

When I was a kid back in the 1960s, the whisper-quiet branch library across the road from the family house was my refuge, my salvation and my inner life-raft, upon which I bobbed across the oceans of time and space, and place and person. After I had devoured *The Cat In the Hat*, the *Famous Five* and *Swallows and Amazons*, and all the other books in the Junior section on the library ground floor, I was presented, at the age of eight or nine, with an Adult Library Ticket, and ushered up the stairs to the first floor, where, organised according to the Dewey System, I discovered shelves of fiction and non-fiction, huge books in braille and rows of encyclopaedias.

After I had tasted the lurid satanic stories of Dennis Wheatley and the derring-do yarns of Wilbur Smith, my gaze settled on the classics of Alexandre Dumas – *The Count of Monte Cristo* and *The Three Musketeers*. And then through the works of Charles Dickens – all of them, apart from *Bleak House*, which was too monumental a task, even for my greedy young eyes. Dickens especially, revealed to me a world full of injustice, of poverty, of class division and interests, of cruel and unforgiving happenstance, of the lives of the desperate, the lonely, the neglected, and the silenced. Of how English society was, and had always been, intrinsically unfair and not right. Not right at all.

In my early teens I developed a nascent awareness that there were things that could be done about all this – so my mother encouraged me to join Amnesty International, to give money out of my paper-round earnings every month and send letters of support for prisoners of conscience. There was lots of racism swirling around and through my life and that of my siblings, growing up in a mixed-race family in London in the 1960s and 1970s. My father, an Indian Muslim from Trinidad, was permanently passed over for promotion at work. Powerless to do anything about it, he took it out on his wife and family. Much later it came to me that my father, along with many of the Windrush generation, had suffered from Post-Traumatic Stress Disorder, simply unable to process the unremitting racism and hostility they encountered. It wasn't an excuse for my dad's behaviour, but perhaps an explanation for it.

For someone born in London, my response to the hatred around me was to grow a massive chip on my shoulder, that I nurtured and fed with a growing internalised anger, unable at that point to channel into the real world. But if righteous anger is not somehow directed outwards, it will eventually eat its way out. My personal epiphany occurred in the unlikely setting of a rainy day in Victoria Park, east London. I learned that anger could force change, if you could somehow harness it.

When in early 1978 I heard that premier punk band The Clash were headlining the Rock Against Racism carnival in Victoria Park, Hackney, on Sunday 30 April 1978, I was a hundred per cent determined to be there, even though I regarded East London as 'a bit dodgy'. The Hoxton area in particular had a very nasty reputation for fascist activity and was regarded as a no-go area for those of us with black or brown skins (unless you were unfortunate enough to live there).

On the morning of the carnival, I marched with my schoolmate Simon all the way from Trafalgar Square to Victoria Park. I can still picture the marchers streaming past the old fascist haunt, the infamous Bladebone pub on Bethnal Green Road where we shouted at a load of boozy demoralised Nazis standing outside. (It's now a Chinese takeaway). I wasn't at all used to seeing Nazis stripped of their menace – it gave me a good feeling and put a spring in my step. By the time we got to Victoria Park it was overflowing, with people even hanging from the trees to try and get a decent view of the stage. The day was full of highlights, including the theatrical moment when a group appeared on stage, draped and masked in white KKK outfits. Then out of the stunned silence rang the unmistakable ding, ding, ding of a cowbell that was the lead-in of Birmingham reggae band Steel Pulse's superb song of resistance 'Ku Klux Klan' – the cue for the group to whip off their pointy hoods, releasing their dreadlocks and launch into the tune, to the roar of the crowd.

Towards the end of the day a team of helpers started going round with buckets collecting for the Anti-Nazi League (ANL) and Rock Against Racism (RAR) and selling the punk fanzine *Temporary Hoarding*. I looked besides, around, and behind me at the sea of mostly white faces, and something clicked. I realised for the first time that there were lots of white people who hated racism and were prepared to fight it. Maybe racist demagogic politician Enoch Powell and fascist National Front skinheads weren't an inevitable part of life and could be fought and perhaps driven back or even overcome? It sounds naïve now as I recount it, but some kind of negative psychological burden was lifted that day in Victoria Park. It changed my life forever.

Looking back, I can see that although the ANL/RAR was necessarily a defensive movement, it did positively change the course of British history, in ways its organisers and participants cannot have imagined at the time. The campaign was both the promise of, and roadmap towards, a radically different future – the opposite of the one Powell and the NF had in mind for us.

The unifying vision that drove the ANL/RAR has been made real in the grassroots, multifaceted multiculturalism from below that had been advancing in London and other cities, despite the efforts of hostile forces to stunt its development and even reverse it. I was unaware at the time of the RAR carnival that the driving force behind both the ANL and RAR were members of the Socialist Workers Party (SWP), a Trotskyist revolutionary party, originally founded by Palestinian Jew Tony Cliff (born Yigael Glückstein) back in the 1950s. I would re-encounter the SWP some years later and come to know Cliff, who I respected immensely.

At the time of the Victoria Park carnival, I was in the sixth form of Sutton Manor grammar school in south London. This was a nearly all-white middle-class establishment. I fitted neither of these categories. My time at Sutton Manor was an alienating, often-times bizarre experience. Many teachers in the 1970s were ex-servicemen who had fought in the Second World War and carried, mental, and physical scars from their conflict experiences. So, amongst my teachers was a Major W who was rumoured to have a plate in his head. He taught Maths and oversaw the school's Combined Cadet Force. There was a Latin teacher Captain R, who had a tin leg, and a former Welsh guardsman Mr M – who masqueraded as a PE teacher. I swear that many of them suffered shellshock, and would fly off the handle at regular, if unpredictable, intervals. Many of these ex-servicemen had fought in the colonial arena – Asia, Africa, and the Middle East. Some also had backgrounds as functionaries in colonial administrations, who, because of the independence movements, found themselves 'back in Blighty', there to be confronted by a small but increasing minority of pupils whose origins lay in those very colonies they had considered until recently to be their own. It was not a happy cultural encounter. I recall a long running teenage insurgency campaign I conducted against Mr M, the Welsh Guardsman. At the start of every PE lesson, he would shout out the register. When it came to me, he would bark: 'Ali'. There would be no answer. He would then glare red-faced at me and repeat 'Ali'. Again, there would be no answer. Eventually I would break the silence: 'My name is *Mahamdallie*, sir'. Enraged, Mr M would hold out his hand. Some dastardly pupil would eagerly hand him a black gym shoe and I would be slippered across the hand. This ritual standoff went on every school week for an entire year, with neither him nor me prepared to cede territory. Perhaps I reminded him of his 'boy' Ali who would bring him coffee in the morning when he had been stationed in Cairo during the campaign against Rommel – or something like that. I don't know. But he refused to be decolonised, whilst I refused to be recolonised.

After leaving Sutton Manor with some rather poor A level grades, I spent two years working in a gambling bookmaker in the horse-racing town of Epsom in Surrey. On the bus to work, at work itself, and on the way home, I would devour existentialist novels by Camus, Sartre, and Genet, as well as working my way through the Heinemann African Writers series that included Chinua Achebe, Ngũgĩ wa Thiong'o, Ama Ata Aidoo, Alex La Guma and Ayi Kwei Armah. I also read Black consciousness leader Steve Biko, who had been killed in South African state detention in 1977, whose writings opened me up to the anti-Apartheid struggle.

I eventually got fed up with the bookies and enrolled to study English and Drama at a college down in Exmouth, on the south Devon coast. I was glad to get out of London, and it was a mostly enjoyable time, apart from occasional run-ins with thuggish Royal Marines who trained at nearby Lympstone Commando training centre, and drank in Exmouth town centre. I arrived back in London just as the Great Miners Strike of 1984–85 was taking place. This was the existential showdown between the Tory Thatcher Government and the most advanced and well-organised sections of the British working-class movement. It was a titanic struggle, and every Friday evening I would chat to SWP *Socialist Worker* sellers who were collecting for the miners, and discuss the progress of the dispute. History was riding on the outcome of the dispute, and we all hated Thatcher for different reasons – for being a racist pot stirrer, for sending the Metropolitan Police into London's multicultural areas as a savage occupying force, for the Falklands farrago, for crushing the London print unions and paving the way for the monstrous Murdoch media empire, for abolishing free school milk, for persecuting Gays and Lesbians. I somehow assumed that the Miners would win out, but as hunger in the pit villages and state violence ground them down they were slowly forced back to work. I realised that 'our side' had lost. I was devastated, with no explanation available to me as to why this had happened. At that point I joined the SWP.

I also managed to get a permanent acting job in a theatre company in Rochdale, Lancashire, a few miles north of Manchester. M6 theatre was then part of a large and vibrant radical theatre movement, that emerged in the late 1960s and early 1970s, specialising in theatre-in-education and community theatre. Two thirds of the year we were performing plays in schools and the other third in community venues in the northwest of England. At the time there were similar companies thriving in every city in the UK. The plays M6 would take into schools would cover social issues including racism and minority rights, and history plays illuminating episodes in past working class and anti-imperialist struggles. The first school play I worked on was called *Diego Garcia*. The title referred to an archipelago of islands in the British Indian Ocean, whose inhabitants had been forcibly expelled by the British in the late 1960s and early 1970s, so the islands could be handed over to the US to build a huge naval and military base. Another school play I acted in was about the political struggle of miners' wives in Chile, and was meant to be a commentary on the role of the British coal-miners' wives during the great strike of 1984–85. So every play was an education for me in the global history of struggle and resistance.

M6 was run as a workers' collective, with every member having an equal say in the running of the organisation. The company was built around a permanent team of what was called actor/teachers, who wrote, rehearsed and performed plays together. Many of the plays would have an interactive element, where the school pupils would take part as participants (quite often cast in the collective role as workers or strikers, who would then come up against 'the boss' or 'the foreman' played by an actor and have to argue with him for their rights to a pay rise or take industrial action).

M6's studio and offices occupied the top floor of a primary school in Rochdale. The catchment area for the school was an area of town where a Kashmiri Pakistani community had settled, whose children made up well over 90 per cent of the school's intake. There were two or three areas of town where the south Asian community were concentrated, due to decades of open discriminatory housing policy by the Labour council and private estate agents, who had deliberately engineered social segregation. In the 1960s, Pakistani men had been encouraged to go to Lancashire and Yorkshire to work in the mills, doing the lowest paid and worst jobs. These immigrants were effectively barred from the council housing where white workers lived because of discrimination and so settled in poor areas with cheap housing close to the mills. Originally the predominantly male Asian workers held to the belief that they would return home after a few years. But this faded, and members of their close families – despite a succession of controls devised to keep them out – joined them over the next decade and a half. The gradual, but still far from total, isolation from white workers arose out of several factors connected not to their desire to live apart, but to their socio-economic position and the racism they endured.

Just a few miles south of Rochdale was the mill town of Oldham that had similar demographics, with the addition of a small African-Caribbean community. On Friday nights myself and my fellow actors would drive to Oldham and spend the night at a Reggae club, dancing, smoking weed, and watching Jamaican Rastafarians sway slowly to heavy floor-shaking dub beats as though caught in a gentle Caribbean breeze. The immigrant area of Oldham was Glodwick, comprising of two-up, two-down rows of terraced housing, packed close together. Asian house buyers were effectively allocated certain contained areas of town. In 1988, when the Commission for Racial Equality (CRE) investigated an estate agent in Oldham, it found that 'the firm tended to recommend white areas to prospective white purchasers and Asian areas to Asian purchasers, to accept instructions from white vendors to deter prospective Asian purchasers and to offer mortgage facilities only to white clients'. Those

Asians who did apply for council housing were hit by racism from the local authority that had a clear policy of racial segregation.

One of the first anti-racist campaigns I was involved with during my time at M6, came about after the killing of a Pakistani lad. In the summer of 1989, Tahir Akram, a fourteen-year-old schoolboy, was walking home through Glodwick when he was shot with an air rifle by a group of whites in a car, who had been driving round taking random shots at Pakistani residents. This kind of act was considered 'sport' by local racists, who acted with impunity, knowing the police literally couldn't be bothered to investigate racist incidents. The pellet penetrated Tahir's eye and killed him. In what is now a familiar story, the police refused to investigate the killing for a racist motive. We petitioned round the area for support for the family and called for a march to pressure the police, but had to retreat in the face of massive pressure put on the family and the local Pakistani community by the combined weight of local police, politicians, and media. I learned that the Northwest of England in the 1980s had aspects more akin to the Deep South of America than the multicultural London I had grown up in.

In the late 1980s the Lancashire cotton mills (and the Yorkshire wool mills) were fatally wounded by international competition; as manufacturers relocated to countries in the Global South where they could maximise their profits by exploiting cheap labour. The Lancashire mill owners attempted to stay in the game by making large numbers of their workforce redundant and driving down the pay of the remaining workers. One surviving mill in Middleton, situated a few miles from Rochdale in the north of Manchester, was hit by a strike, as the workforce, unable to make ends meet, downed tools and asked for a 1.5 per cent pay rise. On the first day of the strike, myself and a couple of SWP comrades fetched up outside the mill gates, expecting a picket line. Instead, we found two huddled groups of workers standing on opposite sides of the gates, leaving a big gap through which scab lorry drivers delivering raw materials thundered through. It was a hopeless situation. On one side of the road stood a group of white strikers, while on the other side, stood a small group of Asian strikers. Perplexed, I talked to each group in turn, asking them why they hadn't thrown up a proper picket line that met in the middle. I asked the Asians why they weren't physically joining up with their white workmates to complete the picket line and stop the trucks. 'We don't know them; we don't think they like us'. I asked the same question of their white co-strikers: 'We don't know them; they keep themselves to themselves you see.' I did see. The mill owners had for decade played a particularly brutal game of divide and rule, that went beyond the workplace, poisoning relations in the wider community itself.

The employers had 'traditionally' given the white workers slightly better paid jobs in the skilled areas of the mill, and doled out the worst paid jobs, such as cleaning, to the Asian workers. The whites worked on different floors to the Asians, and the Asians usually did the night shift and the whites the day shift. The local trade union officials, instead of opposing this industrial segregation of their members, colluded with management in this racist, divisive set up.

I said to the Asian group 'Go find out what you should be doing to keep the strike going'. One eventually sidled across to have a chat with the white union full-timer, and picketing tasks began to be allocated. The next day I got there mid-morning – just as wives of the Asian strikers were turning up with tiffin carriers full of nice food for their husbands. The white workers, clutching crushed cheese baps (large bread rolls), looked on enviously. After a time some of the Asian strikers walked across to their white compatriots. Food was shared and gratefully received.

The next day I came back, a proper picket line, stretching across the factory gates, was in place. The white strikers and the Asian strikers had met in the middle. Years of segregation began to be rolled back, inch by inch. It was a graphic, practical lesson for me, in both the mechanics of institutionalised racism and the potential for workers to overcome it. I would love to report that the strike ended in victory – it did not. After a couple of weeks, the strikers went back to work without their modest demands having been met. And a couple of years later the mill closed its doors – throwing all the workers onto the scrap heap. But I was glad to have witnessed first-hand a glimmer of hope in those rather dark times for the British working class.

In Rochdale itself we were faced at that time with a resurgence of the fascist British National Party, who were recruiting young thugs in the town. In towns such as Rochdale there had been a latent sympathy to fascist organisations going back decades. It was simply part of the town's make up. Sometimes the support was passive, but sometimes it congealed into organisational form. We took on the BNP in Rochdale, facing them down, organising against racist attacks, and so on. Occasionally we would be attacked – one lunchtime I made the mistake of walking into a pub that was notorious for being a 'Nazi pub' and was within seconds jumped by about eight BNP skinheads. They all piled on top of me, and after about a minute of kicks and punches, I felt a pair of strong hands grab my ankles and literally pull me out from under the writhing heap of skinheads and out through the pub doors. A friend of mine, Eddie, son of Polish immigrants who had settled in Rochdale after World War Two, had seen me go into the pub and had followed me, knowing I had recklessly stepped into danger. At one point the BNP found out where I lived – and mounted a demonstration literally outside my front door. From then on, I slept with a machete under my bed. Just in case. To be honest the local Asians were pretty good at pest control – they had an early warning system if any fascists or racist gangs drove into a Pakistani area to cause trouble. The young Pakistani men would wait until the right moment, jump into the road and block the racists in on both sides, and go about them with iron bars and baseball bats. On another occasion, I travelled to an anti-fascist march in Burnley, well known for being a BNP stronghold. It was a miserable day, rainy and windy, and as our small undersized procession made its way through town, we were picked off at the front by the police, and from behind by the BNP. There were a few days like that, where our forces were too small to stop the advance of the far right. My encounters with local fascists also taught me that although they certainly hated Asians and Blacks, at the heart of their ideology squatted a deep-seated, irrevocable anti-Semitism.

One of the highlights of my sojourn in Rochdale was my involvement in the local campaign against the Poll Tax – that had been brought in by the Thatcher government in 1989 in Scotland and 1990 in England and Wales. It was a single rate flat tax on every household, multiplied by the number of occupants, regardless of income. It disproportionally hit the poor and those with large families. In Rochdale, its implementation would have particularly hit Pakistani households, of low income and high occupancy. So I figured I would approach the imam of the local mosque, who, as it turned out, had been facing a steady stream of congregants, who were terrified of not being able to pay the poll tax and being thrown out of their homes. The imam agreed to become the secretary of the Rochdale Poll Tax Union, and led quite a few marches through the town, where shouts of Maggie, Maggie, Maggie – Out, Out, Out!' and 'Smash the Poll Tax!' were interspersed with cries of *'Allahu Akbar!'*. It was a novel sight for the Rochdalians who stood on the pavements looking on rather confusedly as we went by. The Poll Tax would never be fully implemented, with mass opposition not only taking down the tax, but Margaret Thatcher as well. I was present at the huge Poll Tax riot in central London on 31 March 1991, and can still recall mounted police riding pell-mell through Trafalgar Square chasing down protestors, and with the South African embassy billowing with smoke, having been set alight as an anti-Apartheid protest.

I have many good memories of working both for M6 and then its sister company Pit Prop, that was based in Wigan, Lancashire. At Pit Prop I was given the opportunity to write and direct plays, as well as act in them. One play I remember very well from the late 1990s was simply called 'Refugee', specially written for primary school children. In it I played a Kurdish asylum seeker. At a point in the play – that lasted the entire school day and involved the children in various story lines – my character would gather a little huddle of children around him, and explain, with the use of a handful of sand, the history of the partition of Kurdistan. My character told them he was stateless and without a home to go back to. This, the children quite rightly judged was simply not fair. I recall on one particular occasion an eight-year-old girl who took my hand and led me to her classroom window. She pointed across the school playground, across some fields to a little row of houses. 'What are you showing me?' I asked her. 'That's where me and my mum live. We've got a spare room, and after school I can take you to see it. My mum won't mind – we've got room'. She could see what any number of adults could not.

Another play I directed at Pit Prop was a large scale drama called *Dhalta Suraj* (The Sun Sets), mounted in 1993 and involving as amateur actors, members of the South Asian and working class community of Bolton, Lancashire. The subject was the 1919 Amritsar Massacre. Into it I weaved in a contemporary storyline – that of the local Rahman family who were at that time under threat of deportation. For the father, whom I knew well, I wrote a short piece of dialogue about the threat to his family, which he then acted, playing himself. I thought it was a good way of publicising the campaign and making the play relevant. Eventually the family won their fight to stay.

In the early 1990s the theatre movement I was a part of was closed down by sustained Tory government cuts and the imposition of a national curriculum that squeezed out the arts; and so, in 1994, I returned to London. I was offered a job as a reporter on the SWP weekly newspaper *Socialist Worker*, becoming the first person from an ethnic minority to join the editorial team. The pay was terrible but the work was extremely rewarding and allowed me to hone my writing, and discover the particular voice I wanted to write in.

I was assigned, amongst other areas of responsibility, the job of reporting on anything to do with Black history, race, racism, and resistance to it. I worked on the paper from 1994 – 2001, travelling the country wherever there were stories to cover. Much of my time was taken up with covering anti-deportation campaigns, police racism and Black deaths in custody, state injustice, and campaigns against the far right, who were picking up significant and worrying support across the country for the first time since the 1970s. This included me covering the Stephen Lawrence justice campaign into the police's failure to catch the racist murderers of the young Black south Londoner, and the subsequent high profile public inquiry that dropped a bombshell when it concluded that the Metropolitan Police was institutionally racist – a ruling that subsequent British governments have tried, to this day, to roll back. I subsequently worked in the area where Stephen had been murdered, for an anti-racist arts organisation funded by the local council and Charlton Athletic football club, who, to give them credit, wanted to stamp out racism in the community as well as on their terraces.

One of the stories that really sticks in my mind from my time as a *Socialist Worker* reporter, was that of the tragic life and death of a young white working-class man from south east London named Matthew Holmes. Unlike many of the other individuals whose stories I covered for *Socialist Worker*, no one outside of his immediate family knows of or remembers Matthew. I considered that an important part of being an anti-racist is to connect to the wider experiences of the working class as a whole. If you care about all the injustices meted out to black and brown people in our society, you should care about those suffered by white working-class people, who can also be victims in their own right.

I was at my desk at the *Socialist Worker* print shop in east London in late 1997, when I took a phone call from some comrades in Woolwich, south east London. A woman had come up to them on their Saturday town centre paper sale, and told them about her son Matthew, who had recently been found dead in his cell in nearby Belmarsh Prison. I met Ann Holmes at the coroner's inquest for her son. She took out of her purse a blurred photo of her son Matthew, who I could just make out had a facial disfigurement. It was the only photo she had of him, she offered it to me, but I didn't take it off her. The image wasn't good enough to print.

Matthew had not had an easy life. He was born with Melanoma skin cancer of the face that disfigured his features and made him blind in one eye. He had twenty-eight operations on his face. Despite this he did well at school and undertook an apprenticeship. But he was made redundant from a plastics factory after three months, his mother saying, 'it had a bad effect on him'. He then suffered a hit and run accident that seriously damaged his leg. He lived away from home, took to drinking and taking drugs, but he was never a danger to anybody. Matthew ended up behind bars for petty offences. He spent time in Feltham young offender's institution where he slashed his wrists. Then he was put in Belmarsh where again he tried to kill himself. He was released, but without any care or support in place for him. Then, in March 1997, he was convicted of shoplifting and sentenced to another spell in Belmarsh. This was the last thing Matthew needed or deserved. His mother did not find out that Matthew was in prison until two police knocked on her door and told her that her son was dead. She lived just a few minutes from Belmarsh, in nearby Plumstead.

During the inquest we learned that Matthew had repeatedly tried to kill himself in Belmarsh by hanging himself with his belt. After each incident he was given his belt back and taken back to his cell. As well as trying to kill himself he began to bang his head against the cell wall and told prison officers he couldn't take it anymore. He was put on a fifteen-minute suicide watch, but one night he finally succeeded in hanging himself. A pathologist told the inquest it took him one and a half minutes to die. A prison officer checking him had seen Matthew standing, apparently looking out of the window into the night. In fact, he was probably already dead, his body suspended from his belt, that he had knotted around the bars of his cell window. Matthew's mother told the coroner's court that her son was 'normally as bright as a button and cheerful'. Yet in Belmarsh a fellow prisoner observed that Matthew ended his days 'a quiet and sad person'. It was a tragic, lonely, needless, cruel death, and one that remains with me to this day.

Matthew's case had parallels with another case I covered a couple of years later – that of Zahid Mubarek. He was a nineteen-year-old from an east London Pakistani family, who had gone off the rails and committed a series of petty offenses. One of his last offences was shoplifting some razor blades worth £6 (the ones that have the security tags on them at supermarkets). He was incarcerated in Feltham in January 2000, where he was beaten to death with a table leg by his cell-mate, a mentally ill volatile young white man who had openly professed Nazi and racist sympathies. Mubarek was a first-time prisoner and was five hours from the end of a ninety-day sentence. It was a terrible murder, and entirely avoidable as the subsequent damning public inquiry found.

Prisons are terrifying places. I remember travelling in March 2000 to Her Majesty's Prison Full Sutton, a high security jail just outside York, in the north of England. I was there to interview Satpal Ram, a victim of injustice who had been incarcerated since 1987. He was a twenty-year-old waiter in an Indian Restaurant in Lozells, Birmingham, when he had been set upon by a gang of racists. He was verbally abused, attacked and glassed in the face and arm. His main attacker died after refusing treatment for two stab wounds struck by a terrified Satpal with the box cutter he carried with him for his work as a warehouseman. Satpal was convicted for murder, despite the evidence he was forced to act in self-defence. In prison he refused all efforts by the prison authorities to make him accept his conviction and punishment. He had been denied parole on many occasions because of this, serving well over the ten-year term he had originally been given. By the time I got to see Satpal, he had spent time in almost every prison in England, having been 'ghosted' a total of fifty-nine times in a vindictive effort by the prison system to break his will.

Having got off the train at York, I boarded a bus full of relatives visiting inmates for the forty-five-minute journey around country lanes to Full Sutton. There I was searched and my reporter's notebook and pen taken off me before I was allowed into the visitor's room to meet Satpal. After the visit ended, I had to retrieve my notebook, rush out of the prison and write down what he had told me before I forgot it. Satpal was a small compact man by then in his mid-thirties, very softly spoken but with an intense edge about him. He told me that in prison he had educated himself, working his way through literature of the Black revolutionary canon – Steve Biko, Malcolm X, Che Guevara, and Huey P Newton of the US Black Panthers. He recounted how it had become routine for prison officers to torture him at will. Officers would rush him in his cell, handcuff him behind his back and then kick and stamp on him. They would then cover their brutality by putting him on a disciplinary charge. He had spent over four years in solitary confinement, in a cell 'the size of your bathroom'. 'There are things I miss from the outside world', he told me. 'Fresh air, the ability to walk down the street, to be able to cook a meal'. These are the things we take for granted every day, but that had been taken from Satpal because he had stood up for himself and refused to take a racist beating.

After years of surviving the physical and mental torture, he had gradually built up a campaign around himself, and by the time I got to talk to him, he was getting eighty letters of support every week. People would send him books. Rock band Asian Dub Foundation released a fine single 'Free Satpal Ram' and he was also supported by Scottish rockers Primal Scream. He had engaged the solicitor Gareth Peirce who had represented other political prisoners including the Birmingham Six. She had lodged an appeal in the recently established Criminal Cases Review Commission, set up to examine miscarriages of justice. Satpal eventually forced the parole body to recommend his release, but it was blocked by the New Labour home secretary Jack Straw. In a separate case, the European Court of Human Rights, ruled that Straw had no right to block parole decisions, leading to Satpal's release a full two years after he should have been free. Shortly after he got out of jail, I met Satpal for an interview at Rich Mix, an arts venue in east London associated with Asian Dub Foundation. We talked, but I sensed he didn't want to go over the case, or all those years in prison. After that he disappeared from view, presumably to try and pick up his life where it had come to a halt, all those years ago, on that fateful night in a Birmingham restaurant.

There is a central aspect of racism and the way it works that I still cannot get my head around – simply the irrationality at the centre of it – to pick on someone, persecute, disadvantage, beat up, incarcerate, and even kill them, purely because of the colour of their skin. It is this element that I believe leaves the biggest trauma on those who are victims of it.

A few years before he died, I interviewed the Black community activist and restaurateur Frank Crichlow. His name is now well-known because of the celebrated Steve McQueen BBC film 'Mangrove' – about Frank's struggle to keep his West London Notting Hill restaurant open in the face of a sustained racist police campaign to close it down and criminalise him and his customers. Frank had arrived from Trinidad in the early 1950s and opened a small café, where West Indians from the different islands would gather to meet and enjoy themselves. After a while, it also became an unofficial drop-in centre for people who had troubles – particularly with racist police. Frank told me that it was in the late '50s the Notting Hill police started to get a bit 'busy' – framing people under the notorious SUS (stop under suspicion) laws: 'You could tell it was happening. People started to come into the café and telling their experiences'.

Frank recalled for me: 'a good example of that from the early 1960s. They arrested a young man, got him in the station and then took him to Marylebone Court. He comes up from the cells, stands in the dock and he's watching. The magistrate says "So–and-so stand up. You are charged with so-and-so". And the black man looks around as if to say, "are you talking to me?" Not because he's stupid but because of the situation he's in. He's done nothing – so he thinks the magistrate can't be talking to him.'

Frank stared me in the face, shook his head slowly and sighed. He muttered, half to himself: 'That says it all. That says it all'.

MOSSLAND

Robin Yassin-Kassab

Late in 2018 we moved to a place in the countryside of Galloway, in south west Scotland. It was only fifteen miles from our previous residence but it was still an entirely different world.

To reach us you must drive along a winding single-lane road, then through a farm gate (closing it behind you, to keep the livestock in), and half a mile up a bumpy track through fields. These are bare, hard-chewed by sheep, and each contains a ruined stone house beside an elder tree – signs of the subsistence farmers who once populated the countryside much more densely, until they were replaced – driven away to form the industrial working class of central Scotland, or to America, Canada, and Australia – by ovine entrepreneurs.

The immediate topography is of the kind called 'basket of eggs'. It consists of drumlins, small hills like buried eggs or teardrops made of the moraine formed under Ice Age glaciers. The one I see from the window as I write, the closest and biggest, looks more like a well-rounded breast than a teardrop, complete with a stone nipple.

Our land is nestled amongst these welcoming mounds, and provides four acres of diversity amid the sheep-field monoculture. There's a stream, and two ponds connected (we call the larger one by the more dignified title of lochan, which with its untrodden island, its lilies and resident birds, it surely deserves). From the high point overlooking the water, I can see the hills of the Southern Uplands rising south to north beyond the drumlins, and can more or less trace with my eye the hero's journey in S R Crockett's *The Raiders*, a nineteenth-century novel set in the eighteenth century, to rescue his beloved from the clutches of the 'hill gypsies': '…in the wilds of Galloway that look toward Ayrshire, up by the springs of Doon and Dee, there lies a wide county of surpassing wildness, whither resorted all the evil gypsies of the hill – red-handed men, outlaw and alien...'

The woodland around the water includes silver birches, wild cherries, ash, hazels, hawthorns, rowans, field maples, Scots pines, larch, white beams and hornbeam, a walnut, a red oak, a beech, alders, elders, and a thicket of aspens. There are two expanses of marsh which sprout a variety of willows, and on slightly drier land a collection of wild damsons. These along with the cherries put on a show of white blossom in the spring, before drooping with purple fruit in the autumn. More unusually for Scotland, there's a tulip tree, a handkerchief tree, and a katsura tree which in autumn exudes a strong odour of sweet mangoes. It used to annoy me that I could never remember the names of trees or even distinguish clearly between them. Since moving here, however, I can easily recognise most in both summer and winter. It's one kind of knowledge I have gained, even as I have let others slip away.

Surrounding the house there's an ornamental garden which flowers continuously – or more precisely, in consecutive waves – from March to late October. Slightly further away there's a small orchard (apples, crab apples, and plums), and then – fenced and hedged against deer and rabbits – a plot of vegetable beds.

Most of this paradisal arrangement was already laid out when we arrived. The previous occupiers really knew what they were doing. Both taught at the Glasgow School of Art, and brought their architectural, botanical, and design skills to bear on the garden and the house itself.

As for the house – we have a framed faded photograph of the place from the turn of the twentieth century. It shows a rectangle with four doors, like a tiny terrace. Today the structure is divided into three connected parts. A third is still a traditional Scottish cottage, with fireplace, chimney, and thick stone walls. A third is 'the sunroom' – a long, tall space whose entire south-facing wall is a window. And the final third is a partially walled greenhouse, at one end of which grows a prolific adult fig tree. (In *Sura at-Teen* of the Qur'an, the fig symbolises Damascus, as the olive epitomises Jerusalem. We took this as a sign when we decided to buy.)

I won't tell you the property's real name, but will call it Mossland instead, for the moss which grows everywhere on walls and rocks in our damp climate, soaked in the Gulf Stream. (Lichenland would do too, if it sounded less unwieldy – the tree branches are so encrusted with the stuff that it serves as winter foliage.) And I won't tell you how much we paid for it, but I will say it cost several tens of thousands of pounds – and now well over a hundred thousand – less than the average house in London. And the average house in London is a box.

I ask myself sometimes if denizens of the city realise this is possible, that they could swap their boxes for green spaciousness in the countryside. More to the point, do brown and black people know it? Britain's 'minority' populations are overwhelmingly concentrated in cities and towns, and for good historical reason. The employment opportunities which usually brought them here in the first place are in the cities. They form a disproportionate amount of the frontline urban service workforce, one reason why they died of Covid in disproportionately large numbers. And the cities offer the security and comforts provided by already established minority communities. (Our nearest mosque, for example, is thirty miles away, which might bother some.) Still, this is the post-Covid, online, working-from-home era, and many more of us could manage a move to the country, and benefit from the country's own brand of comfort and security, if we wanted to.

I've lived and worked in various cities from Morocco eastwards to Pakistan: London, Paris, Rawalpindi, Istanbul, Damascus, Rabat, Riyadh, Muscat. In the decade before Mossland I lived in a small town nearby, where I'd also spent a chunk of my childhood, but I travelled incessantly, mostly to talk about Syria. Syria burned, meanwhile, and was progressively more and more misrepresented.

So the move here, in one respect, was a very deliberate withdrawal from society. I had travelled too much, used too much jet fuel. I'd certainly used too many words. I was as alienated from the left as much as from the right, somewhat ashamed of some of my pre-2011 positions, horrified by many of the commentators I'd previously admired and, after the collective moral, political, and imaginative failures over Syria, I didn't want to be part of any abstract group. I cut my links to social media, stopped writing about politics, and dug my fingers into the soil instead.

This movement goes against the developmental grain. My paternal grandfather was an illiterate provincial townsman; my father clawed his way to respectability and relative wealth as a successful doctor in the capital city. Now, it seems, I'm de-developing, returning to the peasantry.

In another respect, however, the move to Mossland represents a closer approach to society on a small scale, a healthier, and more intimate reformation of social relations.

Muslims, like almost all post-colonial peoples, tend to valorise the state, whether in Islamic or national format. Our grandparents, seeking liberation from European occupiers, sought to build what appeared to have conferred such astounding power on those occupiers: centralised, tax-collecting, well-armed, bureaucratic states. Even today, decades after the colonial retreat, in many countries the state's repressive institutions – the army, the police – promise the most prestigious careers. Most stories of our past glories – of particular psychological importance to the humiliated – are wrapped up with state narratives which are often skewed towards the fantastical. An obvious example is the romantic focus on the supposed peace, justice, and stability of the Islamic state under the Rightly Guided Caliphs, which ignores the fact that three of these four caliphs were assassinated.

Independence and post-colonial states arrived together, and were often misunderstood as co-dependent. Without strong states, it was assumed, Muslims would lose their freedom and dignity once again. But reality gives the lie to the assumption. The gloriously strong states we created have failed to deter new occupations and persecutions. With all their emergency measures, their nuclear programmes and hyper-militarised polities, Muslim states have failed to deter the repression and dispossession of Muslims in Kashmir or Palestine, or to defend or even offer shelter to the Rohingya. When the Chinese state imprisons, 're-educates', sterilises and enslaves Uyghurs, removes their children, and destroys their historic mosques, Muslim states come together not only to express their support for the Chinese state but even to block motions at the UN calling for accountability.

The states are no better within their own spheres of influence. In terms of education, public health, the economy, and the environment, they have failed. Rather than working to find solutions to civil wars, they have provoked and participated in those wars. Rather than supporting the expression of our rich diversity, they have presided over a lowest-common-denominator homogenisation, and not by 'natural' processes like commerce or increased communications but by brute force. The vast area currently known as Saudi Arabia (whose very name betrays it as a state designed to serve a family rather than a people), for instance, used to contain a wide variety of dress, culture, and religious practice. Today, at least on the surface, it doesn't.

When divide-and-rule politics takes the upper hand, the homogenising urge soon runs out of steam. Far from working to ease religious and sectarian division in Muslim societies, the states have actively exacerbated these cleavages to the extent that they have become the prime motors of sectarianisation – that is, 'the perpetration of political rule via identity mobilisation'. No contradiction here – the states will reliably produce the worst of both worlds. To return to the Saudis, for example: it's entirely possible to pursue authoritarian Islamist policies domestically while deploying Islamophobia to weaken more democratic forms of Islamism abroad.

It's no exaggeration to say that in most parts of the Muslim world, rather than being a defender of its people's rights, the postcolonial state is by far the greatest threat to life, freedom, and dignity. Syria, I'm afraid, epitomises this best of all. The war which the state started has ravaged the country, its economy, its agriculture, even its historic remains, while opening it up to foreign terrorists and imperialists. The state and its backers are responsible for over 90 per cent of civilian deaths, and have played the largest role in the displacement of over half the population from their homes. This experience of statehood has brought Syrians the worst time in all their history, far worse than the French occupation, worse even than the Mongol invasion.

In revolutionary Syria, for a while at least, there was a countervailing glimmer of light. In areas liberated from the state, people set up democratic local councils to manage local affairs, as well as independent trades unions, women's centres, free newspapers and radio stations, film collectives, and theatre groups. Urban gardening projects kept communities going during starvation sieges. The local councils weren't copy-constructed from a fixed ideological model but were negotiated according to the demographic realities and cultural norms of the neighbourhoods concerned. On their own initiative, and in the most difficult of circumstances, Syrians acted cooperatively and creatively. They showed us – if we cared to pay attention – what could be achieved in terms of decentralisation, self-sufficiency, and mutual aid.

And here is the purpose of my anti-statist digression, the reason why despite my resolution I've relapsed into political discourse. Our life at Mossland, on a very modest scale, in a comfortable, quiet, non-revolutionary context, works on these same principles.

Our neighbours, about a mile away, host their own small, ever-changing, international community of WWOOFers – that is, Willing Workers on Organic Farms, who volunteer horticultural or agricultural labour in return for bed and board. There's also a couple sharing their land who grow organic vegetables which are delivered to local consumers by bicycle. This was of course a very useful service, especially for the elderly or immune-compromised in the area, during the Coronavirus crisis. During the same crisis – with the exception of those rare patches when the virus was virulent in Galloway – we formed a local bubble with our neighbours, which meant we were able to do a fair bit of socialising outside, around wood fires. And I taught the neighbours' young children for a few hours when their school was shut, so they've learnt some words of Arabic and covered such subjects as the Sumerians, language families, ancient Syrians on Hadrian's Wall, meditation, slavery, and (naturally) trees – topics not usually offered in primary school. These just happen to be some of my hobby horses, but Aarni and Unti profit from the obsessions of a variety of nearby adults, from trout fishing to poetry composition.

Aarni and Unti's mother used to be a medical professional, and she is our first stop for medical advice. Their father is (at least to my impractical eyes) an engineering genius, and he's the person we call for help when our cars break down or something in the house needs fixing. When I built a lean-to shed against the back of the house (a wondrous structure, if I say so myself, both a tool store and a light-filled art studio in the summer) members of our network contributed technical know-how, tools and labour. When an outside wall crumbled, our friend Bill – an expert dry stone dyker as well as a remarkable artist of landscapes, forests and rockfaces – built it up again in exchange for dinner. When we needed alder poles for stilts on which to construct a marsh hut – a residence for our own WWOOFer one day – we sourced these from a nearby farm, and everybody helped in the felling, sawing, and transportation.

The larger community collaborates too. One example: in the autumn when the apple harvest comes in, there are communal apple pressing events, when everyone shares the apple scrapper and press. The dairy delivery is a local business, as is the roving fish van. We buy eggs from another set of neighbours, and our chickens from a friend who lives higher up in the hills. Everybody exchanges seeds, cuttings, and surplus food. As far as vegetables and fruit are concerned, we are more-or-less self-sufficient, at least in the summer and autumn. Between the greenhouse, the vegetable beds and the fruit cage, we produce asparagus, aubergines and artichokes (both globe and Jerusalem), garlic, onions and shallots, runner and broad beans, carrots, beetroot, potatoes, spinach and chard, leeks, courgettes, pumpkins and marrows, cabbages and cauliflowers, tomatoes, cucumbers and peppers, grapes and vine leaves, figs, peaches and greengages, blackcurrants and redcurrants, strawberries, blueberries, and raspberries. Plus the fruit from the outside trees. Plus the wild stuff – nettles, wild garlic, hazelnuts, and so on – which we gather from the garden and further afield.

The nearest shop, in a one-street village three miles away, is run by a local lady, sells plenty of local products, and orders in whatever the local people ask for. We have no need of police here (we never see any), we associate freely, we feel no distinctions of class. Our life affirms this claim by farmer and political scientist James C Scott: 'a society dominated by smallholders and shopkeepers comes closer to equality and to popular ownership of the means of production than any economic system yet devised'.

Our society at Mossland isn't actually dominated by smallholders and shopkeepers, but by our non-human neighbours. Of which the aforementioned sheep are the noisiest. These are furiously social beasts, fairly constantly roaring and groaning, shouting warnings, disciplining their lambs, quarrelling, and playing. The longer I live with them the more I distinguish the styles of their language. There's so much more to it than simply 'baaa'. Waves of intensity pass through the fields in consonance with woolly current events. Sometimes in the small hours a racket kicks up. To my spoilt rural ears it sounds like closing time at a proximate pub. Faaaack! they yell. Oiii! and Whaaaaat? Which isn't to suggest they don't suffer a delicate emotional life – when not chewing grass or shrieking they nuzzle necks, or butt heads. There's tragedy too: a lamb once spent most of a week waiting quietly by the corpse of its mother, despite the tearing and clawing of scavengers, until there were only bones left. Sometimes disease spreads through the flock, and our nights are punctuated by coughing.

In December, rams are let loose for the tupping. Squat, powerful, insistent beasts, they look a little like hippopotami. Over the winter the ewes grow fatter, more lumbering, and clumsy. In April, they give birth. Bloody placentas litter the grass and also the track connecting us to the road – but not for long. Swooping red kites soon polish them off. In the house (aside from the mice and, in the winter, the weasel, that live in the walls) presides Dusty the cat, who considers herself the real owner of the place. We'd like to think we inherited her with the property from the previous occupants, because she refused to leave with them, but in actual fact she inherited us. She stayed where she was, only her servants changed. Though the transition was difficult – she lived outside for our first seven weeks, scared of our strangeness, and no doubt of our dog. Sometimes we saw a blue-grey streak zapping through distant undergrowth; sometimes we heard a yowling impossible to locate. Then one day when the frost was biting, very thin, she introduced herself at the back door. Thereafter for a while she lived in a cupboard, for security. It was a very positive moment for her when our dog was put down. But the following morning threw up another setback...

You see, I'd buried the dog, a border collie, in the garden at dusk. First thing next morning, a delivery van came down the track. "Is this your dog?" the driver said. "It's followed me down the track." It was a border collie, and from behind looked just like the dead dog. "Erm, no," I replied. "I don't think so." But he was smaller than the dead dog, and emanated a musty stink, and was matted and starving, and also terrified of us, though he wanted to stay on our property. We weren't able to approach him – whenever we advanced, he backed off. So we put food down, and he hung around, and slept the night in the garden. The next day I managed to pick him up (gasping against the stench), and we drove him to the vet. He was health-checked, cleaned up a bit, and his microchip detected.

He came from some miles away. Fortunately for us, he was no longer wanted in his place of origin. Local knowledge told us he'd been on the run for weeks. Various neighbours had tried to feed him, but he'd always run away. Obviously traumatised, he flinched from sudden movements, even from the flutter of birds. We called him Sudfeh, which means 'coincidence' in Syrian Arabic, in honour of his mysterious arrival. Slowly he worked out we weren't going to hurt him, and slowly he relaxed to become an affectionate, playful, almost entirely civilised dog – though he still fears strangers, and young children make him hysterical, and vehicles of any kind, from lawnmowers to trucks, drive him into paroxysms of what appear to be frenzied excitement. The clearest sign of his disturbing past is his obsessive and indiscriminate approach to food. That is, he eats everything. Rather than simply snuffling about in the garden, he hunts voles, or bites at the toads which make him retch. He poisoned himself eating the compost before I properly closed it off. Sheep shit is a favoured delicacy. I don't hold any of this against him because I've come across the phenomenon before. I once met a woman who'd survived a starvation siege in the suburbs of Damascus. She could never stop eating, she told me, though she now lived in Turkey and had a kitchen packed with food. However much she ate, she never felt full. The hunger was embedded deep inside.

Other residents or regular visitors include bats, sparrowhawks, swallows, woodpeckers, a heron, escaped pheasants, wild geese, and a family of moorhens. The occasional red squirrel braves the passage through the fields to steal nuts from our bird table. We've never met the badger but we know it from its sett, and we know the otter once seen at the nearby river fishes in our lochan too, because he leaves his droppings behind. The breast-like drumlin, meanwhile, is pocked with foxholes. The foxes can be seen running amongst the lambs, and sometimes in our garden, peering at us through the glass.

Perhaps our strangest encounter with the non-human communities was in the damp early March of 2019, following a freakishly warm week in late February. For a few days, Mossland became the site of a toad and frog plague or fantasia, some nightmare of a Mexican sex and death fiesta. Sex because pullulating piles of frogs were everywhere coupling or writhing in orgiastic groups. Their spawn (the frogs' in clumps, the toads' in strings) overbrimmed the ponds and puddles. Plenty had missed its watery target and was just dolloped in the grass. And death because their impractical ubiquity meant the amphibians were everywhere stalked by the angel – crushed beneath boots and tyres, and attacked by birds, chewed inside out by the heron and spat down as an alien quivering mass.

So long as the erotic-thanatic fury continued, we began even to fear displacement. Frogs invaded the greenhouse to croak and chirp, and to silently watch us. They entered the drainpipes. Several appeared to be trying to open the front door, raising their hands against it and pushing.

The kites fight aerial battles. The young buzzard that spent a fortnight sitting on our gate was persistently bullied by crows. Furtive creatures skulk from their holes in darkness to rip and tear those slower and more sleepy. The birds eat the worms and the cat eats the birds. Down in the soil a trillion combats ensue.

Everyone's eating everyone else, as in the human world, but here there's no sense that things could or should play out differently. The insects and microbes don't generate propaganda and conspiracy theories to ease their murder. They don't need to act out their most stupid selves. Their behaviour is ordained by their DNA, not by social and spiritual dysfunction. They succeed when they kill, whereas we fail.

Furthermore, cut-throat competition isn't the whole story. As with us, there is cooperation too. See for instance the amalgams of fungi and algae which create lichens, symbiotic beings which sometimes live for centuries. Or the shared mycorrhizal networks by which fungal mycelium connects the roots of plants and trees, allowing them to feed each other, or to communicate warnings. By mutually beneficial arrangement, the roots feed carbons to the fungi, and the fungi feed minerals to the roots.

Mutual aid, it seems, is one of the principles of life. To emphasise the point, anthropologists Natasha Myers and Carla Hustak suggest that rather than evolution, 'involution' – 'a rolling, curling, turning inwards' – "better captures the entangled pushing and pulling of 'organisms constantly inventing new ways to live with and alongside one another'".

And I am one of these organisms living at Mossland. Having never possessed property before, I expected when I arrived that at some point a sense of ownership would settle heavily upon my shoulders. It never did, for precisely this reason. I'm here for a while, profiting from the other organisms – and some of them profiting from me. Instead of ownership, I have a mild sense of achievement, of growth. I'd never considered myself, for example, to be capable of building a shed. (And because the shed was a joint effort, my pride is more communal than individually owned.)

That was the second woodwork project of my life. The first was the compost bin, a cubic metre box shaped by old pallets. Which has since become one compartment in a larger compost complex. It holds donkey manure (which I shovel up from a friend's donkey shed), and the composting now happens in two compartments of two cubic metres each – because the greater the volume of compost the greater the heat it generates, and then the faster it burns rubbish into supersoil. This, of course, is the purpose of composting. We can't bring more sunshine to Scotland, but we can boost our crops by enriching the ground. But I compost obsessively, beyond any purpose. Strange to say, I enjoy for its own sake the act of composing a layered wealth of materials to be decomposed by smaller creatures. Including: kitchen waste, nettles, fallen fruit, seaweed, sawdust, wood ash, comfrey, hair and beard clippings, cardboard, cat fur, coffee grounds, and pond weed. All mixed in with the aforementioned manure, and soon exhaling the sweet mushroomy odour of rotting matter.

The death of matter feeds all the tiny species of the heap. Within the planet on the scale we see are countless microscopic planets, each swarming with life. That's what heats the compost. Life itself. Furious activity.

I experience a hunter-gatherer happiness when I go foraging. That is, I feel myself overtaken by a compulsion deeper than the simple appreciation of getting something for nothing (and it's not nothing in any case – foraging demands plenty of time and effort). I actually feel more properly alive, more fully functional, while scouring the environment for nutrition. This after all is what we evolved to do, and what for at least ninety five percent of our history we spent most of our time doing. The perceptual skills we now use to distinguish between brands, logos, and design schemes were first developed to identify the edible from the poisonous. So, in the garden and surrounding fields, and along the roadside hedgerows, I gather elderflower in June and elderberry in September. Nuts are ready by late summer (nut-picking is as ancient an activity as any

– Mesolithic hunter-gatherers left piles of hazelnut debris in their camps). The richest pickings stretch throughout the autumn: rosehips, hawthorn and rowan berries, blackcurrants, sloes from the blackthorn tree, and chanterelle mushrooms found under mixed woodland. In this season we practise a gendered division of labour – once I have gathered, she prepares the jams, jellies, chutneys, relishes, cordials, sauces, and tinctures which see us through the winter. (I am more than fortunate to live with an excellent cook whose ingenuity extends our self-sufficiency).

Throughout the winter I forage fire wood, sometimes from our garden or from land owned by friends, sometimes from storm-felled trees at roadside. It's another very ancient and inexplicably satisfying activity. Humans have been feeding fire for half a million years, since long before they were Sapiens. After gathering comes sawing, chopping, and stacking. Nothing is wasted – the sawdust joins the compost heap; the bark goes to mulch young trees; and the wood piles which stand for two years drying are visible signs of security more meaningful than any insurance policy.

And we plant trees, partly in penance for the jet fuel previously expended. On arrival at Mossland, I transplanted several ash trees which had sprouted in a friend's garden. I didn't know at the time about ash dieback, a fungal disease which has ravaged Europe's forests and is projected to kill up to 99 per cent of Britain's ninety million ash. Those I transplanted are now dead, and the old ash in our garden (and almost all those in the area) are slowly dying.

More successfully, I added a few birch, a couple more hazels, and some swamp cypress, as well as two hundred metres of hedge to separate us from the sheep, a double row of hawthorn, blackthorn, elder, crab apple, hornbeam, field maple, and in the stretch which is waterlogged in winter, guelder rose and alders – the latter have air ducts in their roots and cork cells in their trunks to keep them aerated when swamped. The purpose of the hedge is threefold: to provide us and the animals with more foraging material, to form a barrier against destructive wind, and to moderate extremes of heat and cold in the garden. The hedge trees are fenced for their first years, to protect them from browsing deer, and because they like rich soil and don't like competing with grass, the ground is thickly mulched with bark, wood chip and leaf mould. In the woodland too, death feeds life. A fifth of all species depend on dead wood.

The best time to plant a tree, so the saying says, is twenty years ago. A loud part of me wishes I'd moved here then, or further back still. It's an illogical wish, of course – twenty years ago, I was another person, and wouldn't have wanted it. Twenty years ago, I think I even expected that in the end I'd settle in Syria, perhaps amongst olive trees in the hills above the coast. In the sunlight. Perhaps with a fig tree too.

How ridiculous that seems today, and how utterly impossible. Not only have I changed, not only would it be dangerous for me to return (having written against the gangsters), but the Syria I knew no longer exists. Neither do the Syrians. It used to be that even if years had passed, you could return to a neighbourhood and ask, for instance, "Where's Abu Ahmad?" and someone would tell you, "he's working in the shop next to the bakery", or suchlike. Everybody could be found again. But not now. Now there's no Abu Ahmad, no shop, no bakery. In many cases, not even a neighbourhood.

Dar al-fanaa. Annihilation, impermanence, flux. Has history been teaching Syrians a spiritual lesson? Is that what this is about?

But we were talking about trees, which when you work with them remind you of your temporality, of your puniness on any grander scale. Some of those I plant may live past my great great grandchildren, and will certainly still be young when I die. For I've lived past a half century now. There's already been sufficient social change to render my early days historical.

My grandfather told me that time moves faster as you age. I can now confirm this unfortunate fact: linear time speeds up relentlessly. There's an element (in my case, a pretty powerful element) of existential terror produced by the constant awareness of the fact. Religion offers some people the reassurance of certainty – *yaqeen* – but I feel less certain with every day that passes. A radical agnosticism blooms in my heart. I fail to comprehend how reality works, or what it is, or what I am, or why. The only thing I know is that I cannot know, no more than a spider can know about Brexit, no more than a fungus can read James Joyce.

My scant reassurance lies in a sensation of the absurd. By which I mean, the faster my life goes, the less solid it seems. It's like watching a film pass before the eyes, a finite series of numberless frames.

And at Mossland, in the absence of human noise, I am conscious of myself as a fragment of the great mystery. It's hard to avoid it, on nights when the galaxy burns across the sky, or in general in the daytime, surrounded by the slowly thrumming trees, the various lives lived at various paces, and confronted everywhere by the ineffable abundance of colour – which is not 'out there' objectively but produced by the human mind, a representation of certain wavelengths of light. The dog sees it differently. The ant in yet another way. So, I am aware that as I watch the world I am also watching myself, and – once again – that there are many worlds contained within the one we perceive.

The insistent momentum of linear time is also, to some extent, soothed by a growing consciousness of cyclical time. If my life is an arrow, it flies among some mighty circles, such as the movement of seasons and months. If it's October, therefore, as well as being a station in my journey towards death, it's time to plant garlic and onions. If it's June, then the air is clouded with midges (Scotland's version of the mosquito), and I have to keep checking my body for ticks. The wood we put in the burner points out another kind of cycle. At present, for instance, we're burning chunks of cherry and silver birch. Both woods are very beautiful, their brightly patterned bark striped with lenticels, mouths for breathing (the greatest art, I have discovered, has no artist behind it, no conscious artistry). These trees were blown down in the storm of September 2018, just before our arrival. As we hand them to the flame, I remember working with Ibrahim, my son, to pull the fallen birch off its sister, who it was leaning on, and working with Ayaat, my daughter, and Sulema, my wife's relative, to saw the cherry into manageable lengths.

Time loops back and forward, never static, always in motion. This realisation has revamped my relationship to the northern climate. Formerly I used to be seasonally affected, thoroughly disordered by the relentless winter gloom. Our sunroom certainly helps (all housing in Scotland should incorporate a south-facing glass wall; access to year-long light should be recognised as a basic human right, like access to clean water). Working outside most days helps too. The task-based approach to time means winter now relents – no longer an interminable sentence, but a brief revolving window in which to read and write.

No state is permanent, all are recurrent – the alternating showers and thin sunlight of spring; or the subtropical miasma of late summer; or the repeated three-day howling storm; or freezing high pressure, spacious, still and clear, as if the earth were meditating.

I have no *yaqeen*, but for all this I feel gratitude. Some people end up in refugee camps. I've ended up here, at least for the time being. I thank God or fate or chance for it, from the depths of my unknowing heart.

ARTS AND LETTERS

DID I REALLY SEE THE TAJ MAHAL?

Boyd Tonkin

Henceforth, let the inhabitants of the world be divided into two classes –
them as has seen the Taj Mahal; and them as hasn't.

Edward Lear, *Indian Journal*

This garden, this place on the river's bank,
These carved doors and walls, this arch, this vault—what are they?
The mocking of the love of our poor
By an emperor propped upon his wealth.
My love, meet me somewhere else.

Sahir Ludhianvi (translated by Carlo Coppola with MHK Qureshi),
'Taj Mahal'

I.

Did I really see the Taj Mahal? Of course, I did. After all, I have the
memories, the photographs, the companions to prove it. Documents,
records, and witness statements could be found. Our driver might have
kept his receipts. The hotel might still have a registration on its books.
Some might suspect, however, that I never properly visited the tomb of the
Mughal empress Mumtaz Mahal and her bereaved husband Shah Jahan at
all. It could be that I sleepwalked through a pre-set sequence of perceptions
and feelings dictated by the millions of travellers who preceded me. The
marble tomb with its floral *pietra dura* inlays; the flanking minarets; the
stately mosque to one side; the manicured *char bagh* gardens lined with
cypresses between mausoleum and gate; the sluggish, depleted Yamuna

flowing behind with the forlorn estate on its far bank – how much do I remember, and how much consists of a pack of mental overlays imprinted by a thousand other images and narratives? In suspicious hindsight, the blazing illumination of discovery may feel like nothing more than a commonplace case of *déjà vu*.

Any biography has its peaks and troughs, its sparkling summits and its dreary plains. And, for the past two-and-a-half centuries, people of some material means – first largely in the West, then around the globe – have come to believe that voyages represent the best, or fastest, way to scale those peaks of experience. I learned to share that often unreflecting faith. I came to want, even need, travel, like any conforming Western consumer. During the pandemic lockdowns I sorely missed it. And with the belief that voyages should punctuate a fulfilled life like exclamation marks goes the conviction that some marks stand taller than others.

The urge to erect a hierarchy of must-see monuments long predates the Enlightenment and Romantic eras that turned travel for personal enrichment into a mass pursuit. The first lists of 'Seven Wonders of the World' began to appear from Greek writers in the second century BCE. Around 140 BCE, the poet Antipater of Sidon drew up the original 'bucket list' of top destinations. He boasted of having set eyes on 'the wall of lofty Babylon' and its hanging gardens, marvelled at 'the huge labour of the high pyramids', admired the Colossus of Rhodes, and so on. The original Seven Wonders cult coincided with the pacification of the Mediterranean and much of the Near East under Roman rule, enforced by Rome's Hellenistic client states. The intimate links between tourism and empires (of various kinds) go back at least two millennia.

A long and winding road leads from such antique travel tips to the enthronement of the Taj by the Raj. By the time that Edward Lear wrote and drew his reactions in his Indian journals of 1874, first-hand acquaintance with the Agra tomb and its gardens had come to be widely accepted not just as a zenith of journeys, but a crown of life. Here, as elsewhere, secular tourism took over the function of sacred pilgrimage for many visitors. That was an odd, double-edged re-purposing, given that the venue in this case consists of a mausoleum with mosque attached. Then again, most historic cathedrals and abbeys in the West now host far more profane than pious travellers (perhaps only at St Peter's in Rome do the numbers of the faithful still rival the lay rubberneckers). At any rate, the quest for personal intimacy with a hallowed site has turned into a modern devotional practice of its own.

In an age of ubiquitous reproduction of the world's most famous places across every medium, physical proximity not only keeps its value. Being there yourself, with Instagram or Twitter to amplify your presence in nanoseconds, seems to matter more than ever. And, when you get the opportunity, spurning the chance to garland your memories with an act of witness can feel a bit like an act of blasphemy. At the same time, the sheer weight of past testimony – all the words, the pictures, the photographs, the films – means that we face Great Wall or Machu Picchu, Empire State or Golden Gate, Pyramids or Taj itself not naked but filtered through lens upon tinted lens of interpretation. No visitor to such a site can ever more hope to behave like an innocent abroad.

On a previous visit to Delhi I had, half-deliberately perhaps, failed to find time to make the routine excursion to Agra. This time, I was taking part in a literary festival. About its events, I remember almost nothing. But I can still feel the bone-chilling aircon of the curved hotel in Delhi where we spent a week, and see the heavy denims and squeaky leather jackets of the smart folk who hung out in the chilled bar. The hotel's hulking concrete bow overlooked the Jantar Mantar – the astronomical observatory built in the early eighteenth century by Jai Singh II, founder of Jaipur, now stranded amid banks and ministries on the edge of Connaught Place. So, I dutifully learned about the celestial mappings and measurements performed by each of the enigmatic instruments that stand like an eerie abstract sculpture park girdled by the honking traffic.

Most of that knowledge has also vanished, although I do remember the noisy throng of demonstrators up from the country who made (and still make) Jantar Mantar their hub in the big smoke. Then, they were protesting against a contested dam project that threatened to displace thousands of villagers and despoil their environment (it duly did). Just now, in summer 2021, farmers are gathering there to resist new laws that will, they say, give corporate agribusiness a stranglehold over small producers. Jantar Mantar still gazes impassively towards the heavens that it tabulated, as it has for three centuries. Around it huddle all the fear and worry of life for those with few resources on this earth.

If I could take an interest in late-Mughal astronomy, why not the Taj itself? My heretical resistance was dwindling. I needed to pay my own homage at last. So, over a couple of hot days in April during the first decade of the millennium, a quartet of festival-goers – M., N., A. and myself – hired a car and driver and set out south down the old, dual-carriageway NH2 from Delhi, that much-clogged artery since supplanted by the six lanes of the Yamuna Expressway. Like any Asian megalopolis, Delhi took an age to leave behind. The yellowing fields of Haryana, then Uttar Pradesh, baked in early-summer haze. Beside the NH2 (in those days, anyway), the odd sad carcass of a wrecked and rusting truck lay as an unheeded warning to the speeding funfair-style lorries – bedecked with fairy-lights, adorned with goddesses, trumpeted by klaxon fanfares – that barrelled past us on this, and every, Indian road. Half-way along the route, we stopped for a *masala chai* and the driver – the first time I had seen this ritual – took care to give a few coins to the insistent posse of transgender *hijras* who waited in the shack-café's parking lot. To shun them, I learned, would bring bad fortune down on this, or any, trip. Our luck held. After the 200km journey to Agra, we toured the Taj and some of the surrounding sites. We stayed in a pretentious tourist hotel, did another stint of sightseeing, and returned to the capital.

2.

Inter-continental travelling, as I write, still feels as remote a prospect as a visit to the stars meticulously charted by Jai Singh's astronomers. The pandemic-era shrinkage of horizons means that, save for a couple of day-trips, I have been almost nowhere for almost eighteen months. So what? Electronic media, not to mention all the older forms of communication, still bring the world to me. But I took to cross-border travel relatively late, then binged on journeys, and have felt their sudden absence like a throbbing phantom limb. My childhood holidays involved no planes or passports. We never crossed borders. Later, I grasped that parents with four children and a single income had wisely chosen to spend precious vacation time in easily-reached places – the Cotswolds, the Welsh borders, the Norfolk Broads, the North Yorkshire Moors – where kids of different ages could roam free in safe and open spaces.

By any decent standards, we were lucky youngsters. To cram us for a week or two into some high-rise hotel on the Costa Brava for the sake of 'going abroad' would have been a futile gesture. Children, though, seldom judge in the light of sweet reason. When schoolmates returned in September with tantalising tales of Greece, Spain, France – sometimes, even, America, India or Israel – I felt embarrassed and excluded. Adolescent snobbery wiped out my real enjoyment of the holidays and replaced it with a vague anxiety that I should have been elsewhere. Briefly, but fiercely, I suffered pangs of social inferiority. All in my mind, of course – but I yearned to catch up as soon as I could.

So from teenage years onwards, foreign travel became an overdetermined object of desire. 'Abroad' shimmered on the horizon, as a symbol of freedom and a proof of self-determination. And with that hankering for elsewhere came a growling fear of disappointment. What if the rest of the planet beyond the English Channel looked and felt much like the land behind the cliffs of Dover did? The observer always has to frame and shape the place observed. In any case, the heaviest item of baggage you will carry on any expedition is yourself.

A lot – too much, perhaps – rode on my travels. They started to feel not just like the expansion, but the validation, of a life. When so much hoping and yearning pivots on such an enterprise, odd outcomes may ensue. The traveller's over-excitement as the pined-for climax of a journey nears even has its own clinical name: Stendhal Syndrome. In 1807, the French writer and adventurer Henri Beyle – who, in print, called himself Stendhal – at last visited Florence. Arrival in the city of his dreams, where he thought 'the civilisation of mankind was born anew', led not so much to instant ecstasy as a kind of breakdown. He reports that 'soon I found myself grown incapable of rational thought, but rather surrendered to the sweet turbulence of fancy, as in the presence of some beloved object.' In the church of Santa Croce he pays homage to the tombs of Galileo, Michelangelo and Machiavelli and, although hardly a conventional believer, finds that 'the tide of emotion that overwhelmed me flowed so deep that it was scarce to be distinguished from religious awe'. That prime touristic mix of erotic and spiritual fervour soon pushes his soul into 'a state of trance'. Then a crisis fells him, and in the porch of Santa Croce 'I was seized by a fierce palpitation of the heart… the wellspring of life was dried up within me, and I walked in constant fear of falling to the ground'. There's a Jerusalem variant of this syndrome, first described by the psychiatrist Heinz Herman in the 1930s. It involves messianic delusions in the over-stimulated visitor on top of hysterical symptoms that Stendhal suffered.

In Stendhal's case, the pressure of prior expectation intensified his swoon. 'So often have I studied views of Florence,' he writes, 'that I was familiar with the city before I ever set foot within its walls.' I too studied guidebooks, pored over maps, devoured travellers' tales, before setting off. I still do. Yet I discovered that, when I finally did make it 'abroad', Stendhal Syndrome never bothered me. If anything, a contrary trouble loomed. If surplus thrills disturb some voyagers, then an 'Is that it?' shrug can lower others' mood. I feared becoming one of those.

Between school and university, I worked through a winter and spring in humdrum agency jobs and then set off with a classmate for a two months' tour around France and Italy in a just-about-functioning old car. Not far into this trip, I remember sitting in the garden beside the fairy-tale château of Chenonceau near the Loire and feeling a blanket of gloom descend. Was I depressed, asked my friend? Certainly, although not for long. Foreign travel had given up its fruits. I couldn't really fault their taste. Straddling the river Cher, its currents reflected in the waters, the château delivered on every guidebook promise. So did nearly every other three-star Michelin spectacle we saw. I realised, though, that a flat, ashen feeling of disappointment could still fall like a dense curtain in front of some storied scene: an Alpine lake, a medieval citadel, a Baroque basilica, a palm-fringed bay. If, consciously or not, I had come to identify foreign travel as a kind of rite of passage into adulthood, then perhaps what disenchanted me was not the place, but the state itself.

The pall of dejection lifted. It has only rarely dropped again. But it did strike the first time I visited South Asia: another barrier breached. During my first night at the impeccably picturesque Hotel Suisse in Kandy, Sri Lanka, where decades before Lord Mountbatten had bargained with the Burmese leader General Aung San (the father of Suu Kyi), I woke up and burst into tears. Jet lag accounted for that, perhaps – or else a passing depressive side-effect of the anti-malarials I took. Perhaps, too, all my preparation tended to seed a sort of reverse Stendhal Syndrome in which first-hand experience could never measure up to the wonders already encountered in images or words. Whatever the cause, though, shadows of sadness darkened the tropical gardens all round into a meaningless wilderness. Then that spasm passed as well.

3.

The further I travelled, the more I noticed that a pattern seemed to emerge. Disenchantment threatened to take hold when the stakes rose higher — a new culture, a distant continent, a global focus of travellers' desire. In that light, a trip to the Taj courted a severe risk of comedown. Here, after all, was a site that had gathered panegyrics as soon as it was built — between Mumtaz's death in 1631, after she gave birth to her fourteenth child, and 1647 or 1648. The Mughal PR machine rapidly moved into top gear. 'This beautiful tomb is a relic left by a king,' wrote the court poet Kalim (pen-name of Abu Talib Hamadani), 'Designed to endure even beyond the end of the world.' His colleague Qudsi (Muhammad Jan) concurred. 'Time has constructed this edifice,' he hymned (in fact, the architect Ahmad Lahauri oversaw the design), 'To display thereby the Creator's glory'. European travellers got in early with their plaudits. By 1670 the French merchant François Bernier could hail 'an astounding work', and set in motion cross-continental tourist comparisons in its favour. 'It is possible I have imbibed an Indian taste,' he reported, 'but I decidedly think that this monument deserves much more to be numbered among the wonders of the world than the pyramids of Egypt, those misshapen masses'. Take that, Pharaohs.

Soon after 1800, when the forces of the East India Company overcame the Maratha rulers of Agra, British officials began to vaunt their new possession. Sir William Sleeman dubbed the Taj 'a faultless congregation of architectural beauties' and, influentially, executed a Romantic-era sidestep from the buildings themselves to the finer feelings of the observer. He fears disappointment — so famous was the tomb by that stage — but 'no, the emotion which one feels at first is never impaired'. From then on, Taj visits have their narcissistic side: with many voyagers, it's all about *me* and my super-sensitive responses. For a few, however, a dazzled humility marked their passage to Agra.

Liveliest, most receptive of nineteenth century travellers in India, Fanny Parkes – wife of a minor Company administrator – visited in 1835. She noticed that 'it is not its magnitude; but its elegance, its proportions, its exquisite workmanship, and the extreme delicacy of the whole, that render it the admiration of the world'. She looks hard, and well ('The veins of grey in the marble give it a sort of pearl-like tint that adds to, rather than diminishes, its beauty'). She enjoys the contemporary life that sprawls around the tomb complex as much as its architectural splendour: during 'the *mela* of the Eed' she delights in the swirl and colour of the fair and contrasts the 'gaily dressed' locals with 'the vile round hats and stiff attire' of European gents. Parkes treats the Taj as 'the highest compliment ever paid to woman' and vows to remember it until 'the lowly tomb of an Englishwoman closes on my remains'.

Some colonial-era accounts let racial ideology befog history. They ascribe the perfection of the edifice to an Italian architect, Geronimo Veroneo – who visited India but did nothing at the tomb. Eventually, sceptics and even scoffers begin to raise voices of dissent. Around 1860 the artist William Simpson deplored 'Taj-worship'. He ranked it far lower than earlier Indian Islamic buildings, and attributed the over-fussy ornament (in his eyes) to the same European intervention that other Westerners had praised. For Simpson, it just wasn't Indian enough.

Come the twentieth century, and a heretical, so-what? Snub to the Taj could signify a rebellious young intellectual on the make. Most eloquent with his punkish dismissal was Aldous Huxley in his 1920s travelogue *Jesting Pilate*. 'I am always a little uncomfortable,' he pretends, 'when I find myself unable to admire something which all the rest of the world admires. Am I, or is the world, the fool?' Of course, he's not uncomfortable at all. He's proud of his nose-thumbing originality. 'Even at sunset,' he crows, 'even reverberated upside down from tanks and river, even in conjunction with the melancholy cypresses – the Taj is a disappointment.' Huxley cherishes his disappointment. He sneers at the 'picturesque' detail and mocks the philistine Raj types who respect the mausoleum for its 'inordinate costliness'. As for the minarets, hyperbole kicks in: they are 'among the ugliest structures ever erected by human hands', while the floral inlays rank only as 'poor and uninteresting'.

Huxley dislikes not just fancy decoration but any monotheistic faith of the kind that raised the Taj. In contrast, in India 'the Hindu architects produced buildings incomparably more rich and interesting' – as if Mughal royal workshops did not employ the best artists and artisans irrespective of their faith. He evidently never ran across the crackpot Hindutva notion – first propagated by a pseudo-historian named PN Oak – that brands Shah Jahan's complex by the Yamuna as a Hindu temple itself: the mythical 'Tejo Mahalaya'. Later, a more convincing critique of the Taj cult came from writers who challenged its status as a homage not to time-defying love and grief but to ostentatious wealth and power. Sahir Ludhianvi (pen-name of Abdul Hayee), both a pioneer of progressive Urdu poetry and a star Bollywood lyricist, bitingly asks in his poem 'Taj Mahal':

Do dead kings' tombs delight you?
If so, look into your own dark home.
In this world countless people have loved.
Who says their passions weren't true?'

In Ludhianvi's perspective, the tomb enshrines a grotesque inequality of memory and mourning.

In the twenty-first century, not only alt-history freaks, smart-alec contrarians and class warriors target the Taj. With Narendra Modi's BJP in power, the relegation of monuments of Mughal culture to relics of Islamic 'oppression' comes from the top. For BJP politician Sangeet Som, the Taj 'should have no place in Indian history'. In 2017, the BJP-run government of Uttar Pradesh notoriously left the Taj Mahal out of a glossy tourist brochure. 'Uttar Pradesh Tourism: Unlimited Possibilities' boasted its title – but strictly limited if a Muslim ruler happened to have ordered a monument's construction. Such stunts only douse the state, led by UP's priest-turned-populist chief minister Yogi Adityanath, in ridicule. More gravely, rampant pollution and urban sprawl have cloaked the banks of the Yamuna in grime. Meanwhile (until the pandemic hit), annual tourist numbers had rocketed – from around 2.5 million when I visited to more than 6 million – without any corresponding boost to the funds available for conservation and repair by the Archaeological Survey of India, the site's custodians. Nearby, almost half of Agra's two million people live in slum districts. Graceful Mughal mansions in the choking centre crumble. *Havelis* decay into hovels. Rabindranath Tagore's fabled 'teardrop on the cheek of Time' now hangs in a partially disfigured face.

4.

All of which might have heightened my risk of crushing disappointment. I need not have worried: the let-down never happened. True, my memories of the tomb itself – not too crowded, bearably warm, with swift-moving queues and hustlers round the gate that A. could bat away with a brisk retort – have some blurring round the edges. No doubt what I've read and seen does now interfere with what I truly saw. The marbles, the inlays, the tombs, the domes, the terraces, the gardens – my own recollections and other people's representations have to a degree bled into each other. Such is tourism in the age not merely of Walter Benjamin's mechanical reproduction, but of a digital proliferation that even he never foresaw. What remains mine, and mine alone, are the surroundings, the outskirts, the fringes that edge the principal event. The peripheries of the Taj anchored my trip in indisputable experience more than the too-familiar 'iconic' edifice at the centre of the picture. The solemn, soothing mosque set at the western side of the tomb, so much quieter than mausoleum or gardens. The scantily visited jewel-casket tomb of Itimad-ud-Daulah (Mumtaz's grandfather) across the cage-like girder bridge over the Yamuna. The solitary dignity – not quite forgotten, but by no means mobbed – of the Emperor Akbar's tomb amid its deer-park at Sikandra, a short drive away in the northern suburbs of Agra. The glimpses of ruined grandeur in smashed latticework or eroded friezes down inner-city alleyways where fleets of scooters squawked.

Above all, no one – thank goodness – had fully coached me about Fatehpur Sikri. Perched on its windy ridge 30km to the west, Akbar's abandoned red sandstone capital, with its elegant but still-enigmatic palaces and pavilions gold-flecked in April sun, did carry me as close to a knee-trembling Stendhal moment as anywhere in the Subcontinent. Crucially, I had read, thought, and seen, relatively little about Fatehpur Sikri before we drove there. Illumination had the chance to ambush me. To be fair to the ever-sarcastic Aldous Huxley, he sensed the place's unsolicited magic too, even if he mistakenly attributes the ghost town's appeal to the 'genuine Hindu vigour' of its designers in the 1570s, as opposed to the Islamic conformity that supposedly governed the Taj. That's unhistorical nonsense: after all, the home, and later tomb, of the Sufi saint Salim Chishti determined Akbar's selection of this site. Still, Huxley does capture the time-frozen, stage-set quality of the russet squares and colonnades as the sun sets over the 'deserted city of coral and ruddy gold'. Because of the clarity and intensity I recall from Fatehpur Sikri, my more mediated – more pre-digested – impressions of the Taj itself begin to feel more substantial, and more personal.

You get the best view of the Taj tomb, I decided, not from the gardens and pool at the front but from the mosque on one flank or the so-called *mihman khana* (guest house) that mirrors it on the other. From there I do – at least I think I do – recall the pearly light that Fanny Parkes evokes. So if you visit the Taj, or anywhere else that wears its reputation like a suit of impenetrable armour, don't rush headlong at the main event. Take time to step a little to one side. Perhaps the same rule – let's call it adjacent revelation – applies to other must-see temples of tourism. Maybe the memorable truth of any life-event that will come to serve as a milestone of individual biography collects around its margins, not its centre. Think of those fruits and vegetables that pack most of their nutrients into tough outer skin rather than soft inner flesh.

If I know that I truly did visit the Taj Mahal, it's not merely thanks to the surprise glamour of Fatehpur Sikri, glowing in the dusty sunlight, as the marble Chishti tomb shone out like a torch against the brick-red ground. It's the courtly, old-fashioned Urdu that delighted A. when he heard it in craft shops near the gate of the Taj. It's the meat-heavy, allegedly 'Baluchi' restaurant in the grandiose Agra hotel that commemorated the Mughal rulers as kings of carnivores – and which duly took its toll on my stomach the next day. Equally, it's the *hijras* who clustered around the car at the roadside café, as ineradicably planted in Indian tradition as any princely monument, and the chants of the Jantar Mantar protesters that carried into the freezing Delhi hotel bar. All such circumstantial realities, not just the long-sought rendezvous with some hallowed shrine, help make an experience your own.

Naive travelling has, like naive living, little to recommend it. All the same, there comes a moment when the guidebook – or, these days, the site about a sight consulted on a phone – may cloud the vision and dull the senses. Try to discard all your cultural baggage and you may experience nothing much worthwhile. But you will often see and feel more with a lighter load. When she visits Santa Croce in Florence, where Stendhal had his Romantic traveller's turn, Lucy Honeychurch loses her Baedeker guide. At first, in EM Forster's novel *A Room with a View*, the young, questing heroine feels panicky and rudderless. 'Of course, it must be a wonderful building. But how like a barn! And how very cold! Of course, it contained frescoes by Giotto, in the presence of whose tactile values she was capable of feeling what was proper. But who was to tell her which they were? She walked about disdainfully, unwilling to be enthusiastic over monuments of uncertain authorship or date.'

Does Lucy really visit Santa Croce? She does when she stops going through the approved tourist-pilgrim motions. Understanding, and enlightenment, arrive not head-on, ready-made and ratified by a star-rating, but sidelong, piecemeal and higgledy-piggledy. No longer cowed by the authority of Baedeker, Lucy begins to enjoy the transient and accidental things: the stern notices about spitting and dogs; the clumsy tourists with their noses red from cold; the stumbling toddlers playing on the flagstones. Soon enough 'the pernicious charm of Italy worked on her, and, instead of acquiring information, she began to be happy'. Around the Taj, if not exactly at the Taj, I began to be happy too.

Some European critics of the Agra tomb, and other Indian architecture, used to scold it for excess incidental ornament and lack of a structural backbone. Even Edwin Lutyens, before he co-designed imperial New Delhi, marked down Indian building as mere 'veneered joinery in stone'. But what if all the marginal decorations, the digressions and the arabesques, were not just optional extras but the heart of the matter? And what if that idea held good not only for monuments, or for journeys, but for the rest of a biography as well? That's what I learned, in retrospect if not quite at the time, when I really saw the Taj Mahal.

BROKEN BISCUITS

Amina Atiq

In her work, Amina Atiq, a Yemeni–Scouse performance artist, explores the conflict and beauty of her dual identity, taking us on a journey to her heartland, Yemen, and her homeland, Liverpool. This is an extract from her first one-woman show, titled 'Broken Biscuits' – a reference to her grandmother's 1970s Liverpool corner shop.

Photo: Amina Atiq

I held Granma's hands in mine like a vessel of the past that feels strange
goodbyes passed the Northern valleys and greeted the Southern blue
waters

In the replacement of the royalist passport, number five issued at Aden on 14th
September 1966, which has been cancelled and retained.

Unlocking the fishermen's Red Sea – colony crown reeked of death
the British empire's protection in the Aden region was an illusion.
buried in my foreign blood –
tea bags for mocha beans. Grenade bombs and rifles overthrown in the
tribesmen hands.
Martyrs will meet life and justice will *dance on the heads of snakes*
ambushed in rocks and the mountains grew eyes. They don't like invaders
who overstayed the hospitability of the three-day rule –
it turned cold quickly, over the Mediterranean.

In bloodshed, English toddlers left the land with Arabic ringing in their
ears, in their first language and memories of an invasion they did not ask
for, strip searching Yemeni fathers with their hands in the air. The intense
rage of the Yemeni people overthrowing them.
They lost the occupation in bitterness. An occupier never admits and
history books written by the victors who dream of victory that deny its
failure, walk home with their shoulder's slouches like a turtle's back.

I'm a dark horse
beating down the door somewhere childhood
escaped the streets etching three syllables of my name beneath the old city
of Bab Al-Yemen
a woman dressed in black found me shackled to the gates, it was my
mother, chewing on her ruby passport
it's time to leave.

Yemeni families made their first appearances in Britain in groups, in the
hands of a revolution leaving a civil war to unravel. They came with
briefcases of gold, milk and honey.

We emptied our homes
unpacked our belongings
but some things we tucked under
our arms until someone else wore it better
because women like me buried home in our bellies
like our father's names,
they call him Mo for short.
Or Danny from the Paki shop
Who is told to: *only speak English here.*

Photo: Brian Roberts

We had moved around twice, left the corner shop and moved to a council house not too far. No-one moves too far, we were hurdled up, promising to leave no-one behind. Outside this home, strangers lurk in the shadows and when they did not like the way you speak, they would look at you differently. My mum kept us close. We kept each-other close.

We lived on top of a newsagent; grandad's corner shop but we never met him – we used the deserted shop as our playground.

We knew nothing of its past but we celebrated birthdays, anniversaries, new births, Eid celebrations, Christmas dinners sprinkled with my mother's spices. My brother and I only played in the summer, we battled with each other, until someone got hurt and the other one cried. We created paper swords and paper hats and when we got bored, we invited my English friend, Tracy down the road. Her mum was Welsh, she had a different language, like us. Mum would make us our favourite, milky English tea and a few broken biscuits and we would sit on the edge of the brick wall in the entry, hanging our small legs.

Photo: Amina Atiq

I was there, in glass windows and brick walls,
begging on the streets for *Penny for a guy*, watching the fireworks display light up your new city, eat a halal Christmas dinner, sprinkle grandma's spices – a taste
we've been trying to recreate, even if we tried. Soon my scouse accent lingered on my tongue,
I wanted to feel wanted like that and I made sure
I did. But I slept with my mother's voice in my ear *Never forget where you came from*.
In my broken Arabic: *This is all the home I need*.

A little ginger boy down road, *'Ey, where do you really come from?'*
I, picking at my skin, scarred with mosquito bites
to remind me what is marked, shall never be forgotten.

In my perfect broken scouse, *I come from here.*
He looks down at his hands, *'But you look different'*.

By sunset, I mapped the world across my body, not finding where to place myself.
We never meant to start a war, so I nodded and smiled and we played piggy in the middle with his friends.
East or West – I had no choice but the piggy was the safest place to be.

Photo: Brian Roberts

Girls like us, settled in a foreign place,
we buried our mother's tongue in our back gardens, to find the roots outgrown even deeper.
A sacrifice that haunts you every time you sing
your mother's anthem. But you keep on dancing.

Photo: Amina Atiq

Dad swore he would never marry a village Yemeni girl. He liked Chantelle, they met at the youth club in Lodge Lane, Toxteth. He said, she was the blonde hair and blue eyes to his soul. I cringed, watching at my mum's reaction over the kitchen table. Mum didn't say nothing, it was never going to happen in our world. Mum comes from a tribe of businessmen who ruled the town. Dad's tribe was a refugee, they had escaped persecution and sought asylum in a nearby village. They say they were related into families of royalties, some connection to queen Sheba and her family. I don't believe him. They are embarrassed to say, they were a farmer's child.

We danced together with my hair in her hands. I turned my face away.
'I don't want to be here mama; your village is my city. My sky is political, its raging and raging'.
My mother chokes up a child-like laughter
and drenches me in olive oil. I hated the smell.
My jet-black hair falling down my back, too thick to carry, too different.
I felt my neck snap. *You think you are liberated, but you are only a visitor in an occupier's land.*
She spreads the excess of olive oil across my pigmented neck.

Photo: Brian Roberts

Searching for home, stranded in wars between two houses.
I broke my voice, the crackle over the phone, this home does not exist without you.

I am sick, homesick.

THREE POEMS

Ruth Padel

Photo: Rehan Jamil

The Pure, Bright Experiment of Rain

Written for Ilhan Çomak, Kurdish poet arrested by the Turkish government in 1994, charged with membership of the banned PKK. Though one of Turkey's longest-serving political prisoners, he has published eight books of poetry from jail. In 2018 he won the Sennur Sezer Poetry Prize for his collection Geldim Sana (I Came to You). Norwegian PEN is helping to translate and publish his poetry in English.

Alone in lockdown, I wake in the dark
and place bare feet on the worn kelim by my bed.
It used to lie at the bottom of my granny's stair

then later on her bathroom floor.
I remember her lifting me out on it,
wrapping a towel around me. Or maybe not –
as you say, in the blazing seas of childhood
we believe every story.
Maybe she hefted me to a cork mat. I remember that too.

Now I pad out in the dark to make coffee.
I know there's a mouse somewhere,
one of secrets of this empty house,

but it's not going to run over my feet.
In the silence, I wait for the water
in a one-cup *vriki*

to make that rushing sound before it boils.
Against the still-black night
our plants on the window sill glow

as they never do in the day
and I wish I could hand you this coffee
walk with you up your stairway

into the heights of life, and talk poetry together,
laugh and stare out, safely out,
to what you call the pure bright experiment of rain.

The Gamble-Fish

My floating face
on which I have to click –
how do you get back, what are the
options in this mystical bedlam

why does each step take me further away
and why do these symbols on the keys
this sunrise, mandala or broken honeycomb
mean what you say
arbitrary as de-cluttering the house
now the children have flown
and finding a nest
of my granny's two-inch fish

cut from the inner mantle
of some marine creature's home.
Wafers of white rainbow
thin as an eyelash

engraved with arabesques and doves.
And overleaf, the tiny faithful crescents of their scales.
Tokens, she always said,
for a Balinese betting game.

She'd lived there in some mysterious past life
and kept them in a drawer
where she kept mothballs, letters, chocolate.
How did they turn up here? They chink

in my hand like *word* and *world*
in the correspondence theory of truth.
I watch the circle of my face
float off, a minnow

through the black water of my screen.
What do I tap to reach the waiting-room?
Where's the right link?
What I am trying to bet on is *hello*.

The Story-Teller, the Bedroom and the Sea

I

A girl sits in a bedroom by a mirror.
Her hair falls through the air like water
her skin is lucent as a plum.
You can see the veins fanning out
like branches against gold sky.
Torchlight flickers
on her dress of flame-coloured silk,
the bed of ivory, the coverlet of white crepe de chine.

There is no turning back.
She's out to save us all.
Her name means *City of the Free*.
A girl, sitting by a mirror
waiting for footsteps of the sultan.
Her mind climbs up like a snake-charmer's flute
remembering stories of the City of Brass.
A dervish, a caliph, a fisherman and a gold ring.

Tiles on the walls behind
painted with black tulips and arabesques
are tunnels into deep space
where shadows gather, trembling in the lamplight
because these shadows have seen it all before
a thousand times - the beautiful girl,
the bed of ivory and the mirror, hung with beads of lapis
which should keep off the Evil Eye, and don't.

Somewhere in the palace
a musician is singing a love song on a tambourine
but the sheikh is fizzing with misogyny.
If he goes on like this, the citizens whisper,

we won't have any daughters left.
Curls of smoke rise
from the bronze incense burner
shaped like a lion
because LION is how the sultan sees himself,
roaring his pain at all women.

Over here is his silver astrolabe
for measuring the heavens
for this sultan is not an idiot
only a wounded narcissistic man.
He has slept with and then beheaded

a thousand girls
who have waited here for him like this.
Eclipse of the moon, eclipse of the sun,
a precipice where love should be
and a thousand frightened faces on the block at dawn.

II

Her father tried to stop her.
Let me go, she said. I have a plan, she said.
But it's a long shot.
The harder you pull, the tighter the rope.
She has put her body in the sultan's power
to reveal to him the riches of her mind.
Her only weapon will be the art
of invention, of *what happens next*.

She is planning to open a window to the sea
we all swim in without knowing,
the sea which gives oxygen,
the Blue Ocean of stories.
Her hair falls through the air like water
and she holds us all in the dark of her mind

where her first story is opening
like blossom in the last rays of sun.
She is relying on her own Aladdin's cave
of echoes from the golden land
of enchantment. Battens of starlight
lie across the floor
but she is seeing a flying horse, a city of magicians,
Sinbad's magical boat
following a hoopoe, the messenger bird,
and a genie crossing the sea in a column of foam.

III

A girl sits in a bedroom
waiting for the door
to open. She imagines the sultan
in a gold belt with a buckle
shaped like two dragons' heads,
tongues touching. What she doesn't know
is what will happen in bed
but she'll go through with it –

and afterwards,
well, afterwards, she'll ask
to see her sister one last time
and hope the sultan will feel sorry for her and agree
so her sister can ask for a story.
She imagines the rustle
of him tiptoeing back
to eavesdrop, to listen.

IV

That girl in a bedroom blooming with shadows –
let's say she's *you.*
You with the blade of an axe on your neck,

you sentenced to die in the morning
setting out on an ocean of stories
to save your life, save all our lives, through art.
Can you stand on the edge of a cliff
and shout YES to the silver of the moon?
Can you go deep within yourself
to where the stories are, the bottom of your heart?
After a night of despair, bruised to the bone,
when you hear the tread of the sheikh,

his hand rattling the door,
put on your flame-coloured silk
to tell your story. Don't beat yourself up
over what you have or haven't done.
Sultans are marching upstairs all the time
all over the world

and if you set out to deal with him, you will have to go
into the most unbearable
feelings you will ever know. Be yourself. Lead
the sultan, whatever shape
he is taking in your life,
to a window looking out to sea.

Let the occurring world empower you
and when you hear his footsteps, don't even dream
of trying to be careful. There are roads you didn't travel
because you chose this path, the path that brought you here.
This is your journey now. Go into the bedchamber,
do what has to be done, and make a story of it.

V

So here is the bedroom, at night,
and two sisters, one telling a story to the other.
Whatever happened, has happened. Now

a disturbed man, a man who has too much power,
more power than anyone ever should have,
is listening behind a screen of filigree and silk
to the voice of a girl
who has no idea if she will be alive next day

but is steering her story
as calmly as if playing the zither.
A girl whose name means 'Free'
telling stories of quest – but also sorrow,
because people have died, a thousand girls,
who cannot be conjured back -
to bring clarity to the sultan's mind
and justice to his kingdom.

As for you, your stories will grow
from what you are going through
like oriental patterns on the couch of Sigmund Freud
or swirls on the body of a bouzouki,
and each moment is a window
opening on the sea
where Sinbad's boat still surges over the sparkling waves.
Look, dolphins are following, laughing in the foam

because no one can take away
your power to make a story from your own
unique adventure of being alive.
Like a magic ring inside a copper flask
or a beating heart in the hand of a surgeon
some enchanted object that was stolen or lost
will be found again, and pass
into the darkroom of your soul.

Don't worry if the story you are telling is true.
What matters is being true to yourself
and that your story has power to enchant.

If you have taken a few wrong turns
in the City of Disappointment
remember Scheherazade,
remember that you *are* Scheherazade,
and there will be a ship for you.

A harbour, a way through.

REVIEWS

}

SAID AND DONE

Faisal Devji

There is a parallel between Timothy Brennan's biography of Edward Said and Said's most famous book. Like *Orientalism* in 1978, *Places of Mind* appears at a time when colonialism and race have once again become subjects of public debate in North America and Western Europe. Reviewers have linked the reception of Said's book and the politics it enunciated to that facing the supporters of movements like Black Lives Matter or Rhodes Must Fall. And it was to find out how we might understand such a trajectory, that I was eager to read the biography. Said was one of the earliest non-European immigrants to achieve fame in the American academy, and I wanted to know how he managed to spark the first new debate on imperialism since its formal dissolution.

That this debate was about imperialism as a form of knowledge, rather than of economic motives or political control, might be due to its posthumous character. For Said argued that orientalist ways of thinking both preceded and outlived colonialism, which made the struggle for freedom an epistemological one, perfectly suited to the university and intellectual life in the West. And the context of this struggle was provided by the 1970s, a decade of immigration from the global south to the north. This movement was no longer defined by the need for labour in post-war reconstruction but the democratic failures of post-colonial states. It created the educated, middle class, and elite diasporas in which Said belonged and whose entry into the professions constituted the sociology of his fame.

As a Palestinian, of course, Said was not fully part of this post-colonial diaspora, dedicated as he was to the achievement of a national liberation whose consequences they had fled. His work on orientalism, colonialism, and the question of Palestine, then, managed to bring together two very different historical trajectories, in which the continuing struggles against

Zionist occupation, like Apartheid, held the possibility of getting nationalism right and correcting the mistakes of decolonisation. Orientalism, in other words, served to name a history of race and empire that remained to be fought, even as many of Said's post-colonial peers were moving towards a critique of the nation-state. His victory was to subordinate the national question to the colonial one as if to begin its history anew.

Timothy Brennan, *Places of Mind: A Life of Edward Said*, Bloomsbury, London, 2021

The post-colonial state was marked by a fundamental ambiguity, liberating the nation from imperialism while inheriting its role. After independence, anti-colonialism was used domestically either to displace conflicts between the new national majorities and minorities, by attributing them to imperialism, or turn such minorities into traitors who had been empowered by it. This was true of Christians and Jews in the Middle East, Indians in East Africa, Muslims in India, and Chinese in South-East Asia. Sometimes, as in India, the anti-colonial narrative was expanded to include the imperial past of minority groups in a way that minimised European dominance. From a national minority himself, Said idealised the unifying force of anti-imperialism and sought to purify its reactionary narrative.

None of these factors finds mention in Brennan's book, which makes Said's emergence as an anti-colonial celebrity in the aftermath of decolonisation inexplicable. There is some attempt to turn him into a solitary genius in the style of the nineteenth century, as the only representative of his people, whether Palestinian, Arab, or non-Western, but this doesn't succeed since *Places of Mind* is neither a personal nor an intellectual biography. What we get, on the one hand, is a bit of pop psychology in which Said is shaped by the desire to escape a domineering father and an adoring mother. And, on the other, an account of his writing that does not take the views of its critics seriously. Not just the orientalists, who are only capable of disputing some of Said's facts rather than his argument, but also Marxists like Sadiq Jalal al-Azm or Aijaz Ahmad writing from the Middle East and South Asia.

As the historian Hussein Omar suggests in an incisive review, Brennan writes out Said's African and Asian predecessors, contemporaries, and even successors, leaving him as the only spokesman in a world whose intellectual life is confined to a dozen Manhattan blocks and one or two Paris arrondissements. Beyond them exists a horizon constituted by the Palestinian-Israeli conflict, with Brennan keen to identify every Jewish thinker Said befriended in a strange echo of anti-Semitic naming practices. But his place in the scholarship from and about Asia and Africa has little to do with New York or Jerusalem. It does not occur to Brennan, for example, that *Orientalism* might owe some of its popularity to the Iranian Revolution, which by 1979 had made Islam a challenge to the West in a way the Palestinian cause never did.

Like other events in the non-European world, the Iranian Revolution also drew upon a critique of imperialism as a form of knowledge that went back to the nineteenth century. Said's success, then, might have been due not to his originality so much as an historical conjuncture. I suspect his career represents the liberal and even conservative appropriation of radical ideas and politics in the US. Brennan seems aware of this when he tells us how Said repeatedly solicited the acknowledgement of famous intellectuals such as Jean-Paul Sartre, Michel Foucault, and Jacques Derrida, only to repudiate them eventually. But while he attributes this disavowal to Said's more serious political and philosophical positions as compared to post-structuralism, post-modernism, or post-colonialism, I think the opposite is probably true.

Much of what Brennan tells us about Said's criticism of academic radicalism is reminiscent of the political right in America. He was against its 'jargon' and considered its theories impractical and 'just hot air'. While such ideas may well have deserved criticism, Said focussed on their lack of easy communicability as well as easy translation into what he considered political action. In Brennan's telling, he was more concerned with their instrumentality than intellectual rigor, an attitude brought out by Said's obsession with appearance, advertising, and public relations. These Madison Avenue concerns were not only evident in the attention he paid his own clothes and image, but to politics as image making, which entailed counselling Yasser Arafat to shave and wear a suit as part of a charm offensive in the US.

Brennan implies that Arafat stopped consulting Said once the State Department signalled its preference for the well-dressed and well-spoken professor as its Palestinian interlocutor. This would make another American professor placed in similar circumstances, the Afghan president Ashraf Ghani, Said's true successor as the designated saviour of his people. Said sought Arafat's recognition as he did that of celebrities like Sartre, Foucault, or Derrida. In his memoir, Said even describes searching for his own books on Foucault's shelves, something one cannot imagine the latter doing. As a result, though much to his surprise, Said was mistaken for a radical and pilloried for sins he never committed. These included not just accusations of terrorism but of relativism and the denial of objective knowledge.

Edward Said appears to have been an intellectual as much as a political version of Forrest Gump, a character present at some of the great moments of history without ever being part of them in any meaningful way. This allowed him both to claim a certain historical influence while at the same time denying its consequences. After assiduously advocating for the PLO to engage with the US, for instance, Said pronounced himself against the Oslo Accords that predictably resulted from such an engagement. Shuttling between left and right while lending a radical glamour to quite conventional positions, he comes across in *Places of Mind* as a split or contradictory subject. And because he cannot explain the phenomenon that Said became, Brennan does little more than rehearse this contradiction.

Said is portrayed as a hugely successful scholar and at the same time a victim of racial and political discrimination. Some of Brennan's descriptions of Said's influence read like they come from a society column, complete with lists of famous people at the parties he attended to demonstrate it. Said himself seemed to revel in such name-dropping, even lying to his future wife about having dated Candice Bergen when courting her. Brennan notes that he was never confident about his own fame, writing that 'well-wishers found his insecurity odd, knowing him well enough to figure out that as he moved about the room, he was quietly torturing himself with the question "What would these people want with little me?"' Perhaps it was the glamour he, too, sought from others.

Brennan does little to illustrate Said's brilliance either as a scholar or a political analyst, and we must turn to his own books for evidence of this. What *Places of Mind* offers, instead, are banal reports of Said's ideas and concerns. In accounts of his conversation, for instance, we are told 'a student would complain that a philosopher made no sense. He would chide, "this is not scholarship...not critical thinking to say something like that."' Or 'one young colleague wrung her hands, looking for commiseration when she wondered whether she was good enough for a fellowship. He responded, "Get good."' We are led to expect epigrams and delivered homilies. The cleverest thing attributed to him is the transcript of a phone message Said left American author and editor, Jean Stein, in 1994, which gives us some idea of his wit.

I have suggested that Said's historical role was to domesticate radical or controversial ideas, from post-structuralism to Palestinian self-determination and make them palatable in America. He did so by importing and translating these ideas into the scholarship on imperialism, helping transform it well beyond his own field of literary criticism. While important thinkers like Mohammad Iqbal in India and Jalal al-Ahmad in Iran had written about imperialism as a form of knowledge earlier, they had neither taken it as their subject nor addressed themselves to the West. Said turned the debate on orientalism into a morality play which then became part of a culture war. But outside Said's own concerns, his work also inspired extraordinary new scholarship on colonial sociologies of knowledge.

Critics like al-Azm and Ahmad understood the scholarship on orientalism arising from the demand of an immigrant diaspora for recognition. They thought it opportunistic and sentimental rather than radical in character, noting that its claim to represent the ex-colonial world was belied by the fact that Said's supporters there tended to be ultra-nationalists or religious supremacists. They also pointed out how Said misread Foucault, his source in conceptualising orientalism as a discourse, by replacing its radical anti-humanism with an emphasis on human agency. But agency, a shibboleth of the time describing the role of women, slaves, and the colonised in history, meant for Said the moral responsibility of the powerful not the politics of the powerless. Nietzsche might have called it *ressentiment*.

Using the term discourse to describe the simultaneous development of orientalist themes in many fields, from art and literature to scholarship and diplomacy, Said was able to define orientalism as a collective project without attributing it to the plan or intentionality of any class or country. As with Foucault, in other words, the consequences of orientalism were structural more than they were instrumental. Unlike Foucault, however, Said did not emphasise the modernity, and so historicity, of this discourse by attaching it to any process of collective regulation or individual discipline. This meant orientalism was famously detached from history and so could be attributed to the West in an almost racial way, while at the same time being blamed on all the individuals deploying it in a travesty of the term agency.

Said claimed that orientalism, never itself a modern discipline, forms part of many Foucauldian regimes of order in fields of scholarship, though without dominating any one of them. It thus remained curiously non-modern or undisciplined, bringing together philosophical speculation, moral reflection, and amateur ethnography in an almost eighteenth-century fashion, which might be why it proves so useful in equally amateurish practices like diplomacy and policymaking. In this way orientalism represents not the disciplinary invention of the Middle East, as Said would have it, but works rather to interrupt and even prevent the emergence of such regimes of knowledge and power. But this also means it is of minor importance in the analysis of power, whose modern forms can do without its othering.

Orientalism's power resides instead in its speculative and fantastical character, one capable both of interrupting and supplementing institutional forms of discipline and regulation. With neither a methodology nor ontology of its own, orientalism may allow for the suspension if not breakdown of disciplinary forms in the modern university. And it is in this sense resolutely non-Foucauldian. If it is neither an art nor a science, orientalism is incapable of constituting its subjects or objects in any institutional sense, with its themes always available for reversal in the way they had been in Montesquieu's *Persian Letters*. But this entails more than seeing Persia as a version of France, or, in the historicist language of the nineteenth century, the contemporary Middle East as a version of Europe's past.

The possibility of reversal means that the alterity which Said describes as being fundamental to the orientalist project, remains something transient and forever threatens to lapse into the identification he wrote about, from Kipling's *Kim* to Lawrence of Arabia. This probably accounts for the orient's celebrated fascination and dreamlike character, something which should not be reduced merely to a form of instrumentality or divided into good and bad versions as Said does. Rather than departing from Foucault, in other words, Said's mistake in *Orientalism* was to stick too closely to his conception of discourse and make it impossible to see the fragmentary and undisciplined role orientalism plays in contemporary scholarship. But such a recognition would disable it from becoming an object of easy moral judgement.

Given his views about orientalism, it is astonishing to see Said engaging in it so fulsomely, with Brennan's biography revealing his liberal use of essentialist terms like the Arab mind. Only a few years before the publication of *Orientalism*, he could claim that 'the characteristic movement of the Arab is circular...Repetition is therefore mistaken for novelty, especially since there is no sense of recognition.' Or that 'the Arabs since Avicenna and Ibn Khaldun (who borrowed from Aristotle) have never produced a theory of mind.' Brennan tells us that he was fond of many of the orientalist texts he criticised. Perhaps Said's contradictions illustrate my argument about orientalism's shift between identity and difference, and thus its inability to constitute either a subject or object of discourse.

By criticising free expression, seen as an excuse for hate speech, progressives have encouraged the creation of thought and language crimes appropriate to Said's notion of imperialism as a form of knowledge. These are then weaponised by far-right states and movements, having been pioneered by Jewish and Muslim groups only to be deployed by Hindu and other activists in Asia and Africa as well as Europe and North America. Often supported by or doing the bidding of authoritarian governments, these activists work to silence criticism in the name of anti-racism and decoloniality. Schools and universities comprise the frontlines of this battle, in which offenses against identity are replacing discriminatory treatment as causes of complaint.

The far-right now operates through the language and procedures of liberal recognition by claiming protection for its historical identity. This should alert us that such battles are all being fought within liberalism rather than between it and some illiberal alternative. When progressives mobilise in such liberal ways for causes ranging from anti-racism to anti-colonialism, they do so at some risk of enabling their own enemies through the legal and disciplinary procedures they demand. And this is in the nature of liberalism as a self-professedly neutral or non-ideological form. The result is often a culture war in which the number of twitter followers and propaganda on social media win battles that diminish the autonomy of academic and cultural institutions in dangerously populist ways.

Historical *ressentiment* and its vocabulary of interdiction offers no ground for progressive politics if it augments the repressive functions of any institution by calling for bans and removals. Such a politics should enable new freedoms instead. When hearing the debates about imperialism that roil campus life on both sides of the Atlantic, I think of the Indian government imprisoning civil rights activists involved in the bicentenary celebration of the battle of Bhima Koregaon, during which low castes fought alongside the British against a high caste dynasty. The violence at this commemoration of imperialism in 2018 led to the arrest of activists, including a disabled academic and a Jesuit priest in his eighties. Campus politics in the West simply cannot grasp the complex reality of empire in such events.

What remains of Said's work apart from his success in turning orientalism into an insult? He was among the American literary critics responsible for making their field into a pacesetting one across the humanities and social sciences. Dependent on translating and introducing continental European scholarship to the US, that moment has now ended, with *Orientalism* stranded on reading lists by the receding wave of literary criticism that reached its high-water mark in the 1990s. His other books are not read. The argument over race and empire has achieved a new lease of life since then. Its activists can learn from Said's career how their progressive claims may be turned into reactionary ones in the end.

ANWAR'S HUMANE ECONOMICS

Mohamed Aslam Haneef

The economic policies of Anwar Ibrahim, the charismatic and rather controversial Malaysian politician, have been repeatedly scrutinised. Anwar's political career spans six decades: from his days as the president of the Muslim Youth Movement of Malaysia (ABIM) (1974–1982), to him joining the ruling United Malays National Organisation (UMNO), during which he occupied a number of portfolios becoming the minister of finance (1991–1998), and deputy prime minister (1993–1998), to his dispute with the then prime minister, Mahathir Mohammad, and subsequent political imprisonment during which he became the leader of *Reformasi*, the reform movement, and the return as opposition leader (2008–2015). So, there is a lot of ground to cover; and trying to understand Anwar's worldview, especially in relation to economics, over this span of time is not an easy task. Khoo Boo Teik's *The Making of Anwar Ibrahim's 'Humane Economy'* is a welcome addition to the discussion, as an analysis of Malaysian political economy and as a contribution to the discussion on 'Islam and economics' seen through the ideas and writings of Anwar. Khoo covers the ground ably.

> Khoo Boo Teik, *The Making of Anwar Ibrahim's 'Humane Economy'*, ISEAS Yusof Ishak Institute, Singapore, 2020 (*Trends in Southeast Asia* No. 18)

He seeks to 'reconstruct Anwar's worldview...and to offer a critical understanding of how he arrived at his ideas of the humane economy' and its implications for Malaysia. Khoo relies on keynote addresses, budget speeches and political party documents. Given that these documents are those of a politician who had various positions and leadership roles in multi-ethnic Malaysia, the findings can often be very complex and seemingly contradictory.

After a very brief introduction to his background, much of the monograph focuses on Anwar's economic views. Khoo, like many other political observers, finds Anwar somewhat an *enigma*. Is he the 'firebrand/radical' Islamist of the 1970s and early 1980s for whom 'economics did not seem to matter?' Or is he the 'economic reformist' — the pro-market reformist he was during the 1990s (as the minister of finance) or is he more the people's reformist he took on from the 2000s to date when he led, and still leads, the opposition coalition Pakatan Rakyat, now Pakatan Harapan?

Khoo is right when he observes that 'there was economics in the young Anwar's Islam and conversely, Islam in the mature man's economics'. But, says Khoo, there is also the period of 'moral ambivalences' in the economic sphere that must have occupied Anwar during the early to mid-1990s 'when growth, prosperity and ambitions were dogged by rent-seeking, corruption and institutional degradation'. This is actually a very interesting period and may require more detailed study. During the early *Reformasi* lectures given by Anwar from 2 September 1998 until he was arrested on 20 September 1998, he did try to present some thoughts on how these seemingly contradictory features were actually tied up to the overall system of patronage politics of the UMNO led government. He tried, but obviously failed to clean the 'shit-tank from within' — a description Khoo quotes from Anwar, but I have also heard the same phrase from the late Tuan Guru Nik Abdul Aziz Nik Mat, *Murshidul Am*, or spiritual leader, of the Malaysian Islamic Party (PAS) who was a strong supporter of working with the opposition Pakatan Rakyat with its reformist agenda. After the death of Nik Aziz, PAS abandoned the reform agenda, adopted a conservative Malay-Islam stand, and joined the 'shit-tank from within'.

The central ideas of Anwar during his phase as ABIM president, and later Malaysian Youth Council president, centred around the pains of 'decolonisation'. Rather than genuine freedom and independence, the neo-colonialists (the ruling elite) were in charge; national development plans, with wonderful objectives were abused to enrich a few at the expense of the many; along with modernisation came the capitalist system and, in the process, exploitation of labour. Khoo quotes Anwar saying 'despite efforts in rural development, oppression and exploitation of farmers by landlords, small businessmen and capitalists in the villages remain'. Khoo refers to this phase of Anwar as the 'angry young man'. But the 'angry young man' had a great deal to be angry about. He was sceptical about the Third World's 'addiction to growth'. He has issue with GDP (particularly from an Islamic ethics approach) and ill conceived definitions of 'growth', 'poverty', and 'wealth'. He had warned of an addiction to unbridled growth, or growth for the sake of growth, without consideration of sustainability or who might be left behind. He is an avid reader. He often quoted the reports of the Club of Rome and *Asian Drama* of Gunnar Myrdal (1968). A favourite example was Adam Smith's *Theory of Moral Sentiments* as a base from which to understand his *Wealth of Nations*. He has a passion for equality and insisted that there was need for a marriage of ethics and economics. He saw that growth was a double edged sword: Malaysia needed growth, but Anwar had the foresight to say, the way we are growing looks good now, but will not look so good in a decade or two.

The young Anwar also criticised attempts to give Islamic justification to development plans, 'to affix the label of Islam to a system that still permits usury and alcohol, exploitation and gambling is an insult to Islam'. Elsewhere, he stated mainstream Western theories of growth and development excluded a moral vision of man from their premises 'only to bring crass materialism, loss of spirituality, decline of morality, and degeneration of character'. However, Khoo sees Anwar's pronouncements, Anwar in his 1980 ABIM Muktamar speech, as one that 'seems to lack a solid Islamic theoretical base'. But it was a period when contemporary Islamic economics was only beginning to make its introductory presence; no detailed theoretical arguments were available even to Islamic economic scholars. However, we can see Anwar's polemics as an action-oriented agenda ideal for a youth movement, something that has carried on with ABIM until today.

Speeches are not meant to lay theoretical foundations of alternative economics. But the term humane economy (that appeared in Anwar's writings in the mid-1990s) does pose a theoretical challenge. What is the humane economy based on? Is it Humane, Humanistic or Humanist economics? All three varieties would then get bogged down with the social, economic, intellectual and political experience of western Europe since the Enlightenment. It would be interesting to see if the use of the Malay phrase *Ekonomi Manusiawi* would be a better phrase to use as it could be understood as a Malay/Malaysian construct. The same challenge also appears in Anwar's call for the creation of *Masyarakat Madani* – Civil Society. One must also keep in mind that, as an avid reader, Anwar's outlook was influenced not only by Islamic scholars, but also from alternative, and sometimes radical scholars, based in the West who were also critical of the liberal market economics of capitalism. The overall emphasis on ethics and morality, good governance, accountability, and free from all forms of exploitation and abuse, with the ultimate aim to establish justice, was very clear in Anwar's ABIM phase.

If the ABIM Phase depicted Anwar as the young angry reformist, his move into UMNO in 1982, not only surprised many, but also required him to 'materialise' his ideas and thoughts into practice. This, according to Khoo, had to wait until he became minister of finance in 1991 when the Malaysian economy was booming, an 'emerging tiger' of the World Bank. Not only were growth figures impressive, but absolute poverty rates also declined. This period also saw an overall reduction in relative inequality measured by the income Gini coefficient. However, as recent research has shown, wealth inequalities and absolute income inequalities saw an increase. Anwar's critique of western models made during his ABIM days were now being seriously reviewed due to the 'success' these pro-market policies may have brought to Malaysia since the late 1980s. As Khoo states it was a period of 'frenzied money making'. Large-scale public infrastructure projects, high levels of private investment, accelerated privatisation, bountiful credit, and rising speculation created opportunities, not least via networks of political patronage, to amass great corporate and individual fortunes. Anwar was caught in between 'the statist ambitions of Mahathir' and the 'Malay capitalist class project' of Mahathir's protégé, former finance minister and businessman, Daim Zainuddin, and could not turn back, even if he wanted to.

In that situation, economic development had to be balanced by 'religiosity and morality'. Striking this balance was the key to good governance. Anwar called for thriftiness and frugality and was critical of wastage in the name of Malay/Bumiputera policies. The plague of corruption was again brought to the forefront, but now, not from the young angry Anwar, but from the then current minister of finance, deputy prime minister and designated prime minister-to-be. The Islamic ideal of establishing 'justice and benevolence' in society was seen as the government's responsibility. There was a call to raise human dignity and to construct a '*masyarakat madani*' or civil society. It should however be noted that Anwar's discourse of *madani* society was not the same as the secular humanistic civil society discourse globally. His was a society that was founded on religion and its universal values from the notion of *madani* sharing the same root word as *din* (religion) and *tamaddun* (civilisation). It was a pluralistic, multicultural notion based on ethics and civilisational values. Hence, Anwar organised numerous inter-faith dialogue conferences with other religious traditions – something relevant for the Malaysian context. This was given a tagline of the 'Humane Economy' in Anwar's *The Asian Renaissance* (1996). Should not, he asked, the 'development that we advance' be 'all-encompassing, infused with the pure value of human life'? 'We cannot build a factory, warehouse and infrastructure while bringing down human morals and dignity'!

This government phase of 'being in power' required 'results', not rhetoric. Hence, within the overall system, Anwar had to bring in the values, ethics and good governance that he talked about in his ABIM and Malaysian Youth Council days. This period could actually be seen as the formation of the main structural features of Anwar's humane economy. It is a 'centrist' position vis-à-vis Islamic economics literature; it is primarily a market economy that recognises both private and public property; acknowledges the importance of material motivation but sees a very important role for the state to provide a socio-economic safety net; strongly encouraging voluntary giving for 'higher purposes'; allows for a mixed market-plan system and promotes mutual consultation for decision-making. Having said that, there would certainly have been challenges in this period, referred so aptly by Khoo as 'periods of moral ambivalences', where both good and bad had to be faced - a test Khoo says Anwar receives an overall 'pass' on.

Some of his statements from prison (1998–2004) made reference to economics and the need for a just humane economy. But the reform agenda was crystallised only after his release and return to active politics between 2006–2015. It was an alternative vision for Malaysia, later to be termed 'A New Dawn for Malaysia'. Anwar was opposition leader in Parliament and the undisputed leader of a 'reform agenda opposition'. The

Malaysian Economic Agenda (MEA), a brief pamphlet of Anwar's party, PKR and later the Pakatan Rakyat manifesto for the 2008 general election, gave a clearer idea of what the Humane Economy 2.0 was all about.

The background of the MEA was the post-1998 financial and economic crisis that saw the decline of the Malaysian economy: growth rates never reached the figures of the pre-crisis years; investment – a very important ingredient for economic growth and development – was nowhere near the 1990s figures; and the government had to keep pumping funds in deficit budgets that increased public debt significantly. While there was acknowledgement of the importance of the knowledge economy, Malaysia did not perform as expected in innovation, research and development but remained an adopter of ideas and technology rarely innovating. The problems were our own making, Anwar declared: 'the government has implemented anti-market policies designed to benefit itself and its cronies, at the expense of ordinary Malaysians'.

The Humane Economy 2.0 continued with its centrist position of a market economy, well and fairly regulated, with good governance by a clean government. It declared, no longer could privatisation be used to enrich a small group of cronies, be it Mahathir's, or those of the succeeding prime ministers, Abdullah Badawi's or Najib Razak. Mega infrastructure projects and government profligacy had caused our future generation to be in unnecessary debt. Corruption was institutional and seemingly uncontrollable, reaching its pinnacle with the 1MDB saga. If aid was given to crony companies it was called incentives for investment, while aid to the poor were termed subsidies, depicting the elite, crass capitalist/materialist mind-set. Good governance was still central; the need to dismantle the ineffective monopolies in various sectors was crucial; a clear social agenda was required; quality public education and health care to the poor and masses was urgent regardless of race. The corrupted New Economic Policy needed to be totally re-written to become an effective affirmative action policy for all Malaysians. It was not possible to continue to use the Malay agenda to enrich a few in the elite corridors of wealth and power. Anwar has a high regard for the late Malaysian sociologist Syed Hussein Alatas's work T*he Problem of Corruption* (1986), where he describes how corruption had become engrained, even normalised, into Asian societies and cultures. He argued that corruption in Malaysia had become cultural, not just an instrument of greed, but it was necessary to succeed in Mahathir-Badawi-Najib's Malaysia.

The shift away from a purely ethnic/race based affirmative action to one that was also more needs based was an important central feature of the Humane Economy. While this needs-based agenda managed to capture the imagination of Malaysians from all ethnic backgrounds, it also led to a new counter force. After the 2008 election, that saw the ruling coalition led by UMNO lose its two-thirds majority in Parliament – and the Chinese Democratic Action Party (DAP) becoming the biggest opposition party in Parliament – there developed a new conservative 'survival of the Malays' sentiment not only from within UMNO but amongst the Malays as a whole, supported by a strong NGO presence. Even PAS, who had committed to a Malaysian reform agenda under the late Nik Aziz, joined this call for the 'survival' of the Malay–Muslim government of Malaysia.

In the last section of the monograph, Khoo attempts to make sense of Anwar's Humane Economy discourse over the last four decades. One aspect is seen as a 'personal' evolution due to his rise, fall, and then rise again in Malaysian social and political life. The ideals that influenced the young Anwar saw him gain the attention of the youth in Malaysia, to a certain extent cutting across ethnic groups although mainly through the ABIM platform. In today's Islamophobic environment, it is very common to see stereotypes being perpetuated by observers and even scholars. However, if one analyses Anwar's speeches during his tenure as ABIM president – not only the Annual General Meeting (AGM) keynote addresses – one would be able to better appreciate how he has always tried to maintain the contextual realities of heterogeneous Malaysia in his views on Islam and especially his ideas on the Humane economy. There is a tendency nowadays to lump together all Islamic organisations and label all and sundry as 'Islamists' as being anti 'plural, democratic and progressive'. However, Anwar has always argued, as can be seen from his speeches, that Islam and democracy are not incompatible, Islam does not need to undergo an 'Enlightenment'; what is needed is to actually understand the Islamic heritage in its entirety and one would see a democratic strand in Islam.

His time within the government needs much more analyses. On the one hand, he rose in the ranks over the sixteen years that he was with the UMNO-BN government. He grappled with the task of having to materialise his views on Islam and the humane economy in a system that was entrenched in a race-based affirmative action that was already being abused. He was the deputy president of the most powerful race-based political party in the country, a party whose leaders – and members to a certain extent – directly benefitted materially from the race-based institutionalised system. In the course of his sixteen years with the government, keeping to your ideals was well-nigh impossible. As the Malay phrase goes, '*mencuci tong tahi dari dalam*', you can't wash the sewer tank from inside. Trying to initiate and undertake reforms from within in what was essentially a 'one party state' proved futile. Nevertheless, this also led to an unintended consequence of developing the buds of a strong opposition.

The Humane Economy 2.0 during the *Reformasi* era provided a new vision for Malaysia. Anwar's assertion that poverty is ethnically blind, and all poor, whether Malay, Chinese or Indian need the support of the state resonated with the young. His call for a move away from a narrow ethnic discourse to an inclusive, pluralistic one has generally been accepted by the majority of Malaysians, especially the younger generations who do not have historical baggage on their shoulders. This generation, by and large, is more Malaysian than Malay, Chinese or Indian. The reform agenda, including the humane economy programme, was finally able to bring down the old UMNO-BN regime in the historic 2018 General Election.

Politics being what it is, things did not work out for Anwar after the 2018 General Election. Betrayals, coups and Malay/Bumiputera alliance between UMNO, PAS and BERSATU, the party formed by Mahathir and now led by Muhyiddin Yassin, managed to topple the democratically elected government. Ironically, this Muhyiddin government lost its support after just eighteen months and saw a relatively lesser known UMNO leader, Ismail Sabri Yaacob, become Malaysia's ninth prime minister on 29 August 2021 after attaining 114 votes out of the 220 MPs What is clear is that a reformist-inclusive agenda must overcome a conservative-exclusive mindset. The COVID-19 pandemic and its impact on Malaysia and Malaysian society has opened our eyes to the stark contradictions in the existing system. The pandemic has made us realise that we cannot allow things to go back to the 'business as usual' mode despite some older rigid-conservatives trying to resist change. If nothing else, the ideas found in the humane economy (and its related areas) can serve as a bridge between the Merdeka (Independence) and Millennial generations. Ultimately, the reformist inclusive agenda must become a people's agenda, a genuine Malaysian agenda.

The Humane Economy may have been Anwar's contribution to Malaysian political economy over the last decades. But it is up to the future generation of Malaysians to see how ethics, moral imperatives and religion can guide economic decision-making in a multicultural and pluralistic Malaysia.

SINGER, SONGWRITER, SUFI

Medina Tenour Whiteman

For many people, folk rock is a genre unto itself, patronised by gnomish white men with mutton chop sideburns nursing tankards of ale, rollie cigarettes, and ambitions to warlockhood, typically found in grimy pubs themed around shamrocks or Stonehenge. Richard Thompson's memoir, *Beeswing,* rather upends that stereotype. A founding member of the acclaimed folk band Fairport Convention, which pioneered the fusion of English folk music with the nascent rock movement of the period, Thompson describes how the band was surprisingly open to a range of influences.

'Surprising' is a word that suits Thompson's music quite well, from the changes in tempo within a single song (often in 5/4 or waltz, which already throw the listener out of the snoozy, predictable binary of 4/4) to unexpected changes from major to minor and back again, 'Oriental'-inspired guitar riffs, or startling – even shocking – lyrics borrowed from the epic ballads of pre-industrial British folk culture.

Thompson is recognised as one of the UK's greatest songwriters, so it's no wonder that the voice we read in his memoir is so fluid and engaging. Songwriting can be seen as acoustically dimensionalised poetry, but traditionally it was also the medium for genealogies, teaching stories, and myth.

Richard Thompson, *Beeswing: Fairport, Folk Rock, and Finding My Voice 1967-75*, Faber, London, 2021

For readers who aren't well-versed in the 1960s–70s British folk-rock scene, some aspects of *Beeswing* might (ironically) fall on deaf ears, being more directed at those dyed-in-the-wool music nerds who want to know which drummer or bassist played on which record, when Thompson switched to a Fender Strat, or what the Zep were like in real life. But even then, there are so many strikingly human, funny, and sometimes tragic anecdotes that the narrative rarely mentions. From descending onto a stage on a rope dressed as a human fly (and not remembering any of it), to the car accident that claimed the life of their drummer, Martin Lamble (as well as Thompson's then girlfriend), the memoir is told through a lens of self-deprecating awareness, of a man who is piecing together the puzzle of his life and offering it candidly to the reader.

The image on the cover is expressive of the person that is revealed in the narrative: a reticent, sensitive, even troubled man, always ready to close his eyes and slip away into a soaring improvisation – the ultimate meditation for a musician, a moment of being fully, fearlessly present. And his lyrics, while often cryptic, are deeply poetic; he says they usually come to him quite spontaneously, the words not necessarily making sense to him at the time. The title of the book is the name of a song that speaks volumes of his songwriting – wistful, raw, and melodious, embracing the horror and beauty and transience of life in this world.

Listening to the songs that the author references gives reading this book a multi-sensory, almost palimpsestic quality. The names he mentions, from the better-known Joan Baez and Nick Drake to Bert Jansch, Vashti Bunyan, or Davey Graham, will enrich anyone's Spotify playlist. While reading *Beeswing*, I rediscovered albums and artists that I'd forgotten about, bringing a rush of familiarity and emotion.

In my teens, as it dawned on me that I could survive the awkwardness of high school on the cachet of musicianhood, I remember being deeply affected by the understated emotion of English folk musicians like John Martyn and Sandy Denny. All make appearances in *Beeswing*. Denny, one of the UK's greatest singer-songwriters, was a vocalist for Fairport Convention. She was another of the tragic characters of the Fairport story; having just sent her husband and young baby off to Australia for a trip, she fell down the stairs drunk and died, at the age of twenty-eight.

As a young musician, Thompson occasionally rubbed shoulders with big names, but generally Fairport Convention – which he describes as a 'happy', 'friendly band' – preferred the less pretentious underground folk rock scene. This was a Britain in the grip of an economic crisis, of freezing, damp houses with useless storage heaters, wild hair (probably the primitive shampoo and feeble boilers had something to do with it), and rampant alcoholism as people 'drank themselves a sweater'. The incipient British folk-rock scene represented a break from the depressing conventionalism of their parents' generation. But instead of going out on a reactionary, psychedelic limb as many bands of the time were doing, Fairport Convention were increasingly interested in reviving traditional songs of the British Isles, tunes and poems that would have been sung to someone's great-grandparents in the cradle. So the band would haunt archives and record libraries, sleuthing out the 'original' folk music of the land, in as much a historical pursuit as a musical one – what would surely now be termed ethnomusicology. From tragic ballads to bawdy dance numbers, shanties, reels, and more, this was true 'folk', in the sense of a human culture carried forward by word of mouth, by people rather than institutions, and seeming to carry a secret code that connected them to the land of their forebears.

However, they also wanted to keep the tradition lively and inventive, so they would mix and match folk tunes with traditional poems, and wrote their own songs that reached back into the old world of folk, but updated with electric guitar solos. Later still, they took their cues from the Beatles' new acid-infused style, playing recordings backwards or at different speeds, or looping tracks many times over, to mesmerising effect. They were also open to international influences, from South African jazz to Indian ragas. Thompson declares that, sometime in the early 1970s, he became 'an orientalist'. This was partly due to his eclectic reading, which often veered in esoteric directions – thanks to Watkins bookstore in Cecile Court, purveyor of esoterica to the rock artists of the era – and led him into Sufi writings. He is quick to point out that this was initially a fairly superficial, abstract thing, something to decorate his home with and read about on the weekends. It's a perspicacious assessment, recognising that at least part of his generation's attraction to Eastern religions was an exoticising curiosity, illustrating the 'white gaze' without using the term specifically.

However, there was something about the stories of Mullah Nasruddin and Sufi writers like Pir Vilayat Khan and Reshad Feild (an Englishman, old Etonian, and erstwhile member of the band The Springfields, wherein Dusty rose to fame) that struck him 'as Zen-like – cryptic as poetry is cryptic, hinting at something greater where words fail'. In 1972, Thompson came across a Sufi community living in Bristol Gardens, in West

London (in what was, in fact, a squat, though he is cautious in how he depicts this period, omitting many of the more hairy circumstances – and I'm not referring to the beards). His account of becoming Muslim is far from the least interesting part of his story for Muslim readers, though coming in at Chapter 13 it might try the patience of a few Muslims who buy the book to read specifically about this episode.

Here he met my father, Ian Abdal Latif Whiteman, and a number of other characters who were involved in the 60s–70s British rock scene, including the photographer, Peter Sanders. Attracted, like my father was, by the music, and the sincere devotion of people sitting together and singing, Thompson was soon taken by the Islamic prayer. 'This all seemed to me like coming home after a long journey,' he says, adding that this was what he had been looking for all his life: to completely surrender his ego. 'There was no conversion', he remarks, 'just affirmation that this was who I had always been.' He began to pray, regularly attended the gatherings of *dhikr* (remembrance of God), and performed hajj in 1972. He describes the 'breathtaking otherworldliness' of the Ka'aba at first sight, seeming to 'float and shimmer and change through the spectrum...I had the feeling that the Kaaba represented my own heart, and that the Haj was a journey to find that out, to travel two thousand miles only to meet my inner self.' Eventually he and his wife Linda – an exceptional singer with whom he recorded several albums – moved to a cottage in Suffolk, where they tried the bucolic life, keeping sheep. It seems a natural continuation of his trajectory, influenced by the neo-ruralist movement of the 1970s. Perhaps, after playing in a band since the age of seventeen, it was a welcome break for him. It certainly dovetails with the Islamic concept of the *fitra*, one that continues to inspire Muslims to seek out lifestyles that are in closer touch with nature.

The Qur'an never commands Muslims to go to great cities and marvel at the spectacular mosques built there – quite the opposite. The cupola we are exhorted to gaze up at is the night sky; here the wonderful engineering is the way birds are suspended in the air, or the mountains pegged firmly into the earth; and the marvellous sights are the rain, the seas, the fruiting plants. Having pondered the mysteries of existence ever since childhood, this is the kind of 'natural mystic' Islam that initially attracted Thompson. He began to think that perhaps 'it was not a mechanistic universe, as traditional Cartesian science would have it, but something far more subtle, complex, and even intelligent. It was impossible to step outside of the universe to understand its origins and purpose by direct observation, so I had to believe – either in science or in an intelligent creator.'

The biggest change in his lifestyle, though, was that he went from drinking heavily (a major feature of the folk music scene, viz. our gnomish folkie above) to going sober overnight – with no desire to drink. His realisation that alcohol had been his way of filling a spiritual void should surprise no-one, but is instructive for anyone working with addiction – an issue that Muslims can't afford to sweep, for the sake of religious decency, under the carpet.

Speaking of carpets, considering that his early interest in 'Oriental' culture came through buying kilims on Portobello Market, it's fitting that Thompson should admit that, over time, he failed to 'weave together the thread of his Britishness and the thread of North Africa that he had adopted'. This painful honesty surely speaks to many third-culture Muslims who struggle to braid these fibres of our being, which sometimes get knotted, and whose untangling is often poorly supported.

But more than any other theme in the book, it's Thompson's comments about music and spirituality that speak straight to my heart. 'I thought our songs were quite open to a spiritual interpretation, and for me, music was like breathing – an everyday, beautiful, life-affirming activity – so why be puritanical about it? Why deny joy to others because you deny it to yourself?' Certainly it's hard to understand how birdsong or a cricket's stridulation constitutes a sin.

While Thompson's comments on this topic are brief, they raise a chorus of questions for me, beginning with the old chestnut of whether music is permissible in Islam. The consensus of scholars from the earliest times declared it to be unlawful, citing several hadiths in which the Prophet Muhammad forbade musical instruments and drinking, and professional singing girls in taverns.

There is not the space here to go into all the details of this discussion. However, Sharia law famously derives its prohibitions from the Qur'an, and it has been pointed out the holy book does not prohibit music specifically. In one commonly-cited narration, the Prophet put his fingers in his ears to block out the sound of a shepherd's flute; interestingly, he did not tell the shepherd to stop, or his Companion not to listen. (Perhaps the shepherd was pitchy.) In another narration, he asked why 'A'ishah did not send a singer to her friend's wedding as a gift.

As a singer and guitarist myself, reading Islamic prohibitions on music today is extremely difficult. Some glibly mention war and slave-girls, while condemning musical instruments and song in the harshest terms. They overwhelmingly associate music with lewd behaviour and intoxicants, declaring that listening to music takes people away from remembrance of God.

Yet I have found a certain kind of music, especially devotional song, to be infinitely better at returning my attention to Allah than activities that are generally assumed to be halal, or are indeed ubiquitous, like working at a computer for eight hours a day in a strip-lit office. I've seen devout Muslims ban their children from listening to music, but allow them to play violent video games until their eyelids are twitching. Something doesn't add up here.

There is a vast gulf between the music industry – largely driven by vanity and greed, and whose excesses are amply demonstrated in Thompson's memoir – and the natural expression of emotion through sound. Singing has an array of proven salutary effects, relieving stress and grief, stimulating immune response, and improving sleep and posture, among other things. Singing in a choir has been shown to synchronise the singers 'pulses, and to give a feeling of togetherness that is hard to find in our times. Music has been with us from our earliest times, voicing jubilation, and coaxing out the tears that everyday decorum obliges us to keep dry.

Sufis have long been known for incorporating devotional music into their practice. Thompson writes about gathering and reciting the Shaykh's Diwan – 'basically songs of spiritual guidance and ecstasy... The different modes, arrangements and sequences of notes were designed to have a measured effect on the human heart.' In Mughal India, the Sufi scholar and master Moinuddin Chishti actively encouraged his followers to play music, as it was a way of melding Islam into the cultural terrain and encouraging conversion. Similarly, Baba Farid 'Ganjshekar' famously challenged the position some deobandi muftis had taken on music and made them retract a fatwa against it. He declared: 'mystic music moves the hearts of listeners and breathes the fire of love into their hearts'.

However, this wasn't the experience that Thompson had of Sufism; the leader of their community came down exceptionally hard on the musicians in their midst. Admittedly, the music that he customarily played was more rocky than your usual *sema*, performed in beer-drenched venues where a whirling dervish would have been somewhat out of place. But his lyrics convey a sense of yearning that echoes the yearning for the Divine that Rumi and others expressed in their poetry – which is, of course, traditionally sung, to musical accompaniment.

The restrictive view of music in Thompson's Muslim milieu ultimately stifled a very important part of who Thompson was. Song was his outlet for joy and sorrow – perhaps even his personal means of worship. It raises an urgent question: can we take a broader view of the ways that people are naturally inclined to express their love of the Divine? Wouldn't this create a more inclusive environment for people who struggle with formal religion? Would there be less fallout?

Another important point is raised here: where are the limits of what a spiritual teacher should command for their followers? Is it right to assume that a *murid* (disciple) should be 'in the hands of their teacher like a corpse in the hands of the one washing them', to use the saying often quoted to bulwark this argument, in order to conquer their egoic desires? It is abuses of this exact argument that have caused many Muslims to have terrible views of Sufis, equating them with cults that rob individuals of their agency and give inordinate power to the one at the helm. Though I see many benefits in Sufi communities all round, I have also seen numerous instances of marriages that are hastily encouraged (which then fall apart, after kids have come along), decisions around work or travel imposed, even divorces ordained between couples that loved one another. This leads to a gradual wearing down of personal sovereignty, to the point where many feel they cannot trust their own intuition or judgement. Little wonder that Richard and Linda, among others, could not stand the pressure and left. The reader gets the sense that they were disillusioned with the pursuit of a wholesome Sufi ideal that began to seem impossible and, more to the point, inauthentic. Richard and Linda separated, and both embarked on solo music careers.

This is the point – 1975 – at which the chronicle ends, but the author continues to mull over what it all means. He doesn't attempt to put the world to rights, and looks back with kindness at the experiences he was given. There's a tone of humility which is gratifying given the famous names that are inevitably dropped.

An unusual addition to this book is an appendix of dreams that are referred to in the course of the narration. Keith Richards tells Thompson, 'you can't play the blues until you've lived in a rainforest', while Jesus sits opposite him on a Tube train and winks at him: 'to follow me…you have to do without.' It's a surreal and quite hilarious addition that makes the memoir all the more endearing, offering a glimpse into the full spectrum of Thompson's consciousness – which, the reader comes to realise, is perceptive, genuine, and trained on the beautiful and the real.

Perhaps Thompson's (literally) sobering experience of Islam helped him to polish this lens. Or perhaps it was always crystal clear.

SUSPICIOUS MUSLIMS

Saimma Dyer

I was standing in a small room in airport security at Heathrow, dutifully emptying my handbag, removing my scarf, jacket, cardigan, shoes. A young South-Asian man was doing the same across from me. The security staff looked bored, going through a checklist with only half an eye on the contents of my bag – travel sweets, hand wipes, lip balm – essential travel items. Suddenly a loud voice interrupted the muted hush of the room: an angry white woman was being herded in, furiously proclaiming in a strong American twang 'You can't do this to me! Do I look like a terrorist to you?! I won't stand for it – I'm going to report you...' The nonplussed security officer replied, 'Don't blame us, it's *your* government that's making us do this.' As she continued protesting, I looked across to the young South-Asian man and we rolled our eyes at each other, a silent acknowledgment of the white woman's privilege – to be so outraged at being singled out for inspection, and to speak that outrage out loud. We quietly shuffled along, our bored attendants waving us through as we quickly put our shoes back on, grabbed our belongings and re-joined the other travellers in the main gate area, going our separate ways. I felt eyes on me, folks who had seen me being taken into the 'extra' security check area, and I felt a flush rise in my cheeks as my husband came up to help take my belongings from my arms. His eyes were tight but we didn't say anything about what had happened. It wasn't the first time that I, a brown woman, had been separated from him, a white man, while at the airport. In fact, it has happened every time we have travelled to the USA. I expect it, almost as a part of the experience of visiting the Land of the Free.

Tawseef Khan, *The Muslim Problem: Why We're Wrong About Islam and Why It Matters*, Atlantic Books, 2021

These, and many more memories have come crashing to the forefront of my mind as I read Tawseef Khan's *The Muslim Problem: Why We're Wrong About Islam and Why It Matters*. It has been a difficult and illuminating read, uncomfortable in highlighting how much of my life experiences resonate with this work, and how I have numbed myself to much of it, primarily as a way to just cope with being a second-generation British-Pakistani woman navigating the world. Khan's own experiences of travelling-while-brown, working-while-brown, living-while-brown, will mirror many – *too many* – brown folks's experiences. And while his book focuses on living-while-*Muslim*, I want to acknowledge the collateral damage of Islamophobia on all bodies of colour, whether they are Muslim, Sikh, Hindu, athiest. As the Angry White Woman said at the airport, *do I look like a terrorist to you?!*

Khan effectively deconstructs five toxic 'myths' of Islam: Muslims don't integrate; Islam is violent; Muslim men are threatening; Islam hates women; and Islam is homophobic. Not only does he share deeply personal reflections from his own life and how these myths have damaged him, he also presents meticulously researched evidence of historical Islamophobia and racism in the Western context. More boldly, he addresses the distortions of the faith within the Muslim world that have contributed to these myths. While some Muslims will applaud Khan's elucidation of Islamophobia, some may not be so keen to look within our communities and at how certain behaviours feed into the toxicity. But again, Khan keenly explores why this is so difficult. As he states in his introduction, 'if the messaging coming from the media about you is negative, or one in which you don't exist at all, it causes untold damage to your self-esteem and how you move through the world.' If we are constantly protecting ourselves from 'outside' attack, we don't always have the tools – or energy – to look 'inside'.

I had written an article a few years ago about my Muslim experience of Christmas, and it had attracted a little negativity online with some Muslims protesting that I was a shameful anomaly, abandoning my faith in exchange for the thrill of an itchy Christmas jumper (how dare they, none of my Christmas jumpers are itchy). I was therefore gratified to read about Khan's family celebrations of Christmas in the chapter on integration. It was wonderful to read how they had embraced this religious observance in their own way, not only in the UK but also with family in Pakistan. And yet increasingly it feels, every year the myth of the 'Muslim problem' with Christmas seems to intensify, Islamophobes falsely claiming Christmas has been cancelled and the oddball fatwas pronouncing the haram-ness and halal-ness of even wishing anyone a Merry Christmas. Why has something that was an occasion for family to be together now become a battleground for the soul of British Muslims? Khan makes the connection about preserving identity and cultural community connections A lot of this hostility, he writes, 'is the voice of traumatised generations of migrants who are trying to hold on to cultural norms that are threatened by living in a society where they're completely minoritised and excluded.'

And whilst on one hand we are indeed being minoritised and excluded, accused of refusing to integrate into Western society, on the other, when we dare to share in the idea of Britishness, we are vilified. Khan shares the example of Nadiya Hussain, the winner of the 2015 *The Great British Bake Off*. Not only was her win a shock to non-Muslim British society, her BBC *Good Food* magazine column sharing Christmas dinner tips only fanned the flames of anti-Muslim hate that she was subjected to.

> Islamophobes can't decide what they want from us. First they claim that Muslims won't integrate... But when we do, Islamophobes complain that we're diluting and undoing the Western way of life... The problem wasn't [Nadiya's] integration. The problem was her existence; the audacity that somebody could feel they belonged, to such an extent that they took up space in our media.

Khan deftly highlights the media's culpability in promoting Islamophobia across the print and digital landscape. The various examples he draws upon very clearly show the bias for anyone who is genuinely interested in seeing how the picture of the stereotypical suppressed hijabi and threatening terrorist is indelibly imprinted on the Western mind.

The chapter un-picking the 'Islam is violent' myth succinctly lays out the political landscape of the modern world, the effect of colonialism, and the rise and impact of Wahhabism. Like everyone else of our generation, I remember 9/11 and 7/7 too clearly. Both occurred while I was working in London, and both affected the way people looked at me, especially my American bosses. I was very good at ignoring the glances, the change in atmosphere – and subject – when I entered a room. But it fed into an underlying rage that I carried with me. Anger at the sense that I was expected – demanded – to condemn the atrocities, anger at the judgement, and also anger at Islam, the religion I was born into but didn't understand and felt more and more alienated by. After 7/7, I particularly witnessed the effect of the 'Stop and Search' policy on the underground. One day as I was passing through Victoria station on my way home after work I saw a young man of South Asian origin being held by two officers as they questioned him and searched through his bag. His fear-stricken face stopped me in my tracks and I stood staring at the scene. Wide-eyed and unworldly, he looked just like my young brothers. Other commuters rushed by, side-eyeing him, and I felt their judgement as much as his. I didn't move until he was released, and only then realised that I was standing there glaring, hands in fists, face red, blood pounding in my ears, on the verge of tears. As I wondered what I could possibly do, they finished their interrogation and he quickly slipped into the crowd, a last glimpse of his face showing that he too looked on the verge of tears. And what could I have done except show my anger? What good would that have done? Surely only made the situation worse. As Khan says, 'Muslims are not allowed to be angry, let alone express that anger in the public arena.' As a brown male, that young man would have been even more at risk if he had dared to show anger or outrage at what he had to endure.

Western societies are deeply uncomfortable with Muslim anger. They don't see us as entitled to it. It destabilises their sense of control. And ultimately, because Western societies also fear the legitimacy of that anger, it's easier to portray it as dangerous and unhealthy.

Muslim men are especially seen as threatening. Khan explores the different facets of masculinity and the multiple hurdles that Muslim men must navigate between faith and society. His words left me wondering about my younger brothers and how different their experience of life has been compared to mine. There is so much that we don't talk about, that we *endure*, and I feel the weight of all that has been unsaid and unshared. After reading Khan's book it's a conversation that I hope to start with them.

Because Muslims are accused of being innately violent, violence against Muslims is taken less seriously. The result is that our suffering is rendered invisible.

This invisible suffering and fear seeps into all aspects of life, especially as women become prime targets. Khan's statistics on Islamophobic hate crimes against women was a part of the book I had to put down for a while. The pain is fresh and real, and belongs to all the Muslim women in my life. One occasion for it was the last UK general election, when the Conservatives won with a majority. The day after was Friday and I was on the phone with my mum when she asked me if it was safe for her to catch the bus into town so she could attend Jummah prayers. My throat tightened as I calmly said to her that I thought she should pray at home that day. I feared that racists would be emboldened by the Tory victory and the thought of my petite, hijab-clad mum travelling on the bus alone petrified me. Coming off the call, I wept tears of frustration and anger.

I am glad that Khan does not fall into the all-too-common rhetoric amongst Muslims that Islam gives women *so* many rights, and aren't we *lucky*, and the West is still catching up to what Muslim women have been granted. While he does in fact show how recent the West's gender equality laws are, he doesn't shy away from how Muslim women are mistreated in their own communities on the basis of faith. And Khan goes further to discuss how the issue of gender equality has been a problem since the time of the Prophet Muhammad who struggled to resolve the issue before his death. This is a rare example of a man discussing this issue so clearly and unequivocally. Along with highlighting the existence of sexist, dubious hadiths that supported the post-prophetic period of clawing back patriarchal control, Khan also connects the issue to wider patriarchy across all faiths and societies, highlighting how this has been, and continues to be, a global problem.

> Some Muslims pine for a return to Islam's foundations, believing that it will resolve the conflict of differing interpretations. But this is based on misguided nostalgia for an imagined Islamic society. They want a society free of all the peculiarities of human behaviour (such as doubt, disagreement, division) that not only exist now, but also existed in the time that they want us to return to. There is, truthfully, no 'reset' button. There are no easy answers.

The diversity of differing interpretations continues to be explored in the final chapter, which looks at LGBT rights. I'll be honest, I wanted easy answers in this area, I wanted to hear my forthright viewpoint echoed back at me: that there is no justification for LGBT discrimination in Islam. Khan gets there cautiously and rightly remains objective, showing the process of movement and flexibility in viewpoints across time and cultures, perhaps keenly aware of how contentious the topic is and how attitudes will shift only with sensitivity around the issue.

As a young woman I had struggled to accept the narrative that I had been taught that homosexuals were outside the fold of Islam and would go to hell. It led to a great deal of confusion and anger at God, and contributed to a time where I didn't consider myself a Muslim anymore. When I encountered a different Islam in my late-twenties, it came with a completely transformed understanding about the faith and a completely different relationship with God, who I now have discovered is loving, compassionate, and inclusive. This God created diversity in every form, including sexuality. When I came across the interpretation of the story of Lot and his angelic guests as being about violent abuse, it finally made sense. Some fractured part of me healed as I found no condemnation of expression of love in the scripture, a text that I was engaging with directly for the first time in my life.

Khan also shares this interpretation of Lot's story and advocates for more direct, personal relationship with the text and 'finding independent answers that align with the equalising spirit of Islam.' He also presents the wide breadth of sexual and gender diversity within Islamic history, starting with the time of the Prophet Muhammad:

> ...during the Prophet's lifetime there is no known instance where an LGBT person was prosecuted or punished simply for who they were. Instead, we know that the Prophet and his wives openly interacted with sexual minorities [who] worked within his household.

The impact of colonialism and Victorian sexual repression on the Islamic world is something that is still being acknowledged and Khan gives various examples where Muslim countries are starting to address discrimination against LGBT citizens. While I personally feel that Iran's support of transgender surgery may have more to do with limiting homosexuality than endorsing diversity, it is still an incredibly positive step of support for the trans community.

What was shocking to read about was what Khan describes as the rise of 'homonationalism' and the connection between LGBT communities and fascism. Khan's research is disturbing, seeing this phenomenon as another form of Islamophobia where LGBT Muslims are ignored and 'suppressed because Western concepts of homosexual identity are predominantly constructed around white gay men.'

Despite all the statistics and research showing the depth of Islamophobia and the struggle to embody an Islam of justice and compassion, Khan remains, at the core of his book, hopeful and optimistic. And this is what carried me through to the end. He clearly and simply lays out the issues and how we can engage with each aspect of our faith, remaining committed to the essence of Islam. He ends with a manifesto which includes his dad's words: 'If there is no mercy, no kindness, no fairness in your practice of Islam, then it is not Islam that you are practising.' Despite acknowledging that 'getting people to understand Islamophobia remains a challenge' Khan remains cautiously optimistic. He looks forward to 'a day when we are free to fail, a day when we are able to be human in the way so many others are permitted to be.' I too hope for that day.

ET CETERA

ON UNIVERSITY, CHANGE AND TRAVEL

Merryl Wyn Davies

From 1984 to 1987, Merryl Wyn Davies was a regular contributor to *Afkar: Inquiry,* the monthly 'international magazine of events and ideas'. The three columns reproduced here provide a glimpse into her style and thought.

Godless of Gower Street

According to the handouts, it was the abode of the 'godless of Gower Street'. Not a bad epithet for the institution founded and still presided over by the dressed skeleton and pickled head of Jeremy Bentham. University College, London, was a product of utilitarian intent whose neoclassical portals were to admit students to an education based on sound modern scientism and rational principles. It was the impact of these ideas on the first generation of students that earned them the title of 'godless' from a shocked society.

The neoclassical portals still remain but scientism and rationalism were merely taken for granted, not something to make a fuss about, question or argue with, by the time I got there.

My era at university was indeed a time when the thought that students could be anything other than 'godless' would have been a severe shock to the average person on the street. For these were the lacklustre years, the tail end of the student protest, anti-Vietnam marches and the still prevalent invitation to drop out into alternative lifestyles and let it all hang out. Or, you could, of course, try to get an education.

One emerged from in depth force feeding on raw facts, which was the pre-university hot house of British 'A' level exams, to the balmy fields of higher education where one was supposed to manipulate and think constructively with facts. In reality, one spent a lot of time being disabused about common place notions, which clearly constituted the wrong way of thinking, in order to acquire a right way of thinking. All in all, one merely substituted one method of blind adherence for another, new set of assumptions and their attendant facts. Critical objectivity was the name of the game.

At the time it felt very much like growing up, like being initiated into a special and rarefied world of the elite – whose creation has been, for centuries, the prime function of universities. There was so much to absorb, so much relish to be gained by grappling one's way into a superior mindset that one could very easily not find the time to stop and question. It is not that the system did not require one to ask questions, questions were definitely the order of the day. It was just that learning the proper range of questions that were appropriate for the bright eyed and up and coming student was the object of the education. What the education neglected to teach, or prompt one to examine, was why these were considered the only appropriate questions.

As a student, I was always vaguely ill at ease. I would master the arguments required, spew out the four essays a week and talk my head off at seminars and be rather disconcerted because it always seemed to me there was a point, a vital fact which I was missing, which would eventually cause me to be unmasked as ignorant and stupid. But it never happened. Nobody ever noticed that while I could make all the logically required elements fit together for public performance, in private I could never make them connect into any meaningful and purposive system. Somehow that did not seem to be the object of the university exercise. Indeed, ineptitude at examinations notwithstanding, I found myself considered to have promisingly passed through the educative process.

Since university turned out not to be the feast that satisfied, rather the fast-food snack that left one still hungry, the desire for knowledge survived my five years at Gower Street as a perplexing conundrum. The university education which I was privileged to undergo (higher education is the province of the minority which confers social advantages, so privileged is the word) was based on hidden agenda. Far from being a bright student, I think I must have been dense in the extreme because it was only years later that I began to fit the propositions thrust upon me into an order which revealed the premises upon which they were based. To be secular was one thing, materialism a problematic and hopefully avoidable problem, but both were demanded by a system which made human reason and its constructed means the only measure of all things. Or, more accurately, there was only human reason, which was knowledge, so one had to be secular and materialist because everything was moveable, going nowhere, though the movement itself supposed to be edifying. Once the penny had dropped, I became ready to be educated.

My stupidity arose from simple mindedness. I went up to university (the conventional phrase indicating a world of significance) with the naively fixed idea that knowledge was a moral tool, it was the means by which moral problems were honed, processed and rendered comprehensible so that moral action could be more clearly and appropriately apprehended and enacted. In other words, I thought knowledge had a normative quality. Being a student of the social sciences, it was always perplexing that the 'society' one studied had norms, but the science one constructed was objective, not normative, to avoid the heinous sin of value judgement.

What one was being taught was a method of abstracting reality, according to the supreme 'gods' of scientism and rationalism, a kind of intellectual sand castle building whose premises were precisely designed to remove norms and values from the academic procedure. Why this was done and how it affected the sphere of one's chosen subject of education was not the subject of education to teach or discuss. It was The Law.

So, what was learned was not the knowledge of reality, but how to construct an artificial reality which approximated to a predetermined set of intellectual rules, where these rules, and only these rules, had validity. I, like many others, am here to testify that one can come through such an indoctrination, even as a secularist, still wanting a morally appropriate application of knowledge. I began to be ready to be educated when I realised the university-based system I had imbibed could never, according to its rules, generate such an end.

Knowledge which detaches itself from values, which are relegated into the concern of some other not very prestigious department, which uses specific but undisclosed values to make objectivity, can perhaps help one distinguish wood from trees. It can never assist in the process of finding a way through the woods, without having to chop down all the trees. As one of the godless of Gower Street what I acquired by way of university education was a precise confusion which was quite irresolvable.

When I began to be ready to be educated what I looked forward to was the creation of a system of university education which critically evaluated information in relation to conceptual values, an education which cherished normativeness not moral neutrality. An open agenda, constantly referred to by open minds, which generated the power to discriminate between good and bad, useful and abusive information, to comprehend more fully the meaning of values, and integrate the two procedures to elucidate appropriate constructive pragmatism. Such an education would never confuse information and methodology for knowledge. It would, of course, require putting God back in Gower Street, or finding somewhere where His Presence was the basis of education.

(April 1986)

Enduring Values

Rummage in any bookshop, leaf through any magazine or journal and the one thing you cannot avoid is change. It is everywhere. The catch phrase of the age is change. Change is being busily studied everywhere, by everyone. Ernest opinions are offered on the significance of change. There is great debate about the need for change. Considered judgements and emotional outbursts all dwell upon the effects of change. Today, the one constant is change.

I had an early traumatic experience with change. My first assignment as a journalist, newly employed by the local weekly newspaper, was to interview a local veteran on the occasion of his eightieth birthday. Swelled with pride at my new status, notebook and pen confidently brandished, entertaining notions of soon growing up to be Woodward and Bernstein, and discovering my first scoop, I ventured forth. I announced myself to the venerable resident and swept on to explain that I wanted to know all about the changes he had witnessed in the local scene. Well, what else could you ask a person who had obviously seen a thing or two in his lifetime? When

I paused excitedly, expecting to be swept along by his fascinating reminiscences of a world entirely altered, the silence was filled by disgruntled growls, on the theme of the nonsense I was talking, and the front door was firmly shut in my face.

Maybe the old man did not approve of journalists. But as I struggled to recover from the first lesson in the school of hard knocks, an even worse thought flashed across my mind: perhaps he couldn't remember anything that has changed. At eighty years of age all the gentleman could notice was that he had grown older – did that amount to anything different? In his youth, the town had waning heavy industry and long dole queues. Now there were factories making ladies stockings and washing machines and threats of redundancy. Absentee owners had merely become multinational corporations, the system rumbled on. True there was now a welfare state to replace the vicarious charity of his younger days – but did the rich still not prosper and the rest make the best of things somewhere further down the order? True they have knocked down half of the town and rebuilt new concrete boxes for people to live in. But it still took four walls and a roof to make a house and the quality thereof decided whether it was a comfortable home. Which, in the case of local publicly financed building, they seldom were.

It is all very well to talk of the shock of the new. But after eighty years perhaps people learn to take the shock in their stride. When one has encountered eighty years' worth of people, maybe one finds them much of a muchness. Perhaps what old people notice is not the change but the way the essentials stay the same. Maybe, under the guise of new-fangled styles, manners and means, what they detect is the old patterns grinding on regardless. A world of all change for no change in which they just get rustier in the joints. A world in which they move more slowly, they have time to see through the frantic pace of activity and recognise that it's not change at all.

Of course, with the door firmly closed in my face and my ego badly dented, I never had a chance to explore these ideas. I merely covered my embarrassment by making a good joke of it when I got back to the office. Which is why the experience has lingered, and made me rather wary of glib assertions about change. After all, change is a pretty relative term. It presumes, does it not, a certain stability in which alteration can be measured. Once in the realms of the relative, is it not just as valid to ask about continuity, things which do not alter, as to chase endlessly after the matters which mark today as different from yesterday.

And yet there is no escape from change, the stock in trade of the twentieth century. This is the age in which to do things differently is considered a positive good in itself - no matter what one does. I just wonder whether a great deal of what passes for change is rather more in the mind of the beholder than an order of the universe.

It cannot be doubted that the twentieth century has some major achievements to its credit when it comes to making a difference. Never before has mankind been able to contemplate evacuating this planet and setting off to new quadrants of the galaxy as a possibility rather than a fantasy. But then never before has the escape route seemed such a necessary insurance policy. Never before has mankind been certain that it could physically destroy themselves, the earth and all that lives upon it. When it comes to change you have to acknowledge that the twentieth century has really made a difference.

As I had cause to learn, the secret of making sense of change is all in the questions one asks. Which brings us face to face with a curious fact. If change is relative, if you mark off today by having some sense of what went on yesterday, the quality of one's insight is decided by the measuring scale employed. When we get down to the onerous task of cleaning up the mess made by the twentieth century, we merely get back to the scale of values which were old when Adam was a tiny boy. A scale of values which have a pretty standard track record at all points in between then and now. The values endure and mankind has a pretty dubious record in the observance department.

Which only goes to prove that when it comes to change, whatever the scale, whatever the scope, whatever the difference, change is not only relative, it is related to everything that went before. All change is not illusion, there is little that is illusory about nuclear power, expect its supposed benefits. It's just that no change takes us away from the same essential questions with which the world began. When every change can be translated into their language, what, may I ask, has changed at all?

(November 1986)

There and Back

T S Eliot once advised travellers to fare forward because they were not the person who had left home, nor the one who would arrive at any destination. I suspect T S had spent a good deal of time on long haul flights from one part of the world to another.

Jet lag is a necessary accompaniment to long distance, high speed, travel. It is thought to be the condition where one's body clock lives on somebody else's time, in another place, which hardly conveys the experience of being at five different parts of the space-time continuum, with several different things to do, all at the same time. It's the sense of urgency and distraction, the surprise at the slow wittedness of everyone else, and out-of-body sensation of super awareness that makes jetlag an experience to reckon with.

My first encounter with the phenomenon was my first return trip from the USA. I had just travelled by bus, nonstop, from coast to coast, across America. I then boarded the plane, at night for the requisite number of hours, and failed to fall asleep. (It must have something to do with the muffled mumbling of the passengers, lost in the engine noise, like having a demented swarm of locusts lost in your head, and the distinctively synthetic air you have to breathe, but I have never learned how to sleep on aeroplanes, no matter how long a journey, how boring the book, film or conversation.) An easy prey for my first jetlag.

So, at London airport there was only the ritual of passport control, long queue (shuffle, shuffle), search for the trolly - there were none - have proper security made of documents and pass on to collect baggage. Personal pack animal mode function on auto pilot, so I manhandle cases, shoulder bag, carrier bag and handbag about myself.

Then a strange thing happens. In front of me is a green doorway leading through customs, into the world beyond. The gateway is clearly visible but going in two directions while my legs seem to envisage at least a three-way option and are capable of walking in four separate directions at one go. My brain, lurking somewhere on the western prairies drinking in all the open space, seems not to observe any discrepancy.

It may have been just a moment, it could have been a few hours, who knows, when I became aware of my surroundings, where I was standing is no longer where I was standing. The transition from here to there is beyond memory or movement, lost in space warp, rather like being beamed into a space ship in those science fiction movies. I find myself accosted by a tall bearded, bespectacled person, anxious to relive me of my multiple encumbrances. As we float along impersonal, anywhere corridors, I try to work out who this person could be, while feeling rather self-satisfied at having accomplished rule one of the international jetnaut handbook: always find someone else to carry the luggage. As we approach the rail terminal, by which time my antennae have turned in to some curiously accented transmissions coming from the bearded person, it occurs to me, this is my brother. I greet him warmly and take no notice of his offhand response. Brothers with frown and short tempers are par for the course.

On the train to my brother's home, I engage in sprightly conversation, relating witty anecdotes of my adventures across the Atlantic. My brother's mood deepens to familiar moroseness. At his home my niece scampers about. A remarkable child who can don exotic presents, rummage in suitcases, and flit from place to place by instant transmigration. Obviously, she is destined to be a traveller herself.

Three days later, somewhat recovered from my journey, my brother expressed relief that the zombie, my good self, had at last been released from the curse of the body snatchers. He explained that holding conversation with a person who speaks like a stuck record at minimum revolution speed, who falls asleep, or retires to another dimension, only to make intermittent earthfall from orbit around Alfa Centori sometime later, and demand, bad temperedly, answers to topics everyone else had dropped an hour before, had proved rather tiresome. Keeping track of the thought sequence of this itinerant nonbeing who conversed in fluent Outer Swahilian-Cantonese, only to become comatose as the answers were supplied had been both a strain and a social liability. Furthermore, he added with venom, undemonstrative brothers frankly dislike being recognised, hailed and embraced as long-lost relatives, at high volume, in public, with monotonous regularity, every ten minutes. Funny, but I was sure I had been lucid, and it was everyone else who was acting strangely.

So that is how I got to know all about jetlag. There are many other helpful hints I could pass on about modern travel, like the great secret is to look as if you know where you are going. Any uncertainty only causes people speaking loud and fast in foreign languages to offer unintelligible advice for hour on end. Or, I could warn you that the entire world is sub artic, at least in those places where they have discovered air-conditioning, so always were at least one thermal vest. Or, I could tell you that when you have arrived anywhere you have at least another hour before you need to reach for your jacket and contemplate standing up, so conserve your energy and enjoy how ridiculous everyone else looks lining the gangway, with nowhere to go. Or, I could tell you my greatest discovery - when in doubt, always follow the car in front, it is usually going towards your destination, or at least somewhere you will recognise and be pleased to have reached.

But these are all minor technicalities. The real experience of modern travel is to be outside-in of Einstein's theory of relativity in four dimensions at once. So, it is no wonder you are not the person who left home, or who arrived wherever it is. It's the re-assemblage of the transmigrated, transmogrified person that adds light years to the time of travel. Just as with your luggage you can only hope they put all the essentials bits on the same plane, heading for the same destination and that you will catch up with yourself the next time round. So fare forward travellers. With luck, maybe you did!

(August 1987)

EIGHT STOLEN AND FABRICATED BIOGRAPHIES

C Scott Jordan

In his 2004 biography, *Alexander Hamilton*, Ron Chernow wrote that Eliza Schuyler Hamilton burned the love letters she wrote to her husband, but claimed that no one knew why. In his 2015 stage adaptation of Chernow's biography, *Hamilton,* Lin Manuel Miranda wrote the song 'Burn' which inferred that Eliza had burnt her letters in a fit of rage about learning of her husband's affair with another woman. Eliza declared she was erasing herself from the narrative, stating the public had no right to know the contents of her heart or her bed. Luckily for Alexander, following his death at the hands of political rival Aaron Burr's bullet, Eliza would defend her fallen husband's legacy until the end of her days, furiously working to preserve his writings and make sure his story stayed alive and could be known today. The whole of Miranda's musical biography centres around a cornucopia of themes, but one stands out: that existential threat of legacy and the immortality found in living a life worthy of being told one day as a story.

Not all can be so lucky as Mr Alexander Hamilton. Unfortunately, the erasure from history of many individuals was quite common in the ages before the internet where seemingly everyone has a place to make their mark and set the record straight. Today the hottest non-fiction sellers often follow the untold lives of those almost lost to history either because society could not fathom certain classifications of humans having the capacity for world changing thought (women, minority populations, or the less than rich and noble). A flurry of films have been adapted from these books and the tales, until recently, left untold. *Hidden Figures*, the 2016 film based on a book of the same name written by Margot Lee Shetterly, follows three African American mathematicians who worked at NASA in the US and played a pivotal role in the space race of the 1960s while confronting the double whammy of racism and sexism. This served as a watershed for a whole host of stories of female scientists (of all ethnic varieties!) on whose backs modern America was constructed, yet their names do not ring out of the heroic tomes of history. In fact, the stereotypical image of a white, balding man in a lab coat wearing horn-rimmed glasses is almost directly contradictory to the image of those who did the maths and science that begot the modern world.

The following list looks at some of the lesser-known instances of those erased from history, covered up, and whose story was stolen by others.

1. Rosalind Franklin

Tragically nicknamed the 'wronged' or 'forgotten heroine' and the 'dark lady of DNA', Rosalind Franklin was a British chemist and X-ray crystallographer whose work was instrumental in our present understanding of the molecular structure of coal, graphite, DNA, RNA, and numerous viruses, including Polio and her last structure, the tobacco mosaic virus. In 1951, Franklin worked at King's College in London with Maurice Wilkins set on determining the structure of DNA, which had triggered a sort of intellectual race. Franklin's X-ray analysis not only showed a helical shape, but led her to determine that DNA was actually a double helix. Interdepartmental office politics created animosity and rivalry between Franklin's colleagues. Max Perutz, without the permission of Franklin, had shared one of her X-ray photos with one Francis Crick at Cambridge who partnered with the American James Watson and also concluded the same double helix structure as Franklin's analysis had demonstrated. While a collaboration was maintained between Watson, Crick, Wilkins, and Franklin. It would be Watson and Crick whose names would go on the first paper, published in three parts in *Nature* in 1953, with the acknowledged 'stimulated by' credit given to Wilkins and Franklin. Dying in 1958, at the age of 37, from ovarian cancer, Franklin would be left out of the nomination that would win the famed 1962 Nobel Prize Watson, Crick, and Wilkins as the Nobel committee generally does not award prises posthumously. Unlike other members of this list, the three Nobel laureates, particularly Francis Crick have maintained Franklin's due credit for the pivotal discovery. Franklin has become a cult feminine icon whose justice and name are continuously fought for to this day.

2. Bill Finger

Until the last decade, the man who had created one of the most iconic comic book characters of all time had almost been entirely erased from history. Bill Finger was born in Colorado, USA, in 1914 and moved with his immigrant family to the Bronx just in time for the Great Depression. Finger went to high school at DeWitt Clinton High School where he met up with a man named Bob Kane. Finger worked as a part-time shoe salesman while writing comic strips for Kane's fledgling studio. In 1938, Action Comics No. 1 hit racks nationwide introducing the world to Superman and the great superhero comic race was on. In collaboration Kane and Finger set out on the idea of constructing 'The Bat-Man' which led to a rough rendering by Kane that would resemble the 1980s tabloid idol Bat Boy. Finger suggested a cowl and cape and the alter-ego name 'Bruce Wayne'. Finger also determined that Batman should be a detective with a knack for the hard sciences. While Finger worked out the details, Bob Kane presented the Bat-Man to a comic producer and made a lucrative deal on the spot – without Bill Finger. Finger went on to write many of the first scripts for Batman which premiered in 1939. Finger also invented his arch nemesis the Joker. For a while Kane and Finger had a good relationship, but after Finger's death Kane would rewrite the history taking most of the credit himself. Kane made another deal to sell the rights for Batman to National Comics (which would become DC Comics in the late 1970s) without Finger, gaining a hefty royalties deal and the mandatory byline which was to be seen on all Batman materials thereafter: 'Batman created by Bob Kane'. Eventually, Finger would go on to work for DC Comics after leaving Kane's studio where he created and co-created numerous iconic characters including the Riddler and the Green Lantern. He died from a heart attack in 1974 and his son Fred and Granddaughter Athena would eventually see his name justly given the creator's credit for the first time in 2015's *Batman v Superman: Dawn of Justice*.

3. Onesimus

The man known as Onesimus was an Akan born in what is today Ghana turned a Coromantee, an Akan individual sold into slavery, at the end of the seventeenth century. Onesimus would come to be owned by the Puritan minister, Cotton Mather in Boston, USA in 1706. Mather had already been famous for his influential writings that led to the execution of Goody Glover, a Catholic washwoman, for witchcraft. His words would also spark a series of trials in nearby Salem which saw the accusation of hundreds and the hanging of nineteen individuals (fourteen women, five men). As the seventeenth gave way for the eighteenth century, a new century required new threat. With witchcraft being so last century, a new invisible 'spectre' was looming in the colonies – smallpox. After being gifted Onesimus, the man would reveal to Mather a vast knowledge of medical techniques being used in Ghana to fight such ailments as smallpox. Onesimus told Mather in particular of a practice where a needle would be inserted into the smallpox pustule of an infected individual and then the needle would be scratched on the skin of young people. The practice would become known as inoculation. When an outbreak of smallpox struck Boston in 1721, Mather hailed the African folk medicine of inoculation as a gift from God to alleviate believers of a disease he saw as punishment for the colonist's sins. To his credit, Mather did give due credit to Onesimus earning him a lot of controversy and clashes with the prototypical anti-vaxxers, a combination of medical science sceptics and blatant racists. One nay-sayer even threw a grenade through the window of Mather's house. Mather's writing to the Royal Society of London and his relaying of Onesimus's explanation of the variolation method used throughout Sub-Saharan Africa would garner him influence and prompt Bostonian physician, Zabdiel Boylston, to inoculate almost three hundred individuals between 1721 and 1722. In 1716, after saving up enough funds to purchase a replacement slave, Onesimus was granted freedom on the condition that he remain available to work on-call and that he payback a sum that Mather claimed he had stolen. What happens to Onesimus after this is lost to history, but Mather's diaries seem to point to the reason for Onesimus's conditional freedom being his inability to get Onesimus to convert to Puritan Christianity. Onesimus's technique would go onto influence Edward Jenner to develop the first vaccine for smallpox in the 1790s, and in 1980 the World Health Organisation would declare smallpox officially eradicated. In 2016, *Boston* magazine gave Onesimus the rank of fifty-second on a list of 'Best Bostonians of All Time'.

4. Margaret Keane

Peggy Doris Hawkins was born in Nashville, USA, in 1927. During a botched jaw operation her eardrum was permanently damaged leading her to read people's eyes to assist with her communication. Drawing since her tenth birthday, her damaged ear influenced her artistic style. All of her human subjects were given over-exaggerated 'big' eyes. She moved to New York City to attend design school and began her career in painting apparel and furniture and then moved on to portraits in the 1950s. At about this time, she took the name Margaret and met the famed real estate mogul, Walter Keane. Walter recounts meeting her in North Beach, captivated by her 'big eyes'. An affair evolved into a marriage in the 1950s. Walter, now retired from real estate, began selling Margaret's portraits almost immediately after their marriage. He was able to sell her paintings to high end buyers. The only problem was that he claimed the art was his. Once Margaret learned of Walter's deception, she was pressured to keep quiet, unsure if her paintings would sell if it was not for her husband's prestige. In the 1960s, Walter developed a mythology around *his* and, to a small part, his wife's art which quickly became some of the most commercially desired art in the country. Even Andy Warhol gave 'The Painting Keanes' his blessing. By the end of the 1960s, their marriage had fallen apart and in 1970, Margaret went public on a live radio broadcast claiming her husband did none of the paintings. A reporter for the *San Francisco Examiner* arranged for a paint-off competition between Margaret and Walter in San Francisco Union Square, but Walter was a no show. The showdown would again be staged in 1986, but this time by a judge when Margaret sued her ex-husband and *USA Today* for running a story defending Walter. Walter refused to draw, sighting a sore shoulder, but when Margaret was able to recreate a Big Eyes portrait in the court room, in fifty-three minutes, she was awarded $4 million in damages. In 1990, a court upheld the defamation suit, but overturned the damages reward; Margaret was less concerned with the money than the fact that justice was upheld. Margaret Keane's doll-eyed style would influence countless artist, toy, and cartoon designs. She continues to paint and relax in California, her name and style rightfully hers.

5. Margarete Steffin and the Women of Bertolt Brecht

Margarete Steffin was a German actress and writer who had a rough start, getting fired from low level jobs for her Communist political leanings in the Weimer Republic. Her pathway into the theatrical arts began when she took dictation lessons with the famed actress Helene Weigel, the wife of the famed playwright and poet Bertolt Brecht, who would go on to be the revolutionary patron saint of the arts for East Germans. As Weigel and Steffin developed a deeper friendship, Brecht found a muse in Steffin and eventually took her as a mistress. Steffin, adept at writing and editing, was not Brecht's only mistress, nor muse. According to the American scholar John Fuegi who researched Brecht's biography, Brecht kept a factory like assembly line of young, attractive women who wrote the great works he would take credit for. Brecht was an 'ideas' man who was described as unable to sit still and focus long enough to put a piece together, so instead he would throw out ideas and framings, then leave it to his entourage of literary women to put together and pen the plays and poetry to which his name would be affixed. One of his most prised mistresses was Elisabeth Hauptmann who would even gain a few credits of her own and was offered bylines on some of Brecht's later works in their most recent editions. It is said that Hauptmann wrote more than 80 percent of *The Threepenny Opera* which first brought Brecht to fame in 1928. Fuegi dug through the archives and managed to find witness testimony from the descendants of Brecht's women, that he rarely gave credit to, his factory of editors he controlled using manipulation and sexual politics to maintain competition within their ranks, and prevent anyone from challenging him. A similar model was used to build up the theatre cultures that followed him. With the Nazis coming to power in the 1930s, Brecht was forced into exile first in Denmark, then in Sweden, and finally Moscow waiting for Germany to become his dream of a democratic socialist utopia. Several of his literary women followed him maintaining the machine that kept Brecht producing through the atrocious twentieth century. Margarete Steffin followed Brecht all the way to Moscow where she died from tuberculosis waiting for a visa to the US. Brecht's plays would go on to influence countless other works of art, music, and film into the contemporary period. He died not knowing the Berlin Wall fell, resting peacefully in a Berlin cemetery with a stake nailed into his heart as per his instruction (as he had a severe fear of being buried alive accidentally). Fuegi claims the reality of Brecht is the best kept secret in German literary circles who maintain the 'official' history with mafia-like discipline. The descendants of Brecht's women fight for their ancestor's justice in the courts to this day.

6. Margaret Mead and Culture of Samoa

Margaret Mead was a twentieth century American cultural anthropologist whose name is not only synonymous with her field of study, but also with the scepticism she faced over her methods and conclusions of her research. Studying at Columbia University in New York, Mead read under Franz Boas, the German-American anthropologist often given the moniker the 'Father of American Anthropology', and the American anthropologist and folklorist Ruth Benedict. Aside from being prominent social scientists in their own rights, Mead and Benedict challenged sex norms by being women working in a 'man's world' particularly in an area overrun with the male perspective and patriarchal vestiges. A young and rising star, Mead set out to Samoa to do fieldwork for her PhD which would lead to the writing of her first and most well-known book, *Coming of Age in Samoa: A Psychological Study of Primitive Youth for Western Civilization*. The work opened a window into a totally new society diverging from any the Western dominated anthropology of the day had encountered with rampant premarital sex and a new look at social interactions and societal construction. Mead's work was applauded for diverging from the common genetic based anthropology that dominated the 1930s, where evolution and eugenics overruled the observe and report investigative style Mead used. A couple of problems have since arisen in review of much of Mead's work. First and foremost, Mead spent very little time within the civilisations she was studying, instead electing to conduct interviews with a few representatives of the culture. Sample size alone calls her conclusions into question, but there is a complication. A common custom in Samoan culture held that the young women Mead interviewed had been joking with her or leading her astray. Some claim Mead was aware of this cultural quirk, but a New Zealand anthropologist Derek Freedman would visit Samoa fifty years later and arrive at vastly different conclusions concerning sexual norms and even tracked down some of Mead's sources, which she left anonymous for their protection, seeking to debunk her conclusions. A final issue with Mead's methods is that she had a propensity for challenging Western norms with regards to sexuality and gender and so the question must be asked, did Mead go in with an open mind and draw conclusions or did she have conclusions in mind she was seeking to justify. Debate over the veracity of Mead's work is still hotly debated to this day but much of it is a fight for all the wrong reasons. However history will remember Margaret Mead, it is ultimately the people as subjects of anthropology who lose out in the end and a major blow is dealt toward higher understanding and the bloody road of anthropology as colonial tool and orientalism is allowed to continue in the wake of such controversy. Anthropologists, both past and present, are bewildered by such episodes.

7. Stephen Glass

Stephen Glass is a name often synonymous with the death of journalistic integrity, back when it was blatant and not the sham we see today in the age of post-truth. Between 1995-1998, Glass worked for the progressive political magazine *The New Republic* which declared its creed as 'a liberalism centred in humanitarian and moral passion and one based in an ethos of scientific analysis'. During his time at *The New Republic*, it was determined that twenty-seven of his forty-one articles contained fabricated elements. It began as minor complaints from organisations Glass had demonised in articles including the drug awareness advocacy group D.A.R.E., the College Republican National Committee, and the Center for Science in the Public Interest (CSPI), a Washington-based watchdog organisation. Adam Penenberg, a writer for *Forbes*, served as the tipping point as he tried to follow up on a lead in a famed article by Glass, 'Hack Heaven', about a fifteen-year-old 'hacker' who made a lucrative deal with a made-up tech company whose security he had breached. Glass attempted to claim that the alleged 'hacker' had tricked him into the story but when the hacker, the tech company, and the convention he was supposedly attending, all turned out to be completely made up, he had been found out. A 2005 film, *Shattered Glass*, dramatises the events around the scandal. Following the scandal, Glass elected to start anew and attended Georgetown University Law Center, graduating magna cum lade with his JD. Despite passing both the New York and California Bar Association examinations, he was refused certification. Moral fitness and ethical concerns were cited as reasons for his denied certification. The California Bar Association found in their investigation into his application that a total of thirty-six articles written for *The New Republic*, three for *George*, two for *Rolling Stone*, and one *Policy Review* article were in one way or another fabricated by Stephen Glass.

8. Henrietta Lacks and the Unknown Other

1951 began with Henrietta Lacks going to Johns Hopkins, the only hospital in the area that would treat black patients, with what she referred to as the pain of a knot in her womb following the birth of her last son. By the end of the year, the cervical cancer that had caused the pain had metastasised and she would die in the hospital after numerous blood transfusions and treatments. She would be buried in an unmarked grave that remains a mystery to date. It is believed she was buried near her mother at Lackstown, the name given to the land that used to belong to the slave owning family of Clover, Virginia who owned Lacks's ancestors. While metaphorically she lived on in the memories of her children, physically she wasn't exactly gone either. While she was being examined, two samples of her cervical tissue were taken without her permission or knowledge. The samples, one cancerous and one not, were given to George Otto Gey who cultured the tissue and created the HeLa immortal cell line, well known in biomedical research. At the time Lack's cancer cells were of the fastest growing cells known. And eventually the HeLa line would become widely available and used in labs around the world. Shortly after Lack's death, her cell line was used to help in developing a treatment and the eventual eradication of polio. Her name faded until in 1974, when Michael Rogers with *Rolling Stone* stood at a urinal in a San Francisco medical school library bathroom and saw "Helen Lane Lives!" written in felt pen on the wall in front of him. This led him down the rabbit hole to eventually learn that Helen Lane was a misnomer accidentally leaked from a confidential medical file for Henrietta Lacks. Rogers would travel to Baltimore and learn the story of the HeLa cell line and even trace down Lack's husband to learn that the same medical hospital had been unethically taking blood samples from Lack's family to build an entire genome in the hopes of answering the question as to why Henrietta's cancerous cervical cells grew so fast and continued to live to this day. Rogers wrote a bittersweet peace for *Rolling Stone* in 1976, but the story went cold shortly after. It wouldn't be until the 1990s, when medical institutions began recognising Lacks for her contributions to science. In 2010, a colleague of George Gey would donate a headstone to commemorate Lacks. Throughout the early 2000s, Rebecca Skloot began researching the history of the HeLa cell line and eventually wrote the book *The Immortal Life of Henrietta Lacks* which would be adapted into a film in 2017. Today she is receiving the credit due to her, but the tale of her, her family, and her cells exists as another sad chapter of unethical medical practice, particularly between the medical establishment and the black community of the US, echoing of the Tuskegee Syphilis experiments and numerous experiments conducted in the name of science that began with slaves as subjects and has continued uncomfortably to today creating a major trust deficit between medical professionals and the black community that shows in numerous statistics. This apartheid in medicine, as the American medical ethicist Harriet A. Washington refers to it, is on the same level as genocide throughout history. Perhaps less blatant and slower in its delivery, but no less bloody or wrong. Erasure is not a historical problem, but a problem occurring at this very moment. Most readily seen in history as the plight of the indigenous peoples of the Americas to today with Palestine or with the Uighurs in China and the Rohingya in Myanmar, the stealing of one's biography, one's name, or one's life is not always the act of one dastardly moustache twirling villain, but in its most real and terrifying form, the social ignorance of the masses, implicit in its perpetration and unaware of what is being lost. It is up to us the story tellers, the speakers and writers of words to make sure that the great story lives on and all stories have the right to be told.

CITATIONS

Introduction: CM@Ten by Ziauddin Sardar

On the role of criticism in early Islam, see, for example, Franz Rosenthal, *The Classical Heritage of Islam* (University of California Press, 1975); and Marshall Hodgson, *Venture of Islam* (University of Chicago Press, 1972). The quotes are from: Abdullah Saeed, *Islamic Thought: An Introduction* (Routledge, London, 2006) p103; Mohammad Arkoun, *The Unthought in Contemporary Islamic Thought* (al-Saqi Books, London, 2002) p13; Sadakat Kadri, *Heaven on Earth: A Journey Through Sharia Law* (The Bodley Head, London) p87; and Toby Huff, *The Rise of Early Modern Science: Islam, China and the West* (Cambridge University Press, 1993) p222-236. My Royal Society, London, lecture, 'Islam and Science: Beyond the Troubled Relationship', was delivered on 12 December 2006 and an abridged version was published in *Nature* 448, 131-133 (12 July 2007).

Books mentioned include: Ziauddin Sardar, *Desperately Seeking Paradise: Journeys of a Sceptical Muslim* (Granta Books, London, 2004) and *Reading the Qur'an* (Hurst, London, 2011); Robin Yassin-Kassab, *The Road From Damascus* (Hamish Hamilton, 2008); Mohammad Iqbal, *The Reconstruction of Religious Thought in Islam* (Oxford University Press, 1932); Al-Nadim, *The Fihrist of al-Nadim*, translated by Bayard Dodge (Columbia University Press, New York, 1970) Ibn Khallikan, *Biographical Dictionary*, translated by B Mac Guckin de Slane (Allen and Co., London, 1836; reprinted by FreedomBooks.com, 2017); Medina Whiteman, *The Invisible Muslim: Journeys Through Whiteness and Islam* (Hurst, London, 2020) and Hussein Kesvani's *Follow Me, Akhi! The Online World of British Muslims* (Hurst, London, 2019).

On postnormal times, see The Postnormal Times Reader, edited by Ziauddin Sardar (IIIT, London, 2018); and on transmodernity see Ziauddin Sardar, 'Afterthoughts: Transnormal, the "New Normal" and

Other Varieties of "Normal" in Postnormal Times' *World Futures Review* 13
(2) 1-17 June 2021.

Biographies of the Prophet by Shanon Shah

Of the many contemporary biographies of Muhammad in print, I relied on
the following for this piece: Karen Armstrong's *Muhammad: A Prophet for
Our Time*, 2006, Harper Collins; Lesley Hazleton's *The First Muslim: The
Story of Muhammad*, 2013, Atlantic Books; Martin Lings' *Muhammad: His
Life Based on the Earliest Sources*, 1991, Islamic Texts Society; Maxime
Rodinson's *Muhammad*, originally published in 1961 and reissued in 2021
by the New York Review of Books; Barnaby Rogerson's *The Prophet
Muhammad: A Biography*, 2004, Abacus; and Ziauddin Sardar's *Muhammad*,
2012, Hodder Education.

The critical scholarly works on *Sira* and modern biographies of Muhammad
referred to were: Kecia Ali's *The Lives of Muhammad*, 2014, Harvard
University Press; Tarif Khalidi's *Images of Muhammad*, 2009, Doubleday
Religion; Omid Safi's *Memories of Muhammad: Why the Prophet Matters*,
2010, HarperOne. The Ibn Qayyim excerpt is from Khalidi's *Images of
Muhammad*.

Also referred to was Fred Donner's *Muhammad and the Believers*, 2010,
Belknap Press of Harvard University Press.

Danièle Hervieu-Léger's work on religious transmission and bricolage are
best appreciated through her book *Religion as a Chain of Memory*, 2000,
published by Rutgers University Press and her 1998 article 'The
Transformation and Formation of Socioreligious Identities in Modernity:
An Analytical Essay on the Trajectories of Identification', *International
Sociology*, *13*(2), pp. 213–228.

My discussion of the Comaroffs' work is based on excerpts from their
chapter, 'The Colonization of Consciousness', compiled in *A Reader in the
Anthropology of Religion* (Second Edition, 2008, pp. 464–478), edited by
Michael Lambek and published by Blackwell.

My article on Muslim vegans and vegetarians is in *Critical Muslim 26: Gastronomy* (pp. 86–102).

Merryl by Ziauddin Sardar

Merryl Wyn Davies books are: *Knowing One Another: Shaping an Islamic Anthropology* (Mansell, London, 1988), *Darwin and Fundamentalism* (Icon Books, Cambridge, 2000) and *Introducing Anthropology* (Icon Books, Cambridge, 2000); as co-editor, with Adnan Khalil Pasha, *Beyond Frontiers: Islam and Contemporary Needs* (Mansell, London, 1989); with Ziauddin Sardar, *Faces of Islam: Conversations on Contemporary Issues* (Berita Publishing Sdn Bhd, Kuala Lumpur, 1989), *Distorted Imagination: Lessons from the Rushdie Affair* (Grey Seal, London, 1990), *Why Do People Hate America* (Icon Books, Cambridge, 2002), *American Dream, Global Nightmare* (Icon Books, Cambridge, 2004), *Will America Change?* (Icon Books, Cambridge, 2008), *The No-Nonsense Guide to Islam* (New Internationalist, Oxford, 2004); and With Ziauddin Sardar and Ashis Nandy, *Barbaric Others: A Manifesto of Western Racism* (Pluto, London, 1993).

The citations from her works include: convert quote is from 'Living Out the Faith', *Inquiry* November 1994, p52; Wales quotes are from 'On the Green, Green Grass of Home' *Critical Muslim 19: Nature*, July-September 2016, p241–249 and 'The Glow Linger On', *Inquiry* September 1986, p25; the Aberfan disaster quotes is from '9/11 and All That', *Critical Muslim 2: The Idea of Islam*, April-June 2012, p271-277; the Rugby quote is from 'The Game's the Thing', *Inquiry* August 1986, p25; the BBC quotes are from 'Wink, wink, nudge, nudge: This is the BBC', *Inquiry* November 1985, p25 and 'Programme Accidents', *Inquiry* January 1986, p51-52; each month quote is from 'The Arrogance that Slew', *Inquiry* June 1986, p28; the Chicago Conference quote is from 'Thinking About Relevance', *Inquiry* August 1985, p62-63. The Nigeria quote is from her unpublished 'Annual Community Relations Lectures', given in June 2005, at the Kensington and Chelsea Council. Her article on Pir Sabaq was published as 'The Spirit of Enterprise', *New Internationalist* September 2011, p26-27. The Indian Ocean World quote is from her unpublished work.

Merryl Wyn Davies many articles in *Inquiry* include: 'The Legacy of Maududi and Shariati', *Inquiry* October 1998 34–39; 'Towards an Islamic Alternative to Western Anthropology' *Inquiry* June 1985 p45–51; and 'Re-Designing a Discipline', *Inquiry* April 1986 p45–49. The article on Malaysian writers, 'Writing About Malaysia' was published in September 1987, p50–55.

For more on Merryl Wyn Davies, see Ziauddin Sardar, *Desperately Seeking Paradise* (Granta, London, 2004). See also, Ziauddin Sardar, *The Consumption of Kuala Lumpur* (Reacktion Books, London, 2000), and Tariq Modood an d Fauzia Ahmad, 'British Muslim Perspectives on Multiculturalism', *Theory, Culture & Society* 24 (2), Special Issue on Global Islam, which can be downloaded from: http://www.tariqmodood.com/uploads/1/2/3/9/12392325/british_muslim_perspectives.pdf

The Puzzling Memoir of Hanna Diyab by Robert Irwin

The main source for 'The Puzzling Memoir' is Hanna Diyab, *The Book of Travels*, 2 vols. (Arabic and English) translated by Elias Muhanna and edited by Johannes Stephan (New York, 2021). But there is another translation, *The Man Who Wrote Aladdin* (Edinburgh, 2020). This was done by Paul Lunde for his own amusement and was edited and posthumously published by Caroline Stone. The degree to which the orphan stories of the *Nights* may have benefited from Diyab's personal input is carefully discussed by Paul Lemos Horta in his *Marvellous Thieves: Secret Authors of the Arabian Nights* (Cambridge Mass. 2017) pp.1–87.

Asad, The Neglected Thinker by Josef Linnhoff

Muhammad Asad's books include *Unromantisches Morgenland: Aus dem Tagebuch einer Reise* (Frankfurt am Main, 1924); *Islam at the Crossroads* (1934); *Sahih al-Bukhari: Translated from the Arabic with explanatory notes and index* (Srinagar, Kashmir: The Arafat Publications, 1935); Asad, *The Road to Mecca* (Louisville, Ky., 2000 (1st ed., New York, 1954)); *The Principles of State and Government in Islam* (Berkeley, CA: University of California Press, 1961); *The Message of the Qur'an* (Gibraltar: Dar al-Andalus, 1980). Muhammad Asad and Pola Hamida Asad, *Homecoming of the Heart (1932-1992): Part-II of the Road to Mecca*, edited by M. Ikram Chaghatai (Lahore: Pakistan Writers Cooperative Society, 2015). Many of the articles of Asad's 'one-man' journal *'Arafat,* published between 1946 – 48, have since been republished in *This Law of Ours and Other Essays* (Gibraltar: Dar al-Andalus, 1987). The complete collection of articles plus texts from other speeches are found in Volume II of M. Ikram Chagatai, ed. *Europe's Gift to Islam: Muhammad Asad (Leopold Weiss) Volumes I and II* (Lahore: Sang-e-Meel Publications, 2006).

The quotes are from: Asad, 'The Outline of a Problem', *'Arafat* 1:1 (September 1946), in M. Ikram Chagatai, *Europe's Gift to Islam: Muhammad Asad (Leopold Weiss) Volume II* (Lahore: Sang-e-Meel Publications, 2006), 748; Asad, 'Is Religion A Thing of the Past?', *Arafat* 1 / 2 (October 1946), in *Europe's Gift II*, 764-8; Asad, 'This Law of Ours', *'Arafat* 1:5 (January 1947), in *Europe's Gift (II),* 840; Explanatory footnotes on Q3:49 in *The Message of the Qur'an;* Rashid Ahmad Jullundhri, 'Review of The Message of the Qur'an: A New Translation with Explanatory Notes', *Islamic Quarterly* (London: July-September 1968); 11; Asad, *The Road to Mecca* (1954), 47; Muhammad Arshad. 'Muhammad Asad: Twenty-Six Unpublished Letters', *Islamic Sciences* 14 (Summer 2016), 53; Judd Teller, 'A Jew in Islam,' review of *The Road to Mecca*, by Muhammad Asad, *Commentary* (Sept. 1, 1954): 282; Compare pages 177 from 1954 and 1973 editions of *The Road to Mecca.*

For studies on Asad's life and thought see Gunter Windhager, *Leopold Weiss alias Muhamm ad Asad - Von Galizien bis Arabien 1900-1927* (Vienna: Bohlau, 2008); Dominik Schlosser, *Lebensgesetz und Vergemeinschaftungsform: Muhammad Asad (1900-1992) und sein Islamverständnis (*Berlin:E-B Verlag, 2015). In French, see Florence Heymann, *Un juif pour l'islam* (Paris: Stock, 2005). The most useful articles in English include Martin Kramer, 'The Roads from Mecca: Muhammad Asad' in *idem*, ed. *The Jewish Discovery of Islam: Studies in Honor of Bernard Lewis* (Tel Aviv: The Mosche Dayan Center for Middle Eastern and African Studies, 1999); 225-247; Abdin Chande.

'Symbolism and Allegory in the Qur'an: Muhammad Asad's Modernist Translation', *Islam and Christian-Muslim Relations* 15:1 (2004); 79-89; Furzana Bayri, 'Li-qawmin yatafakkarün (Q. 30:21): Muhammad Asad's Qur'anic Translatorial *Habitus', Journal of Qur'anic Studies* 21:2 (2019); 1-38; Abraham Rubin, 'Muhammad Asad's Conversion to Islam as a Case Study in Jewish Self-Orientalization', *Jewish Social Studies: History, Culture and Society* 22:1 (Fall 2016); 1-28; Yosef Schwartz, 'On Two Sides of the Judeo-Christian Anti-Muslim Front: Franz Rosenzweig and Muhammad Asad,' *Tel-Aviver Jahrbuch für deutsche Geschichte* 37 (2009); 63–77.

Munshi Abdullah by Hilman Fikri Azman

The edition of Munshi Abdullah's autobiography referenced in this piece is Abdullah bin Abdul Kadir, *Hikayat Abdullah* (with annotation from R. A. Datoek Besar and R. Roolvink) (Djakarta/Amsterdam: Djambatan, 1953); One of the more comprehensive biographical studies of Abdullah used for this article is Hadijah Rahmat, *Abdullah bin Abdul Kadir Munshi: His Voyages, Legacies and Modernity,* vol. 1 (Singapore: World Scientific, 2021);A catalogue of a large number of Abdullah's books and some manuscripts has been compiled by M.A. Effendi, Raja Hamzah Yunus et al. in *Re-Inventarisasi Naskah Naskah Yang Tersimpan di Mesjid Pulau Penyengat* (Kantor Wilayah Departemen Pendidikan dan Kebudayaan Propinsi Riau, Bidang Permuseuman, Sejarah dan Kepurbakalaan, June 1981);

For more on the opinions of Abdullah's contemporaries see John Turnbull Thomson, *Translations from the Hakayit Abdulla (bin Abdulkadar), Munshi* (London: Henry S. King and Co., 1874); John Bastin, 'The Missing Second Edition of C. H. Thomsen and Abdullah bin Abdul Kadir's English and Malay Vocabulary' in *Journal of the Malaysian Branch of the Royal Asiatic Society*, vol. 56, no. 1(244), (1983); Frank Athelstane Swettenham, *The Real Malay* (London: John Lane, 1907); andWalter Henry Medhurst, *China: Its State and Prospects, with Especial Reference to the Spread of the Gospel* (London: J. Snow, 1842) For more contemporary explorations of Abdullah see C. Skinner, 'Transitional Malay Literature: Part 1 Ahmad Rijaluddin and Munshi Abdullah,' in *Bijdragen tot de Taal-, Land-en Volkenkunde* 134, no: 4 (1978); Yusof A. Talib, 'Munshi Abdullah's Arab

Teachers' in *Journal of the Malaysian Branch of the Royal Asiatic Society*, vol. 63, no. 2, (1990); Mohd Daud Mohamad, *Tokoh-Tokoh Sastera Melayu Klasik* (Kuala Lumpur: Dewan Bahasa dan Pustaka, 1987); Kassim Ahmad, *Kisah Pelayaran Abdullah* (Kuala Lumpur: FajarBakti, 1981);H. F. O. B. Traill, 'Aspects of Abdullah 'Munshi' in *Journal of the Malaysian Branch of the Royal Asiatic Society*, Vol. 54, No. 3 (241) (1981); Ismail Hussein, *Sastera dan Masyarakat* (Kuala Lumpur: Penerbit Pustaka Zakry Abadi, 1974);

For more on the influence of the printing press and the modern evolution of Malay thought and language, Farish A. Noor, "Of Rajas, Maharajas, Dewarajas and Kerajaan: Four Thousand Years of Feudal Politics from Majapahit to Malaysia Today," in *What Your Teacher Didn't Tell You* (Selangor: Matahari Books, 2014); Syed NaquibAl-Attas, *Islam dalam Sejarah dan Kebudayaan Melayu* (Kuala Lumpur: Angkatan Belia Islam Malaysia, 1990); George Cœdès, *The Indianized States of Southeast Asia* (Honolulu: East-West Center Press, 1968); Ian Proudfoot, *Early Malay Printed Books: A Provincial Account of Materials in the Singapore-Malaysian Area Up to 1920* (Kuala Lumpur: University of Malaya, 1993); Ibrahim Ismail, "The Printing of Munshi Abdullah's Edition of the Sejarah Melayu in Singapore" in *Kekal Abadi*, issue 5, no. 3 (September 1986); Shaharuddin Maaruf, *Malay Ideas on Development* (Selangor: Strategic Information and Research Development Centre, 2020).

Aamer by Taha Kehar

Aamer Hussein's collections of short stories are: *Mirror to the Sun* (Mantra. London, 1993); *This Other Salt* (Saqi. London, 1999)/*aka The Blue Direction* (Penguin India, 1999); *Hoops of Fire: Fifty Years of Fiction by Pakistani Women* (Saqi, London 1999) (ed) (republished as *Kahani: Short Stories by Pakistani Women* (Saqi, 2005); *Cactus Town: New and Selected Stories* (Oxford University Press. Karachi, 2002); *Turquoise* (Saqi. London, 2002); *Insomnia* (Telegram. London, 2007); *Electric Shadows: Selected Stories* (Bengal Lights. Dhaka, 2013); *The Swan's Wife* (Ilqa/Readings, Lahore, 2014); *37 Bridges and Other Stories* (HarperCollins. Delhi, 2015); *Love and its Seasons* (Mulfran. Cardiff,

2017); *Hermitage* (Ushba. Karachi, 2018); *Zindagi Se Pehle* (Ushba, Karachi, 2020) and *Restless: Instead of an Autobiography* (Forthcoming Ushba/Reverie. Karachi 2021).

His novels are: *Another Gulmohar Tree* (Telegram. London, 2009) and *The Cloud Messenger* (Telegram. London, 2011).

DNA: A Personal Story by Jeremy Henzell-Thomas

I have referred to the following sources: Jeremy Henzell-Thomas, 'Out in the Open', Introduction to *Critical Muslim* 19, *Nature*, July-September 2016 (Hurst, London), 3-24; 'British and Muslim: A Personal Perspective.' Presentation at a Symposium on *Islamic Studies in Britain*, British Academy, 23 March 2010; 'British and Muslim, or just Human... and what about Welshness? Some Reflections on Identity.' Presentation in the Public Lecture Series organised by the Centre for the Study of Islam in the UK, Cardiff University, in association with the Muslim Council of Wales, Muslim Youth Wales and the Cardiff University Islamic Society, 8 February 2011; 'British and Muslim: Holding Values to Account through Reciprocal Engagement', *Arches Quarterly* (Spring 2011), 30-43; Adam Rutherford, 'How Accurate Are Online DNA Tests?' *Scientific American,* October 2018. See https://www.scientificamerican.com/article/how-accurate-are-online-dna-tests/; Bryan Sykes, *Blood of the Isles* (Bantam Dell, 2006) published in the United States and Canada as *Saxons, Vikings and Celts: The Genetic Roots of Britain and Ireland* (W.W. Norton); Chris Rojek, *Brit-Myth: Who Do The British Think They Are?* (Reaktion Books, London, 2007), 8; David Derbyshire, 'Most Britons Descended from Male Farmers who Left Iraq and Syria Ten Thousand Years ago' (January 2010). See http://www.dailymail.co.uk/sciencetech/article-1244654/Study-finds-Britons-descended-farmers-left-Iraq-Syria-10-000-years-ago.html#ixzz0hI9sjTLx; Andrew Marr, 'GOD: What do we believe?' *New Statesman*, 4 February 2008; Roger Scruton, *England: An Elegy* (Continuum, London, 2006); Stephen Fry, contribution to the debate initiated by the British Ministry of Justice in their consultation on 'What does it Mean to be British?' This debate, which ended on 26 February 2010, was part of the consultation process around the Green Paper, *Rights and Responsibilities:*

Developing our Constitutional Framework (March 2009). See http://governance.justice.gov.uk/join-the-debate/british/humanist-philosophers-group/ ; W.J.P. Burton, 'Commander James Liddell', paper read before the Royal Cornwall Polytechnic Society, June 18, 1928.

Mossland by Robin Yassin-Kassab

The quote on Sectarianization is from Nader Hashemi and Danny Postel, editors, *Sectarianization: Mapping the New Politics of the Middle East* (Hurst, London, 2017); the James C Scott quote is from *Two Cheers for Anarchism: Six Easy Pieces on Autonomy, Dignity, and Meaningful Work and Play* (Princeton University Press, 2012); anthropologists Natasha Myers and Carla Hustak are quoted in Merlin Sheldrake, *Entangled Life: How Fungi Make Our Worlds, Change Our Minds, and Shape Our Futures* (Bodley Head, London, 2020);

Compost devotees will enjoy Bob Flowerdew, *Composting* (Kyle Cathie Limited, London, 2010). The domestication of fire (and plants, animals, and humans themselves) is covered in James C Scott's *Against the Grain: A Deep History of the Earliest States* (Yale University Press, 2017. See also: Peter Wohlleben, T*he Hidden Life of Trees: What They Feel, How They Communicate* (William Collins, London, 2017).

Did I really see the Taj Mahal? by Boyd Tonkin

Edward Lear's *Indian Journal* is out of print but Jenny Uglow follows his Subcontinental travels in *Edward Lear: a Life of Art and Nonsense* (Faber & Faber, 2017). Sahir Ludhianvi's 'Taj Mahal' can be found on the SOAS website at http://mulosige.soas.ac.uk/taj-mahal-sahir-ludhianvi/. Antipater of Sidon's epigram on the Seven Wonders appears in Book IX of the *Greek Anthology*; a reproduction can be found at https://warburg.sas.ac.uk/pdf/ekh112b2445785v3.pdf. For Jai Singh's Jantar Mantar network of observatories see https://www.jantarmantar.org, and for the *hijras* of India, Zia Jaffrey, *The Invisibles* (Weidenfeld & Nicolson, 1997). Stendhal's swoon in Florence is recounted in his *Rome, Naples and Florence* (translated by Richard N Coe; John Calder, 1959). Early accounts of the Taj Mahal are collected in WE Begley & ZA Desai, *Taj Mahal: the Illustrated Tomb* (Aga

Khan Project for Islamic Architecture/University of Washington Press, 1989). A succinct, enjoyable account of the Taj's creation and reputation appears in Giles Tillotson, *Taj Mahal* (Profile Books, 2008) and a more extensive scholarly survey in Ebba Koch, *The Complete Taj Mahal* (Thames & Hudson, 2006). Selected by William Dalrymple, an edited version of Fanny Parkes's entertaining Indian chronicle of the 1820s and 1830s is published as *Begums, Thugs and White Mughals* (Sickle Moon Books, 2002). Aldous Huxley's strictures appear in his *Jesting Pilate: the Diary of a Journey* (Chatto & Windus, 1926). For the Taj's recruitment into India's culture wars, see Harrison Akin's 'How Hindu Nationalists Politicized the Taj Mahal'; *The Atlantic*, 27 November 2017. Sashi Tharoor rebukes the rewriting of Taj history in *Why I am a Hindu* (Hurst & Co, 2018). For an account of the recent pressures on the site, see Damayanti Datta, 'Losing the Taj', *India Today*, 10 September 2018. *Agra: the City of Monumental Contradictions*, Ashima Krishna's 2012 report for the Global Heritage Fund, situates the historic estate in its frayed urban context: http://ghn.globalheritagefund.com/uploads/documents/document_2096.pdf. A thorough, myth-free history and guide to Fatehpur Sikri appears in Lucy Peck's *Fatehpur Sikri: Revisiting Akbar's Masterpiece* (Roli Books, 2014). First published in 1908, EM Forster's *A Room with a View* is a Penguin Classic title.

List: Eight Stolen and Fabricated Biographies by C Scott Jordan

For more on Rosalind Franklin see the editorial "Rosalind Franklin was so much more than the 'wronged heroine' of DNA," *Nature*, 21 July 2020. (https://www.nature.com/articles/d41586-020-02144-4); For more on Bill Finger see Don Argott and Sheena M. Joyce's documentary *Batman & Bill* distributed by *Hulu*, 6 May 2017; For more on Onesimus see Erin Blakemore's "How an enslaved African man in Boston helped save generations from smallpox," *History*, 1 February 2019. (https://www.history.com/news/smallpox-vaccine-onesimus-slave-cotton-mather); For more on Margaret Keane and her Big Eyes see Eliana Dockterman's "The True Story Behind *Big Eyes*," *Time*, 25 December 2014. (https://time.com/3632635/the-true-story-behind-big-eyes/); For more on The Literary Woman of Bertolt Brecht see Imre Kovacs's "Ghosts of Brecht's women lay claim to his plays," *The Independent*, 7 February 1998. (https://www.independent.co.uk/news/ghosts-brecht-s-women-lay-claim-his-plays-1143276.html); John Fuegi's *Brecht and Co.: Sex, Politics, and the Making of the Modern Drama*, (Grove Press, New York, 2002); For more on the controversy behind Margaret Mead see Alice Dreger's "Sex, Lies, and Separating Lies from Ideology," *The Atlantic*, 16 February 2013. (https://www.theatlantic.com/health/archive/2013/02/sex-lies-and-separating-science-from-ideology/273169/); John Horgan's "Margaret Mead's bashers owe her an apology," *Scientific American*, 25 October 2010. (https://blogs.scientificamerican.com/cross-check/margaret-meads-bashers-owe-her-an-apology/); Same Dresser's "The meaning of Margaret Mead" *Aeon*, 21 January 2020. (https://aeon.co/essays/how-margaret-mead-became-a-hate-figure-for-conservatives); For more on Stephen Glass see Buzz Bissinger's "Shattered Glass," *Vanity Fair*, September 1998. (https://www.vanityfair.com/magazine/1998/09/bissinger199809); Stephen Glass's *The Fabulist*, (Simon & Schuster, New York, 2014).

For more on Henrietta Lacks and medical apartheid in the US see Rebecca Skloot's *The Immortal Life of Henrietta Lacks,* (Crown, New York, 2010); Michael Rogers's "The Double-Edged Helix" *Rolling Stone,* 25 March 1976. (https://www.rollingstone.com/culture/culture-news/the-double-edged-helix-231322/); Harriet A. Washington's *Medical Apartheid: The Dark History of Medical Experimentation on Black Americans from Colonial Times to the Present*, (Anchor Books, New York, 2008)

CONTRIBUTORS

Amina Atiq is a Yemeni–British activist, writer and performance artist ● **Hilman Fikri Azman** is an emerging Malay intellectual torn between academic scholarship and fighting for democracy ● **Merryl Wyn Davies** was a writer and anthropologist with a terrific sense of humour ● **Faisal Devji** is Professor of Indian History, University of Oxford ● **Saimma Dyer** is the co-creator of RAY of God, a non-profit organisation that promotes feminine spiritual wisdom ● **Mohammad Aslam Haneef** is Professor of Economics at the International Islamic University Malaysia, Kuala Lumpur ● **Jeremy Hanzell-Thomas** is a Research Associate and former Visiting Fellow at the Centre of Islamic Studies, University of Cambridge ● **Robert Irwin** is the author of numerous books and novels, including *Ibn Khaldun: An Intellectual Biography* ● **C Scott Jordan** is Executive Assistant Director of the Centre for Postnormal Policy and Futures Studies ● **Taha Kehar** is a novelist, journalist and literary critic based in Karachi, Pakistan ● **Josef Linnhoff** is a Research Fellow and Editor-in-Chief at the Institute for Advanced Usuli Studies, Columbus, Ohio, USA ● **Hassan Mahamdallie**, playwright and senior editor of *Critical Muslim*, is the author of *Crossing the River of Fire: The Socialism of William Morris*, which has just been republished ● **Shabana Mir**, an anthropologist, is Director, Undergraduate Education, at American Islamic College, Chicago ● **Ruth Padel** is a celebrated British poet ● **Bina Shah** is a Pakistani writer, columnist and blogger living in Karachi ● **Shanon Shah** teaches at the University of London's Divinity programme and is the director of a faith-based UK charity working to address the climate crisis ● **Boyd Tonkin** is a writer and literary critic ● **Medina Tenour Whiteman** is a writer, musician, and many other things ● **Robin Yassin-Kassab** is the co-author of *Burning Country: Syrians in Revolution and War*.